THE POLITICAL IDEAS IN THE PAÑCAMAHĀKĀVYAS

Mangala Mirasdar

Department of Sanskrit
University of Poona
Poona

EASTERN BOOK LINKERS
DELHI : : INDIA

Publishers :
EASTERN BOOK LINKERS
5825, New Chandrawal, Jawahar Nagar,
Delhi-110007 Ph.: 2520287

First Edition : 1995

ISBN : 81-86339-10-8

Rate

Laser Typesetting & Printing at
UNIQUE PRINT MEDIA
Phone : 7252362

PREFACE

This publication viz 'Political Ideas in the Pañcamahākāvyas' is a humble attempt to present the political concepts and ideas reflected in the Sanskrit Pañcamahākāvyas. The work is largely based on my thesis of the same title.

It would be interesting for the students of political science to know the concepts and ideas prevalent in the ancient times in India. The readers can judge how far these ideas are relevant in the modern or present day context.

I take this opportunity to acknowledge my indebtedness & gratitude towards my guide Dr. V.G. Rahurkar.

I am greatly indebted to Eastern Linkers Delhi, for kindly taking up the book for publication.

Mangala Mirasdar
Department of Sanskrit
University of Poona

TABLE OF CONTENTS

ABBREVIATIONS

AB	Aitareya Brāhmaṇa
AP	Agni Purāṇa
BG	Bhagavad Gītā
BORI	Bhandarkar Oriental Research Institute
BR	Bṛhadāraṇyakopaniṣad
KA	Kauṭilīya Arthaśāstra
KN	Kāmandakīya Nītisāra
Kirā	Kirātārjunīyam
Ku	Kumārasaṁbhava
MS	Manu Smṛti
Nai	Naiṣadhīyacarita
NP	Nārada Purāṇa
NS	Nārada Smṛti
NV	Nītivākyāmṛta
R	Rāmāyaṇa (Vālmīki)
Raghu	Raghuvaṁśa
ŚB	Śatapatha Brāhmaṇa
Śiśu	Śiśupālavadha
ŚN	Śukranīti
SP	Śantiparvan (Mahābhārata)
VP	Vāyu Purāṇa
YS	Yājñavalkya Smṛtti

INTRODUCTION

This treatise attempts to study critically and interpret various aspects of the political ideas dealt with in the *Pañcamahākāyas*. The five *mahākāvyas* are Raghuvaṁśa and Kumārasaṁbhava of Kālidāsa, Kirātārjunīyam of Bhāravi, Śiśupālavadha by Māgha and Naiṣadhīyacarita by Śrī Harṣa. A historical span of these five mahākāvyas is from 4th Century A.D. to 12th Century A.D. The scope of ancient Indian Polity reflected in this period is wide. The *Pañcamahākāvyas* reflect a good deal of political concepts in the classical Sanskrit literature.

Indian and Western scholars with their profound study have offered a lot of information and a valuable contribution to the political history of ancient India. There are also some recent scholarly efforts presented by modern scholars who dealt with the political thought in Sanskrit literature. But the two important classical *mahākāvyas* viz. Kumārasaṁbhava and Naiṣadhīyacarita are altogether neglected from the political point of view, by the scholars. I have tried to do justice to these two *mahākāvyas* along with others in this work. Though Naiṣadhīyacarita and Kumārasaṁbhava are love poems, there are some significant aspects of political considerations from the view point of ancient polity which are difficult to be neglected. For instance Kumārasaṁbhava clearly exhibits the merits and requirements for a post of commander-in-chief, which is significant from the political point of view. Along with the glimpses of the political thoughts in Naiṣadhīyacarita it alludes to the important duties and missions of an envoy, which is a significant factor in polity.

My approach towards some of the important aspects of the subject from different standpoint is quite new and original and I am sure, has not been dealt with so critically by the scholars in this field. While discussing the three traditional powers of the king, I have made a special mention and dealt with due details, the 'magical power' of the king, which influences to a considerable extent the king as an administrator. This power is employed by the kings as a weapon against the distressing enemies, evil powers and also for the welfare of the subjects. Due to the king's origin from the particles of the divinities, many of the supernatural powers are attributed to the kings. This point is discussed while stating the theory of divine kingship, but inspite of the magical boons offered by the divinities to the king, we come accross some allusions where the effects take place by the influence of the magical power of the kings themselves. While investigating the magical powers of the kings in the *Pañcamahākāvyas,* I have caught a thread which reaches to the theory forwarded by G.J. Frazer in his 'Golden Bough'. He states the king's origin from a magician, in the period before religion. In Naiṣadhīyacarita, I found that the rain-making and controlling power of Nala, might be a relic of the magical power in the age before religion emerged. The whole of the Frazer's theory and discussion of the exact link between these two is not attempted by me as it would be subject matter of a separate topic; but I have tried to show that in addition to the three traditional powers of the king, there exists a magical power of the king which can not be mixed with the supernatural power offered by the divinities.

While discussing the merits and duties of the rulers in the *Pañcamahākāvyas,* the merits are exhibited, showing their political significance. For instance, while describing the merit of truthfulness, the relative aspect of truth-fulness in the political field is discussed. The virtue of charity of the kings, reveals the fact that it does not remain as a personal merit of the ruler but it is closely connected to the welfare of his subjects. The ruler distributes his acquired wealth among his subjects through the virtue of charity. The virtue of acquiring a control over the senses is directly connected to the ambition and success of a conquering monarch. The poets of The *pañcamahākāvyas* describe with due emphasis the necessity of the control over the senses to the conquering monarch.

As, kingship was a regular and dominent form of government reflected in the *Pañcamahākāvyas*, it gives ample scops to describe the merits, demrits, duties of the kings with due details. The shining merits of the kings in the *Pañcamahākāvyas* reflect the fatherly touch of affection of the kings towards their subjects. While discussing the merits of the kings, the vices are considered as the red signals to the rulers.

The prudent rulers in the *Pañcamahākāvyas* exhibit various aspects of their administration. If one analyses with critical acumen and studies different political concepts casually referred to by the poets, one is struck with wonder with the fund of scientific information. An employment of the four political expedients, six guṇas, necessity of acquiring a friend-power, policy towards enemies, counsel and assistance of prudent ministers, an empolyment of spies and a significant mission of envoys, importance of royal assembly, all these aspects offer an ample scope for discussion and investigation of different view-points. In the political field, the unjust tactics empolyed by the ememies are to be reacted by the kings, so the beholders of righteous means were also experts in the knowledge of unjust means and were aware of this black aspcet of polity.

The two *mahākāvyas* viz. Kirātārjunīyam and Śiśupālavadha exhibit a poetic representation of the purely political ideas. We come across a lot of data of the political principles in them. I have tried to forward a comparative study of these two *mahākāvyas* and to investigate some advanced features in them. For instance, compared to Yudhiṣṭhira's arguments in Kirātārjunīyam, Uddhava's arguments in Śiśupālavadha hold a definite plan for political actions. Yudhiṣṭhira's speech, backed by nīti, seems to be a speech of a righteous administrator who is not ready to apply a 'tit for tat policy, while Uddhava, a prudent politician and counsellor does not hesitate to advise the application of seditious means to uproot the strenght of the enemy and his arguments seem to be of a confident diplomat and counsellor.

The political study of the *Pañcamahākāvyas* cannot be completed without considering the social background in which the society was situated. The social order of the Hindu Society was based on the double division of four castes and four life- stages which was known as '*Varṇāśramadharma*'. The duties of *varṇas* and *āśramas* were strictly observed by the rulers and the subjects. The rules and regulations were able to regulate the life of an individual as well as of the society through the strict observance. It is worth considering that the duties of *Āśramadharma* lead to a smooth succession of the royal throne because kings, the strict observers of *āśramadharma,* bestowed the royal throne to their able sons.

It was a peculiarity of the ancient Indian polity that the idea of '*dharma*' has been immensely imbedded in it. The concept of dharma was invariably connected with the concept of polity. That is why, the scope of the concept of dharma and its influence on the political field is an important topic. The religious sacrifices performed by the rulers had a political significance. The performance of sacrifices were connected with the ambition of the monarch on one side and a welfare of his society on the other side. The political motives behind the performance of sacrifices are discussed in due details. The priests and preceptors were not only the beholders of dharma, but were like a shield before the king to protect him and his kingdom from the human and natural calamities. The priest as a head of the religious institution, had to perform public and political duties. The priest was not directly designated in the administration, but the framework of Hindu Society had inevitably offered him a prominent place in the state polity. A pleasant co-operation of the *Brāhma* and *Kṣātra* power was always a topic of admiration by the poets of the *Pañcamahākāvyas*. So we cannot depict and evaluate king's administration without mentioning the position of the priest.

An observance of penances was inveriably connected to increase the *kṣātra* power of the kings. Arjuna's efforts of acquiring the divine missiles through the observance of penances reveals the fact. So the performance of sacrifices, observance of peanances were not only the religious aspects but were unavoidable parts of polity.

Frequency of wars occurred in the *Pañcamahākāvyas* offered a chance to investigate the motives behind the wars, preparataion of war, ethics of war, precaution to be taken before the commencement of war, rites to be performed before the expedition, army and its constituents, various weapons and missiles to be employed, skill in archery, modes of righteous and unrighteous warfare etc. All these topics are discussed in due details. A part played by Commander-in-chief was significant in the wars. He was not only a working officer of the army but divine qualifications were attached to him. The poetic muse of Kālidāsa stimulated him to compose a poem on the birth of a divine commander-in-chief. It exhibits the merits and qualifications of an able commander-in-chief who gets victory over the enemy by his prudent leadership.

While considering the political ideas and concepts in the *Pañcamahākāvyas,* we cannot neglect the fact that the political concepts are immensely influenced by the political treatise of Kauṭilya and the Smṛṭies. For instance, the classification of allies and enemies occurred in Śiśupālavadha (II. 36)) is clearly a reflection of the classification forwarded by Kauṭilya (VI. 2. 19/20) The principle of sixfold policy stated by Kauṭilya (VII. 3.1) is followed in Śiśupālavadha word to word. Śiśu II. 93). The rulers in the *Pañcamahākāvyas* clearly mention their treading of the path directed by Śāstras (Raghu IV. 13 XVII. 77) and also by the path directed by Manu (Raghu 1.17; Kirā I. a) So I have frequently referred to the allusions and quotations from these traditional treatises.

Thus a graphic picture of the administration of the rulers in the *Pañcamahākāvyas* is drawn with the significant aspects of polity. The political considerations to their acts are specifically discussed which are appealing from the five poetic compositions.

SOCIO POLITICAL INTENTIONS OF THE POETS OF THE PAÑCAMAHĀKĀVYAS :

Before discussing the political thoughts in the Pañcamahākāvyas it would be worthwhile to consider the social and political background (in the period of the poets) which inevitably reflects in the compositions. The poets are the best interpreters of their age. Naturally a definite political background in the particular age is seen in the great treatises. So it is interesting to discuss in brief the period of the Indian history and the political considerations which stimulated the great poets of the *Pañcamahākāvyas* to compose their poems.

The earliest historical mention of Kālidāsa is found in the Aihole Inscription dated 634 A.D. According to the opinions of the scholars like Dr. Bhandarkar, V.V. Mirashi and Prof. Keith, it is now an accepted fact that Kālidāsa was under the patronage of Candragupta II, who was entitled as Vikramāditya and who ruled in 380 A.D. to 413 A.D.

Kālidāsa wanted to make an ideal of kingship through the ideal reign of Gupta dynasty. Due to the peaçe and prosperity in Gupta period, it was known as the Golden Age of India. The well- known traveller Fie-Yan had wondered hundreds of miles in North India but met with no danger from robbers. This peaceful reign is reflected when Kālidāsa describes the reign of the kings like Dilīpa and Atithi in Raghuvaṁśa. In the reign of Atithi the travellers were fearless and for, the merchants the rivers were just like their home wells.[1]

Kālidāsa, while describing the merits of the Raghu kings actually refers to the virtues acquied by his Gupta patrons. While describing the expeditions of conquests, it is clear that Samudra Gupta was before his eyes.

Before 3rd Century A.D. the kings were not able to recreate *Hindu dharma* because of the aggressive powers like Śakas and Hūṇas, but this task was undertaken by the world conquering monarchs like Samudra Gupta, Chandra Gupta II. Raghuvaṃśa clearly refers to Raghu's conquest of Hūṇas. The ideals of *Cakravartin* was well recognized by Kālidāsa. The descriptions of the horse-sacrifices performed by the kings of the Raghu-race clearly reveal the fact that Gupta kings performed the horse-sacrifices which were a symbol of imperial sovereignty. The coins in the Gupta age had an imprint of sacrificial horse on them. When Kālidāsa refers to Āsamudrakṣitīśānām (Raghu I.5) as remarked by Dr. R.N. Dandekar, "this is also a punning reference to the line of Gupta kings up to *samudra,* that is upto the reign of Samudra Gupta".[2] So the description

1. Ragu XVII.64

of the conquests were not a mere imagination but a poetic reconstruction of the military undertaking by Samudra Gupta. It also reveals the fact that the princes were entrusted with some responsible duties to test their abilities. The political tactics adopted by the Gupta kings also are reflected in Kālidāsa's works. Increment of the friend power by matrimonial relationship was the policy of Gupta kings as reflected in the description of Kuśa's marriage with the Nāga princes Kumudavatī in Raghuvaṁśa (16th canto).

Kālidāsa seems to be an exponent of popular Hindu religion, which was immencely flourishing during the reign of Guptas. Kālidāsa's deep devotion towards God Śiva is clearly seen in his works. Dr. R.N. Dandekar explains - "From among other deities belonging to Śaiva pantheon, Kārtikeya, a son of Śiva and the commander-in-chief of the gods seems to have been perticularly popular with Guptas. Kumāra and Skanda which are the other names of this god were proudly borne by the two great Gupta emperors. Kālīdāsa has devoted an entire epic-poem to the subject of the birth of Kārtikeya, The martial ambitions and achievements of the Gupta Emperors would seem to explain their special affiliation to the Divine General"[3] It is true that a poetic muse of Kālidāsa created a desire in him to compose Kumārasaṁbhava, but political considerations also impressed him. When his country was being attacked by Hūṇas, there was a necessity of a strong savior. It was his patron under whose leadership the country became safe. So this kāvya seems to be a combination of fact and imagination. It is also a matter of gratifying the

---

2. R.N. Dandekar, The Age of the Guptas and other essays, Ajanta Publications, Delhi, 1982; p. 113
3. R.N. Dandekar, the Age of the Guptas and other Essays; Ajanta Publications, Delhi, 1982; p. 81

legendary young Kumāra to Kumāra Gupta in order to turn him into an invincible national hero.

From Kālidāsa's period when we turn to Bhāravi's Kirātārjunīyam (510 A.D. to 580 A.D.) we meet with somewhat different background. Though in Kumārasaṁbhava a difficult task like producing a divine commander-in-chief was to be accomplished by the gods, they were not altogether adverse to the war against their enemy. They wanted only an able leader who could give them victory against the *rākṣasas*. But in Kirātārjunīyam Bhāravi had to prepare a ground for the hero to 'lift him up for the diligent power for a *ksatriya*. This nature of repose from the duties of a *kṣatriya* and from the worldly life influenced Hindu society long before the time of Mahābhārata also. Among the four aims of human life, salvation, the last aim was the extreme rest for the human being, who is afficted by the worldly griefs, and this aim was acquired by diverting one's mind from worldly life. The model arrangement of four *āśramas* in which the first three human ends were duly set aright have been set aside for the obtainment of the shortcut of salvation. It was being forgotton that every person is basically a member of society in which he lives; and it is proper for him to give an equal justice to the humane aims which are not only for the personal interest but for the nourishment of the whole society.

It does not mean that salvation was of less importance, but the misplaced order of the ends spoils the instinct of valour of *Kṣatriyas,* which is harmful for the whole nation. The responsibility of preparing the Pāṇḍavas for the exhibition of their valour and making them enthusiastic is secured by Bhāravi. The great sage Vyāsa in Kirātārjunīyam, praises the high qualities of Yudhiṣṭhira and emphasizes the political truth of the necessity of increase in strength and arms to win the enemies. He urgefully states that a success in battlefield is gained only through powerful weapons and not by only good merits. It was the great influence of the advice by Vyāsa which enabled Yudhiṣṭhira to obtain the divine missile from Lord Śiva.

The special effort put in by Bhāravi clearly seems to stimulate the Vaolour of kṣatriyas and their ambition of acquiring valour and also regaining the lost kingdom. The anger of Draupadī, the spiritual queen of Pāṇḍavas, was influenced by the information about the prosperous reign of Duryodhana. The lady with self-respect censured Yudhiṣṭhira for his peace policy, who was bearing insults from his enemy, Draupadī reminds Arjuna of the insults by enemies and prays him to behave like a kṣatriya whose strength lies in his arms. Arjuna, who was impressed by the stimulating advice by Draupadī, exhibits valour in the fight with lord Śiva in the guise of Kirāta and acquires his desired fruit.

Alongwith the quality of valour, a knowledge of polity is very essential for an administrator. We see a fine poetic representation of the purely political ideas in the consultation of Uddhava, balarāma and Śrikṛṣṇa in Śiśupālavadha of Māgha. While selecting one of the equally important undertakings of attacking the enemy Śiśupāla attending the sacrificial ceremony of Yudhiṣṭhira, the discussion of the political situations takes place. According to Uddhava one should react the enemy's attack considering all the pros and cons of the situation. In the consultation, all important aspects of the science of polity are discussed.

The fifth epic poem is Naiṣadhīyacarita, written by Srī Harṣa. He was a protege of king Jayacandra, who ascended the throne between 1163 A.d. to 1177 A.D. So the date of the composition of Naiṣadhīyacarita is the latter half of the 12th century. Though Naiṣadhīyacarita is a love story of Nala Damayantī, many of the political glimpses are reflected in it. The appealing characters of Nala and the golden swan as a *dūta,* provides the minute details of the mission of envoy and an ethics of messengership. Nala as a messanger advocates with all his zeal and sincerity the case of gods before his beloved. Damayantī insists on him to communicate his name and family (IX. 36), but he conceals his identity as a real diplomat. Here he does not seem to reconcile his own self- interest with duty. His anxiety is how to reconcils his honour with the failure of his mission.'

The description of *Swayaṁvara* depicted in Naiṣadhīyacarita reveals the fact that Harṣa had experienced the swayaṁvara before his own eyes.[4] Dr. K.N. Watve remarks - "Śrī Harṣa wrote this poem to commemorate the swayaṁvara of Sañyogitā, which was celebrated by her father Jayacanmdra, the patron of Harṣa who might have seen this *swayaṁvara* with his own eyes".[5]

Thus the great poets of the *Pañcamahākāvyas* had definite political background experienced by them through which they depicted the ideal kings with their ideal administration.

A thorough study of the *Pañcamahākāvyas* provides us a lot of data of the political concepts. Though there seems to be a repetition of the verses and ideas at various places, that repetition serves the purpose of giving inclings into the various aspects of polity, and throws a flood of light on the political conditions of those days.

---

4. Nai X.55
न यक्षलक्षैः किमलक्षि नो वा सिद्धैः किमध्यासि समाप्तशोभा ।
सा किंनरैः किं न रसादसेवि नादर्शि हर्षेण महर्षिभिर्वा ॥

5. K.N. Watve, Sanskrit Kāvyāce Pañcaprāṇa, Manohar Granthamala. Pune 1947; p. 277

appealing characters of Nala and the golden swan as a [illegible] [illegible] provides the minute details of the mission of envoys sent [illegible] messengers. Nala is a messenger [illegible] advocates with a [illegible] zeal and sincerity the case of gods before his beloved Damayanti [illegible] to communicate his name and family (IX. [illegible]) but he conceals his identity as a real diplomat. Here the poet [illegible] to reconcile his own selfishness with [illegible] [illegible] failure of his mission.

In [illegible] poem [illegible] is depicted [illegible] reveals the fact that [illegible] had [illegible] before his own eyes. [illegible] XVII [illegible] wrote this poem to commemorate the [illegible] which was celebrated by [illegible] the [illegible] might have seen this [illegible] with his own eyes.

Thus the great poem [illegible] political background [illegible] by [illegible] [illegible] the ideal kings with the [illegible]

A thorough study of the [illegible] presents [illegible] of the political concepts. Though there seems to be a repetition [illegible] verses and ideas [illegible] various places [illegible] served the purpose of giving [illegible] into the various aspects of polity and throws a flood of light on the political conditions of [illegible]

CHAPTER-I

KINGSHIP

ORIGIN OF THE KING'S OFFICE :

Though other types of states existed in ancient India, Monarchy was the most common form of government. The necessity of the king arose from the want of security and protection of the people. In the primitive times when the society was in its tribal form, peace and security were often in danger. Because of the frequent internal quarrels and external attacks, the people certainly needed a rule of a strong person who could assure them safety and peaceful life. The accounts from the stories quoted in Vedic literature clearly show that the origin of kingship in India was out of a military necessity. In *Aitareya Brāhmaṇa* the account of war, between gods and demons indicates the inevitability of an able leader to the divinities also. In one of the stories, the gods recognized the reason of their constant defeat against the demons as the absence of a leader. When they approved *Soma* as their king they obtained success against their enemies.[1] More details about the origin of the king are given in the Śānti Parvan of *Mahābhārata*. In one account Bhīṣma narrates Yudhiṣṭhira about the creation of the king. He says - 'when the society was formed, the people were happy and they pursued the path of dharma and conducted themselves towards one

1. AB I.14
अराजतया वै नो जयन्ति राजानं करवामहै इति ।

another in a righteous manner. But in course of time poverty and delusion captured the minds of the people and due to the conflicting instincts of the dominating people, the weak remained without asylum. The gods also became subjected to fear and appealed to *Brahmā* for help and grace. The 'Creator' created a son named *Vijaras* as the protector of the people and composed a code of law for the social advancement and well-being of the world. This code of law required an authority to enforce its practical application and from it the institution of kingship came into being.[2] Another account in *Śāntiparvan* states that people suffering from anarchy requested *Brahmā* to appoint a person who could protect them. Manu was appointed by *Brahmā* to secure the responsibility. But Manu realized the responsibilities of overlordship and expressed his unwillingness to rule over the people addicted to untruth and all other sins. On this, the people agreed to give 1/6th of their agricultural product and 1/10th of the merchandise to him. In return they asked for peace and protection. Manu accepted the office, people took to *Swadharma* and the social welfare of the world was accomplished.[3] Kauṭilya also has mentioned a similar account about the origin of the king. Under the storm and stress of anarchy the people elected Manu as their king. The terms on which the office was conferred on him also were given. The people promised to pay him one sixth of the grains and one tenth of the other articles of merchandise, besides a portion of gold in their possession. Such wages to the king were in return for his guaranteeing to the people their protection and welfare.[4] These accounts clearly indicate the need of an efficient ruler for the confused society and the intention behind the

2. ŚP (Critical Edition by BORI) 59.13 to 28.
3. ŚP (Critical Edition by BORI) 67.18 to 23
4. KA - I. 13.5/6/7

origin of kingship lies in the need of the protection of the people. The king's office was created to ensure security and justice for the mankind against the law of jungle. The weak and the poor could co-exist in the society with the strong and rich, only when law and order were maintained by the ruler. So king's office was created to hold the best guarantee of the public security.

It was a beneficient institution, a fact proved not only by the views regarding an origin of kingship, but also by the account of the plight to which the people could be reduced if there was no king. In the absence of king, a strong sense of insecurity prevails. This peculiar kind of state is called *arājaka,* means a state without a ruler. The condition of the subjects becomes deplorable without their master.

Not protected by a ruler, the state becomes a target of internal and external dangers, The poets of *Pañcamahākāvyas* depicted the danger of kingless state. In Raghuvaṁśa it is described that after a sad demise of king Daśaratha, the subjects became devoid of a ruler, due to the absence of the princes. So the ministers sent a message to prince Bharata to attend the Kingdom, because a kingdom without a king becomes a prey tc the enemies who are vigilant in seeking holes.[5] In *Rāmāyana*[6] *we* come across a detailed account of the condition of he kingless state which reveals that the agency of the king was deemed extremely necessary for the state. The subjects without a king was like the cows who perish in want of protection, without a cowherd.[7] *Śāntiparvan* in its 67th chapter, narrates a detail account of the kingless state.[8] If a ruler, holding daṇḍa is absent,

5. Raghu - XII.11/12
6. R-II. 73.9 to 25
7. R- II.69.29
8. ŚP (Critical edition by BORI) 67.3 to 17.

the stronger roasts the weaker as a fish on a spit. Life becomes unsafe. A man cannot enjoy the possession of his person and property. The wicked rob the weak and the innocent of their wealth, and themselves also suffer in their turn. The atmosphere is pervaded by an all-round darkness and the subjects cannot depart a peaceful life in the absence of an able ruler. Manu[9] also states the similar condition of the kingless subjects and the necessity of the ruler to offer the people protection and welfare. Seeing the confused condition of the people dispersing in all directions through fear, *Prajāpati* created the king for the protection of the people.[10] A significant advice is given in *Śāntiparvan* in the connection that one should obtain first, a protector of wife and wealth and then acquire wife and wealth; because there is no guarantee of the security of life and wealth if there is no protector.[11]

It would be interesting to mention the various theories in brief, stating the origin of the king. A careful look into the abovementioned accounts, stating the origin of the king, reveals the fact that various motives and purposes are seen behind the creation of kingship. The above narrated story in *Aitareya Brāhmaṇa* indicates that due to the absence of a king, the gods had to accept a constant defeat from the demons. So they elected *Soma* as their king and they conquered all the directions. The account declares the necessity of a king from the want of a military leadership. A theory of

---

9. MS VII.20/21
यदि न प्रणयेद्राजा दण्डं दण्ड्येष्वतन्द्रितः ।
शूले मत्स्यानिवापक्ष्यन्दुर्बलान्बलवत्तराः ॥
अद्यात्काकः पुरोडाशं श्वा च लिह्याद्धविस्तथा ।
स्वाम्यं च न स्यात्कस्मिंश्चित्प्रवर्तेताऽधरोत्तरम् ॥

10. MS VII. 3
अराजके हि लोकेऽस्मिन्सर्वतो विद्रुते भयात् ।
रक्षार्थमस्य सर्वस्य राजानमसृजत्प्रभुः ॥

11. ŚP (Critical Edition by BORI) 57.41

contract is seen from the accounts in *Śāntiparvan Kauṭilīya Arthaśāstra* etc. which suggests a contractual relationship between the ruler and his subjects. In this theory the idea of protection and taxation is mutually connected. This theory seems to be reflected in Raghu. (1.18.) Third is the theory of the divine origin of the kingship which pervades prominently the *Pañcamahākāvyas* and which is the important aspect to be discussed here in details.

DIVINITY OF THE KING :

Generally, most of the ancient politicians had discussed the divinity and divine origin of a king. In Vedic literature, we come across many allusions and parbables mentioning a divine origin of the king; but the doctrine of the divinity of a king was unknown to the Vedic period. A.S. Altekar remarks "When a Samiti could depose a king, the theory of latter's divinity was not likely to take root in the society. But the atmosphere in the *brāhmaṇa* period was favorable to the idea of divinity of the king. *Brāhmaṇas* were claiming divinity for themselves and were not disposed to deny it to the king, who was expected to uphold their privileges."[12] In *Smṛties, Purānas* and afterwards in the epics, the doctrine of the divinity of a king seems to be deep-rooted. Agni Purāṇa strongly supports the theory mentioning that a king, princes, the sages and gods are 'Hari-incarnate', whether their names are included in the list of the incarnations or not.[13] Vāyupurāṇa states that monarchs are born through the particles or Viṣṇu.[14] The theory of the divine origin of the king

12. A.S. Altekar, State and Government in Ancient India (1962) Published by Motilal Banarasidas) p. 89/90.
13. A.P. 276.25
14. VP 57.12
विष्णोरंशेन जायन्ते पृथिव्यां चक्रवर्तिनः।
मन्वंतरेषु सर्वेषु अतीतानागतेषु वै ॥

exhibits its two aspects. One of them mentions the divine origin of the king from the elements of the divinities while another aspect supports only the functional resemblance of the divinities with the king. In this second view a king himself is not go incarnate but his functions are similar to that of the gods. The *Smṛṭis* and Purāṇas are not the rigid supporters of any one of the views; but these two aspects are intermixed by the ancient politicians. When Manu states the divine origin of the king out of the elements of divinities,[15] he also alludes the functional resemblance of the king with that of the divinities.[16] Agnipurāṇa while declaring the first aspect also mentions the second aspect viz. the functional resemblance of the two.[17] These two aspects are visible in *Śāntiparvan* also. It warns that the king should not be dishonoured as a common person because a great divinity lies in the form of a king; further it adds the functional resemblance. It points out how the king resembles Fire, because he burns the wicked by his power; the god Sun, because he sees everything through his spies and so on.[18]

The notion of the divine origin of kingship and the divinity of the king is fully developed in the *Pañcamahākāvyas*. The great poets of *Pañcamahākāvyas* describe divine births of the kings and their obtainment of the supernatural power from the divinities. The queen Sudakshiṇā bore an embriyo having contained the lustre of the guardians of the directions.[19] The divine birth of

15. MS VII.5
यस्मादेषां सुरेन्द्राणां मात्राभ्यो निर्मितो नृपः।
तस्मादभिभवत्येष सर्वभूतानि तेजसा॥
16. MS VII. 7/9; IX. 303 to 311
17. AP 225.16
18. ŚP (Critical Edition by BORI) 68.41 to 45.
19. Raghu II. 75

Rāma was nothing but an incarnation of Lord Viṣṇu. At the accomplishment of the sacrifice performed by king Daśaratha, a divine person appeared from the sacrificial fire and offered an oblation, through which the queens bore embriyos having the particles of Lord Viṣṇu.[20] The queens, in the dreams saw an incarnation of Viṣṇu bearing lotus, sword, disc etc. The king Daśaratha was very much pleased by obtaining the fathership of the lord of the three worlds;[21] and the Lord, in his turn, the source of three worlds was desirous for offering fathership to the king owing to his eminent merits.[22] In Kirātārjunīyam the ascetics in hermitage recognized Arjuna as an incarnation of god Viṣṇu, the destroyer and creator of the world.[23] Nārada in Śiśupālavadha, in the lists of incarnations, mentions that Rāma though 'Aja' took birth in *Mānavakula*.[24] The might of Nala, the king of Niṣadha was composed of the particles of the divine lords of the regions;[25] and it was the foundation of the arguments of Damayantī who denied the proposal of gods and says that marrying to a mortal king Nala\would be equivalent as marrying the gods, from whose eternal elements the king is born.[26] Thus the divine origin of the king is distinctly seen in the above allusions.

The second aspect of the theory viz. the functional resemblance in that of the king and the divinities, frequently occurs in the *Pañcamahākāvyas*. The king Atithī is described as a fifth in addition to the four lokapālas.[27]

20. Raghu X.56/60
21. Raghu X.66
22. Raghu X.53
23. Kirā XII. 33, XV.53
24. Śiśu I.67
25. Nai I.6
26. ibid VII.94, III.89, VI.94, XIV.99, XIV.43
27. Raghu XVII.78

He was like a Sun, destroying sin by his mere sight and removing darkness (ignorance) by establishing truth.[28] King Nala was as great as the divine lords of the regions of the sky. His impartiality was greater than that of Yama and Kubera.[29] Daśaratha as a king equated to Yama, Kubera and Varuṇa respectively by his equal justice, by his showerings of wealth and by his chastising the wicked and by his splendour, he resembled the Sun.[30]

The doctrine of the divine kingship with its two aspects, effected through want of protection to the people, distressed by the state of anarchy. This governing motive behind the origin of divine kingship is clearly expressed in the *Pañcamahākāvyas*. The motive behind the birth of Rāma in Raghuvaṁśa, Kṛṣṇa in Śiśupālavadha and Kumāra in Kumārasaṁbhava[31] is the need of protection of the subjects from the wicked. When Daśaratha began to perform a sacrifice for the birth of a son, at the same time, the gods oppressed by Rāvaṇa went to Lord Viṣṇu, who assured them that taking birth as a son of Daśaratha, he would kill Rāvaṇa with the sharp arrows.[32] In the praise of the gods they clearly revealed the intention of the incarnation of the Lord, as a human king. There is nothing unattainable and any necessity to attain it but it is his act of favour to the people that he condescends to take birth and acts like human beings.[33] A similar solicitation was

---

28. ibid XVII.74
29. Nai XVII.143; XIII.12
30. Raghu IX.6
31. The birth of Kumāra is referred in another context. it is mentioned here only to note a motif behind it.
32. Raghu X.44
33. ibid X.31

prayed by the people, who requested lord Viṣṇu to incarnate himself for the destruction of the haughty and oppressive Kañsa and Śiśupāla and to protect the subjects from their harassment.[34] The gods, who were oppressed by the demon Tāraka, prayed the Creator and the divine birth of Kumāra, the commander-in-chief of gods took place. Arjuna and Kṛṣṇa both were the divinities and at the request of *Brahmā,* they were living in a human form to wipe out the evil beings.[35] This notion of incarnation of the Lord as a human king and its purpose reminds us of the famous maxim in *Bhagvaḍ Gītā.*[36] Thus the king, having the divine elements, assures the subjects with the sense of security and protects them with his divine powers. As A.S. Altekar quotes - "It was probably felt that the theory of the divinity of king would enable him to discharge his duty better."[37]

Due to the divine origin and having contained from the eternal particles of the divinities, a king achieves a favour and support of the divinities, through which he sets in motion the productiveness of the earth, life and fruitfulness of all the classes of beings and objects. The divinities help the righteous and dutiful king in many ways. In the prosperous reign of king Duryodhana, the Earth yielded of her own accord plentyful treasures to him, the merciful king, whose merits were comparable

---

34. Śiśu I.38

35. Kirā XII.35
अयमच्युतश्च वचनेन सरसितरूहजन्मनः प्रजाः ।
पातुमसुरनिधनेन विभू भुवमभ्युपेत्य मनुजेषु तिष्ठतः ॥

36. BG IV.8
परित्राणाय साधूनाम् विनाशाय च दुष्कृताम् ।
धर्मसंस्थापनार्थाय संभवामि युगे युगे ॥

37. A.S.Altekar, State and Government in Ancient India (published by Motilal Banarasidas, 1962); p.92

to Kubera.[38] Arjuna obtained the victorious missiles from the divine guardians Indra and others by the inspiration of Lord Śiva.[39] Indra offered a victorious chariot to Rāma to equate with Rāvaṇa who was mounted on a chariot.[40] In Naiṣadīyacarita the rival kings could not fight against Nala who was possessed with the divine weapons by virtue of boons by the divinities.[41]

Nature also participated in the tasks of the righteous rulers. The five great elements were as if the slaves of Arjuna's lustre.[42] The path which was troden by Rāma and Lakṣmana to perform the mission of protection of the sacrifices was decorated by showering water and flowers.[43] An auspicious augury by the Nature proved that the birth of the kings like Raghu was for the benefit of the world.[44]. The divine birth of Kārtikeya proves that not only the king's divine origin but the divine origin of an army commander-in-chief also was a great work by the divinities. Apart from the poetical aspects around the theme of Kumārasaṃbhava, from the political point of view also, it may be stated that the essential requirements for an army-chief were obtained by Kārtikeya through a divine origin.

It is notable that the divinities offer their full co-operation, their lustre and valour to the earthly king who is their essence. By the bright and dazzling zone of divinity behind the king, he controls and protects his subjects; and the subjects also are not transgress the commands of thinking him a mere human being,

38. Kirā I.18
39. Kirā XVIII.46
40. Raghu XII.84/85/86
41. Nai XIV.96
42. Kirā VI. 33
43. Raghu XI.3
44. ibid III.14

as says Manu.[45] People offered respect to the child-king Sudarśana like their father and a well known title 'Mahārāja' was rightly applied to him, who was only six years of age.[46] king's divine image in the society made it easier for him to rule and control over the subjects. As the king was conceived to be a deity in human form, the subjects also did not incurred his displeasure because his anger was able to burn all the family with its hoard.[47]

A divinity offered to the king was a valid chance for him to seek good of the people. "It required that he should in reality possess a godly nature" as N.N. Law quotes- "The king's divinity does not place him above the observance of obligations attached to his office."[48] Inspite of his divinity he was bound by his duties to secure the needs of his subjects. Even Manu, who advocates the divinity of the king in an extreme form, warns that the king will suffer and meet with punishment in his very life, if he misbehaves or misgoverns. A divine power of *Daṇḍa,* which is created by the Lord for the use of the king for the protection of the creatures, destroys the king himself with his relatives for the miscarriages of his duties.[49] So the

---

45. MS VII.8
बालोऽपि नावमन्तव्यो मनुष्य इति भूमिपः ।
महती देवता हयेषा नररूपेण तिष्ठति ॥

46. Raghu XVIII.39/42

47. MS VII.9
एकमेव दहत्यग्निर्नरं दुरुपसर्पिणम् ।
कुलं दहति राजाग्निः सपशुद्रव्यसंचयम् ॥

48. N. Law, Aspects of Ancient Indian Polity published by Orient Longmans, 1960 p. 153

49. MS VII.28
दण्डो हि सुमहत्तेजो दुर्धरश्चाकृतात्मभिः ।
धर्माद्विचलितं हन्ति नृपमेव सबान्धवम् ॥

king's divinity does not exempt his from his performance of duties or from punishment for his misrule.

But there is one exceptional school of thought which takes the king on the head. According to them the kings are above the laws of *dharma* and above punishment though they transgressed the law.[50] Disobeing the king, results in the destruction of a person. Even a weak and undeserving king must be honoured and obeyed, A man who attacks the king though sinful, should be roasted on a spit and he should be counted as a killer of more than hundred brāhmaṇas.[51]

But we are of the opinion that such incidentally pronounced views should not be given much importance and they should not be taken as a rule. The ancient politicians who strongly supported the king's divinity, also had restricted it, binding the kings with the duties instructed by the laws of dharma. They had not blindly taken the king's on their heads. Even Manu, the absolute supporter of the king's divinity offers a middling rank of the status to the king, caused by *'Rajas'* (activity), inspite of his divinity.[52] Only a virtuous king should be supposed as divine; on the other hand he is demon's portion who behaves oppresive towards his subjects.[53] In *Śānti Parvan* also it is mentioned that if the king

---

50. ŚB V.4.7
तं दण्डैर्घ्नतो दण्डवधमतिविनयन्ति ।
तस्माद्राजा दण्डयो यदेनं दण्डवधमतिनयन्ति ॥

51. NS XV.31
राजनि प्रहरेद्यस्तु कृतागस्यापि दुर्मतिः ।
शूले तमग्नौ विपचेद् ब्रह्महत्या शताधिकम् ॥

52. MS XII.46
राजानः क्षत्रियाश्वेव राज्ञां चैव पुरोहिताः ।
वादयुध्दप्रधानाश्च मध्यमा राजसी गतिः ॥

53. ŚN I.70
यो हि धर्मपरो राजा देवांशोऽन्यश्च रक्षसाम् ।
अंशभूतो धर्मलोपी प्रजापीडकरो भवेत् ॥

observes the dharma he attains the dignity of a god and if he acts unrighteously, he sinks into hell.[54] These allusions declare that only the righteous king claims divinity and not others.

Secondly *Varnāśramadharma* a protection of which is accepted as the prime duty of the king; and it is also supposed to be having a divine origin.[55] So though divine, the kings had to observe the duties of *Varnāśramadharma*. If a king failed to observe the duties, the subjects had to suffer; and the people had a full right to question the king as a defaulter. In this connection the 'Śambūka incident' in Raghuvaṁśa is representative of the above point under discussion. A certain *brāhmaṇa* lamented in the gate of the royal palace carrying in his arms his dead infant child. He reproached Rāma that deprived of the benign rule of Daśaratha, the Earth has passed into hands of Rāma and got such miserable condition. Hearing the calumnious words of the *brāhmaṇa,* Rāma immediately searched out the reason of the mishap that a Sūdra named Śambūka was securing a penance, which was prohibited for a Śūdra.[56] The king Rāma corrected his mistake by killing the *Śudra* and repelling the evil practice in the *Varṇśramadharma*. So accepting king's divinity also, there was the controlling power of 'duty' which stood above the divinity of the king. People expected justice from their divine protector. The *brāhmaṇa* in the above instance praised Rāma as protector even from the god of death.[57] So king's divinity was restricted in this sense that only good and pious kings were regarded as divine and they were respected

54. ŚP (Critical Edition by BORI) 91.4
55. Nai XVII. 104
56. Raghu XV.42 to 53
57. ibid XV.57

by the subjects; on the contrary bad and impious kings were meant as an essence of devil to stay in hell.[58]

The kings in the *Pañcamahākāvyas* having the essence of divinities, were aware of the prime duty of protection of subjects. They were strong enough to maintain the social order of *Varṇāśramadharma* and the prescribed duties. The intention behind the theory of the divine origin of kingship, expected by the ancient law books and politicians is dully fulfilled by the rulers in the *Pañcamahākāvyas*. The writers believed in maintaining the status-quo about the duties of *Varṇas* and *āśramas*, in the privileges of the respective castes and in the progressive deterioration of *dharma* in the ages to come and wanted a strong king to preserve the social order; therefore the king was raised to divinity and an absolute obedience to his orders, was demanded. People accepted divinity in a king so far as he conducted himself properly and in a constitutional manner in the affairs of state.[59]

SEVEN CONSTITUENTS OF THE STATE :

We have metioned the prominent motives behind the origin of the state. The state for the protection of which, the king was appointed was comprised of seven constituents. The state is said to possess seven limbs, each discharging its particular function. The seven constituents of the state which are mentioned by almost all the ancient authorities on Polity[60] are well acquainted

---

58. ŚN I.87
गुणिजुष्टस्तु यो राजा स ज्ञेयो देवतांशकः ।
विपरीतस्तु रक्षोऽशः स वै नरकभाजनः ॥

59. MM P.V. Kane, History of Dharmaśāstra (Vol. III) p.27 published by BORI, Poona 1946, p.27

60. KA VI. 1.
स्वाम्यमात्यजनपददुर्गकोशदण्डमित्राणि प्रकृतयः ।
KN IV.1 ; AP 225.11, 233.12, 239.1 MS IX.294
स्वाम्यमात्यौ पुरं राष्ट्रं कोशदण्डौ सुहृत्तथा ।
सप्तप्रकृतयो हयेताः सप्ताङ्गं राज्यमुच्यते ॥

with the *Pañcamahākāvyas.* In Raghuvaṁśa in the very first canto, the sage Vasiṣṭha asked king Dilīpa about the well-being of his kingdom comprised of the seven constituents. Clear mentioning of the seven constituents of the state is seen in Dilīpa's reply. He says "The existence of prosperiey and happiness in the seven departments of my state, is a matter of course, since you are the destroyer of all the calamities divine and human."[61]

The seven constituents referred above are the king (*Svāmin*), the minister (*amātya*), the territory (*janapada*) the fort (*durga*), Treasury (*Kośa*), Army (*daṇḍa*) and ally (*miṭra*), Though these elements are separately mentioned, they work as a whole. Each of the seven limbs is complementary to others and an administration of the state gets hindrance even if one part is defective.[62] So while stating the unobstructed prosperity of his state, King Dilīpa specifically mentions the seven constituents of the state. The state is like a chariot having the seven parts contributing to one another. The seven constituents with their individual excellence, work harmoniously which is very helpful for a prosperous state. In Naiṣadhīyacarita, in the context of the poetic description of Damayanti's beauty, it is mentioned that, when these seven constituents are strong and pure, a powerful enemy also is unable to become successful over the king and his state.[63]

These limbs are linked together as to form one single whole. In Śiśupālavadha the constituents of the state are compared to the organs of human body. As a human body works through its various organs so also the king administrates the state with the seven limbs.[64]

---

61. Raghu I.58
62. KN IV.2
63. Nai VII.81
64. Śiśu II.82

As the disease of a single organ ruins the whole body so also a distress of even one part can destroy the whole state. So a ruler should be very watchful about the defects in the limbs of the body-politic.

It is difficult to point out an importance of each of the seven elements due to their merits excelling each other. Like the limbs of a body, all the seven constituents are essential for the normal working of the state; but at different times, a different element assumes importance over others. According to Manu, like a triple staff of an ascetic, no one excels each other, as the merit is concerned.[65] All the limbs are specifically important and co-operative to others and they help the whole administration of the state. In Śukaranīti a beautiful anology is metioned in connection of state organism. The state is compared to a tree, of which, the king is the root, the ministry the trunk, the military offices the branches, the army the leaves and flowers, the people and territory, the fruits and seed respectively.[66]

An exaltation of one of the seven parts of the state is seen to be stated in some ancient works. According to Kāmandaka, a territory, with all the other constituents should be protected, because all the constituents depend upon territory; the king gets the highest prosperity through the protection of the territory.[67] Agni Purāṇa states the exaltation of the kingdom over all the other elements of the state.[68]

---

65. MS IX.296
सप्ताङ्गस्येह राज्यस्य विष्टब्धस्य त्रिदण्डवत् ।
अन्योन्यगुवैशेष्यान्न किंचिदतिरिच्यते ॥

66. ŚN IV. 1256/57
राजवृक्षस्य नृपतिः मूलं स्कन्धाश्च मन्त्रिणः ।
शाखास्सेनाधिपाः सेनाःपल्लवाः कुसुमानि च ।
प्रजाः फलानि भूभागाः बीजं भूमिः प्रकल्पिता ॥

67. KN IV.76

68. AP 239.2
राज्याङ्गानां वरं राष्ट्रं साधनं पालयेत्सदा ।

Inspite of all these opinions it is clear that Swāmī or king is prominent among the seven constituents; Because He is the impelling agent of the other elements; He is attributed as *Aṅgin'*[69] and by his excellences prospering the other elements, he becomes exceptional among all other kings.[70] According to Kauṭilya also king is the state. It means that the king being the soul of the body- politic represents all the elements of the state.[71]

Thus, with a ruler who rules over the people living in a certain definite territory, having some administration and economic system, an Army for defence, a state is established. An analysis of state into seven elements means the state as an organism with an ideal ruler was well known to the five *mahākāvyas.* So we are going to handle for discussion all these elements, if not in their due order, beginning from the important element, viz. king.

THE RULERS IN THE PAÑCAMAHĀKĀVYAS : THEIR MERITS AND DUTIES :

We have seen that an intention behind the origin of the king was to give the best guarantee of security and protection to the subjects. Though the notion of divine kingship was established and deep rooted in the society, the divinity did not help an unworthy king to survive from disaster, even from his subjects. Without worth and personal merits of the king, his divinity was not respected by the people. That is why much emphasis was laid on the kingly qualities by the ancient *Hindu* writers and thinkers.

---

69. Śiśu II.94
70. ibid II.82
71 KA VIII.2
राजा राज्यमिति प्रकृतिसंक्षेपः ।

An account of the qualities and merits of the ideal kings narrated by the poets of *Pañcamahākāvyas* reminds us of the kingly qualities enumerated in *Arthaśāstra*. The standards of merits required for a king are - "Born of a high family, godly, possessed of valour, seeing through the medium of aged persons, virtuous, truthful, not having a contradictory nature, grateful, having great aims, enthusiastic, not addicted to procrastination, powerful to control enemies, of resolute mind, having an assembly of ministers of no mean quality and possessed for a taste of discipline.[72] In the commencing canto of Raghuvaṁśa, the merits of the ideal kings of Raghu-race are narrated by the poets. The depiction is of the line of monarchs who maintained the purity of birth; who carried on their undertakings till they were crowned with success; who held sway over the whole earth bounded by the ocean; whose chariots ran unhindered upto the gates of heaven; who performed the sacrificial rites to the fire according to rule; who honored the prayers of supplicants by gifts according to their desires; whose punishments were proportionate to the crimes; who were roused into action at proper time; who collected wealth only for the acts of charity; who spoke in a deliberate manner in order to preserve the vow of truth; wished to extend their conquest only for fame; entered upon a married life only for issue; who devoted themselves to the acquisition of knowledge in their childhood; who saught pleasures in their youth; who led an ascetic life in declining age and finally closed their lives in a state of contemplation."[73] This graphic picture of the merits of the solar kings clearly

---

72. KA VI. 1(3)
महाकुलीनो देवबुद्धिसत्त्वसंपन्नो वृद्धदर्शी धार्मिकः
सत्यवागविसंवादकः कृतज्ञो स्थूललक्ष्यो महोत्साहो दीर्घसूत्रः
शक्यसामन्तो दृढबुद्धिरक्षुद्रपरिषत्को विनयकामः ।

73. Raghu I.5 to 8

reveals the required qualifications for an ideal ruler. Some of the qualities of the rulers in *Pañcamahākāvyas* are noted below.

PURITY OF BIRTH: It was an established belief that the ruler of the subjects should have born in a pure dynasty. King Dilīpa,[74] Aja[75] Atithī[76] are described as born in a good family. In the *Swayaṁvara* of *Indumati*, her friend, while describing the kings, particularly stresses their illustrious race (Raghu 6.63). King Nala in the Naiṣadhḥyacarita is described to be sanctifying the family of king of *Vidarbha* with his pure lineage.[77] While stating a desire for an offspring, Dilīpa pointed out that a child born of a pure family gives happiness both here and hereafter.[78] It was also believed that birth-rites, if properly performed lend sanctity to the child-born. Purity of birth, was meant to be an essential requirement for an ideal king to command respect from his subjects.

ELEGANCE : Though, elegance was not an essential requirement for a ruler, the poets of the *Pañcamahākāvyas* had depicted the heroes of their poetic treatises, as having charming and handsome personalities. When king Nala came to Damayanti as a messenger of gods, she was surprised to see his cupid-like form and suspected him for Aśvin.[79] Her hidden feelings were aimed only at one person, Nala whose beauty was beyond the range of speech.[80] The handsomeness of Aja seems from the minds of the princes gathered for

---

74. Raghu I.12
75. ibid VI.79
76. ibid XVII.4
77. ibid XVII.4
78. Raghu I.69
79. Nai VIII. 29
80. ibid XI. 129

the *swayaṁvara* of Indumati, who became hopeless about the obtainment of Indumati, seeing prince Aja who resembled the god of love.[81] The minds of the residents of Mithilā were drinking with their eyes the two princes, Rāma and Laksmaṇa, who appeared like two *punarvasūs* came down to earth from heaven.[82] Arjuna in Kirātārjunīyam is described as having a charming form.[83] The hero of Kumārasaṁbhava is not a king, but an army-chief, also possesses the quality of handsomeness. Thus, the natural virtue of elegance is prominently visible in the kings of the *Pañcamahākāvyas*.

VALOUR AND PROWESS : We have already seen that the origin of kingship was from the need of protection of distressed people. So a valorous ruler was able to protect his subjects from the internal and external calamities. 'Valour' was not only an ornament of the ruler but it was an essential need for him. The rulers were not only valorous but their ambition of conquering the sea-girt earth through their valour proved they they were able conquerors of the earth. We come across frequent allusions revealing the valour of the kings in the *Pañcamahākāvyas*. The Kings had a great belief in the prowess of their arms. Bhima in Kirātāarjuniyam, to rise up Yudhiṣṭhira from inactivity, urges that no enemies will be able to withstand in battle as the four brothers are renowned in all quarters[84] and who had already displayed their valour.[85] He states the impor-

---

81. Rahgu VI.2
82. Raghu. XI.36
83. Kirā VI.1
84. Kirā. II.23
85. ibid. II.17
द्विषता विहितं त्वयाऽथवा यदि लब्धा पुनरात्मनः पदम् ।
जननाथ ! तवानुजन्मनां कृतमाविष्कृतपौरुषैर्भुजैः ॥

tance of valour that prosperity abides only in valour and not in despondency.[86] In the fight between Kirātarāja and Arjuna, Arjuna shared a great deal of enterprise and he was not hesitated by the row of arrows dischared by Kirātarāja.[87] The followers of Kirāta lost their glare by the valour of Arjuna.[88] In the eighteenth canto, when Lord Śiva in the disguise of Kirāta revealed his real form, he was much pleased by the valour expressed by Arjuna more than the propitiation of his penance.[89] The solar kings obtained the attribute 'Vira' by the valour of their own arms.[90] There was nothing impossible for the kings who were dependent upon their bows (Ragu III.6). We come across a vast description of the valour of Prince Raghu in the occasion of the horse sacrifice performed by Dilipa. Even Indra was pleased to see the heroism of Raghu.[91] His brightness was compared to the scorching heat of the sun.[92] When Raghu started for the expedition of conquest, his prowess was directing his fourfold army.[93] In the southern direction, even the bright rays of sun became dim but the princes could not stand before the lustre of Raghu.[94]

In the battlefield king Nala showered a rain of arrows from the cloud of his flashing bow. He became

---

86. Kirā II.15
87. ibid. V.44
88. ibid. XIV.43
    यथास्वमाशंसितविक्रमाः पुरा मुनिप्रभावक्षततेजसः परे ।
    ययुः क्षणादप्रतिपत्तिमूढतां महानुभावः प्रतिहन्ति पौरुषम् ॥
89. ibid. XVIII.14
90. Raghu. II.64
91. Raghu III.55
92. ibid IV.15
93. ibid IV.30
94. ibid IV.49

radiant as the fires of his might which burnt up the cities of his enemies. His fame of military heroism was spread even in the regions of sky.[95] He is addressed as an 'abode of might' (Nai 13.10). In the Swayaṁvara of Damayanti the valour of the Mahendra king is described in details.[96] Kārtikeya, the divine army chief of the gods, in Kumārasaṁbhava destroyed the demon Tārakāsura, through his valour. In the fight, the demons could not face the army chief of only 'six days' of age as a darkness cannot stand before the sun.[97] He felt of war like a pleasure-game. His military skill made the missiles futile, thrown by the demon.[98]

Thus, valour seems to be a prominent aspect of king's merits. Though the kings, having a strong ambition of acquiring the title *'Cakravartin'*, expressed their valour against the enemies, they were aware of the second side of the valour, that the proper use of their strength and valour consists in its application to remove the calamities of his subjects.[99] Their army was kept ready to maintain peace.[100] So the king's valour was only for the protection of the distressed and not to harass anybody.

CONTROL OVER THE PASSIONS : An important aspect of the king's qualifications was a control over his senses. It was the first step to attain success in the sphere of politics.

---

95. Nai III.39
यशो यदस्याजनि संयुगेषु कण्डूलभावं भजता भुजेन ।
हेतोर्गुणादेव दिगापगालीकूलंकषत्वव्यसनं तदीयम् ॥
96. ibid XII.25
97. Ku XV. 34
98. ibid. XVII.12
99. Raghu VIII.31
बलमार्तभयोपशान्तये..... ।
100. ibid. I.19

The solar kings in Raghuvaṁśa were self-controlled and their self-restrained minds were totally aversed from the passions.[101] the worldly enjoyments had no hold on them.[102] The tendencies of their minds were averse to sin. They knew that the external enemies stay in a distant place, so before turning towords them, they had to conquer the six internal enemies, residing very near to them.[103] The eminent politicians advocate that a king who forsakes the six internal enemies becomes happy.[104] According to Manu, after controlling the senses and mind and not afflicting his body by external means, one can achieve his desired objects.[105] King Kuśa, who had controlled himself, thought his single self as more than one because of his noble, brave and self-restraining son.[106] King Rāma revealed a great evenness of mind, when he put barkgarments at the time of exile for fourteen years, as well as, at that time of wearing the auspicious slik garments proper for this installation ceremony and the subjects was benumbed to see the self-restrained king.[107] the king Aja had obtained an even stage of mind, thinking gold and clod of equal value.[108]

---

101. Raghu XVI.8
102. ibid. I.23
103. ibid. XVII.45
104. ŚN I.142
कामक्रोधस्तथामोहोलोभोमानोमदस्तथा ।
षड्वर्गमुत्सृजदेनमस्मिस्त्यक्तवते सुखी नृपः ॥
105. MS II.100
वशे कृत्वेन्द्रियग्रामं संयम्य च मनस्तथा ।
सर्वान्संधायेदर्थानक्षिण्वन् योगतस्तनुम् ॥
106. Raghu XVII.4
107. ibid XII.8
108. ibid VIII.21

Damayanti's friend describes King Nala as a self-restrained king practising the religious austerities in conformity with rules.[109] In the field of politics, the control over the senses or steady-mindedness has a unique value. A success, as if impelled by eagerness, comes to those, who do not allow their minds to be uneasy.[110]

While describing an ideal reign of Duryodhana, the messenger of Yudhiṣṭhira informs - Desirous to reach the line of conduct laid down by Manu, Duryodhana has conquered the six internal enemies and he behaves with due regard to policy[111] A king, though powerful, does not resist an attack of ignorance sprung from anger, destroys all the regal powers; as the dark half does all the digits of moon.[112] That is the very reason that the great sage Vyāsa praises the even mindeness of Yudhiṣṭhira who bore the yoke of righteousness due to his unshaken steadiness even in difficult days also.[113] The result was favourable for Yudhiṣṭhira because the enemies by their fraudulent efforts brightened his unshaken merits.[114] In the propitiation of penance by Arjuna, to gain the divine missiles, his self-control is

---

109. Nai XIII.17
मित्रप्रियोपजननं प्रति हेतुरस्य संज्ञा श्रुतासुहृदयं न जनस्य कस्य ।
छायेदृगस्य च न कुत्रचिदध्यगायि तप्तं यमेन नियमेन तपोऽमुनैव ॥

110. Kirā III.40
यशोधिगन्तुं सुखलिप्सया वा मनुष्यसंख्यामतिवर्तितुं वा ।
निरुत्सुकानामत्रिभियोगभाजां समुत्सुकेवाङ्कमुपैति सिद्धिः ॥

111. Kirā I.9
कृतारिषड्वर्गजयेन मानवीमगम्यरूपां पदवीं प्रपित्सुना ।
विभज्य नक्तं दिवमस्ततन्द्रिणा वितन्यते तेन नयेन पौरुषम् ॥

112. ibid, II.37
बलवानपि कोपजन्मस्तमसो नाभिभवं रुणाद्धि यः ।
क्षयपक्ष इवैन्दवीः कलाः सकला हन्ति स शक्तिसंपदः ॥

113. ibid, III.15

114. ibid, III.6

clearly visible. The spring-season full of prosperity of flowers could not hesitate his mind and he protected himself through his self-restraint.[115]

So a control of passions which is a key to success on the part of king, is an idea repeatedly stressed by the poets. A king, who has subdued his internal enemies is able to conquer the whole world; on the other hand a person without self-control becomes subordinate to others.[116]

INTELLECT : Sharpness of intellect was an essential requirement for an ideal king and it was much praised by the poets of *Pañcamahākāvyas*. An intelligence of king Dilipa was so sharp that it entered deep into the Śāstras without any obstacle.[117] His appearance was befitting to his wisdom and his wisdom was befitting to his personality.[118] Due to the high intellectual capacity the great sage Vyāsa offered the wisdom of Yoga to Arjuna the fittest recipient.[119] Steady wisdom is necessary for an administrator; because a steady wisdom wins everywhere.[120] Wise people who have possessed a steady wisdom, like a four-leged bed-stead and rely on it never get weariness.[121] Their sharp intellect touches the target very little from outside but rushes very deep inside of the object; on the contrary the wisdom of the

---

115. Kirā X.35
116. ibid. XI.33
    परवानर्थ संसिद्धौ नीचवृत्तिरपत्रपः।
    अविधेयेन्द्रियः पुंसां गौरिवैति विधेयताम् ॥
117. Raghu I.19
118. ibid. I.15
119. Kirā III.26
120. Śiśu V.47
    निर्धूतवीतमपि बालकमुल्लन्तं यन्ता क्रमेण परिसान्त्वनतर्जनाभिः।
    शिखावशेन शनकैर्वशमानिनाय शास्त्रं हि निश्चितधियां क्व न सिद्धिमेति ॥
121. ibid.II.77

dull personalities touches the larger part of the target outwardly but cannot pierce it.[122] So a ruler with sharp intellect is able to take correct decision and acquires ability to overpower his enemies.

STUDY OF ŚĀSTRAS : The power to control the senses, which was an important requirement for a ruler, was achieved through the study of *Śāstras*. The study of science enlightens a proper way to the mind. According to Kauṭilya whole science prescribes control over senses.[123] The study of sciences shows the way like a lamp to the wise persons also, when their minds are confused in the forest of controversies.[124] In Raghuvaṃśa it is described that King Dilīpa's intelligence entered deep into the Śāstras without any hinderence. He had mastered all the branches of learning.[125] The king, who was skilled in the art of words had the same expectation from his child that he should go to the other end of learning and prince Raghu also, after the tonsure ceremony learnt the letters and entered into the great ocean of learning. By his intelligence he gradually got across the four lores resembling the oceans.[126] The study of *Śāstras* is comprised of the four lores viz. Ānvikṣikī, *Trayī, Vārtā* and *Daṇḍanīti*. These four disciplines are covered by the term *'Rājavidyā'*[127] Because humility which is a root of all the political framework, is to be achieved by king

122. Śiśu II.78

123. KA I.6
कृत्स्नं हि शास्त्रमिन्द्रियजयः।

124. Kirā, II.33
मतिभेदतमस्तिरोहिते गहने कृत्यविधौ विवेकिनाम्।
सुकृतः परिशुद्ध आगमः कुरुते दीप इवार्थदर्शनम्॥

125. Raghu, I.23

126. Raghu, III.30

127. NV. V.55
आन्वीक्षिकीत्रयीवार्तादण्डनीतिरिति चतस्ओराजविद्याः।

through the study of the *Śāstras*. The study of sciences leads to the control of senses and helps the king to protect his kingdom.[128] Thus the education of the *Śāstras* is very essential for an administrator.

SENSE OF SELF-RESPECT :

Self-respect is indispensable for a king, This quality is prominently stressed in the *Pañcamahākāvyas*. A person lacking the sense of self-respect and dignity gets the condition of a mere grass which bows down by mere breezes.[129] That is why the heart of the dignified hero like Arjuna was broken by the insult by enemies as he was not free to take revenge of the enemies by his own arms.[130] Draupadī's mind suffers the same grief by the distressed condition of Pāṇḍavas due to the lack of the self-respect.

An obtainment of many other objects is possible only through the sense of self-dignity. A man enjoys prosperity and steady fame.[131] Even an unattainable peak of mountain creates desire to attain it only through the sense of self- respect.[132] An anger of the self-respected persons is able to burn the enemies into ashes, like a fall of thunderbolt on a dry grass.[133] Such person gets an imperishable glory at the cost of perishable life and the fruit and unsteady wealth become

128. A.P. 238.3
नयस्य विनयो मूलं विनयः शास्त्रनिश्चयात् ।
विनयो हीन्द्रियजयस्तैर्युक्तः पालयेन्महीम् ॥
225.22
आन्वीक्षिकी ञ्चार्थविद्यां वार्तारम्भांश्च लोकतः ।
जितेन्द्रियो हि शक्नोति वशे स्थापयितुं प्रजाः ॥

129. Kirā, XI. 59; Śiśu II.50

130. Kirā XI.57

131. ibid. XI. 61

132. ibid. XI.60

133. ibid. XI.65

the object of secondary consideration.[134] Thus relying only on the valuable quality of self-respect a person becomes able to get through all the obstacles in the path of success. having a sense of dignity a person bears obstacles but not humiliation.

A self-respected person cannot bear any insult from others. Even a dust when beaten by feet climbs on the head, so dust also is better than a person who is at ease after an insult[135] As the high-spirited persons have attained the depth of ocean and a height of a mountain, no one dares to overstep them,[136] That is the very reason that *Rāhu* swallows the lustrous sun after a long time but the mild and gentle moon in a short time.[137]

The Solar-kings are attributed as "the kings who march ahead of those to whom self-respect is wealth."[138] Thus, for a *'Vijīgiṣu'* self respect is a fundamental quality, by which, though less in valour and means, he acquires the desire to get the highest position among the other kings.

CHARITY : Charity is not only a merit of the king but it is very essential requirement for a king. It is proper for a ruler to distribute the acquired wealth in the conquests among his subjects seeking their welfare.

---

134. ibid. II.19
अभिमानधनस्य गत्वरैसुभिः स्थास्नु यशश्चिचीषतः ।
अचिरांशुविलासचञ्चला ननु लक्ष्मीः फलमानुषङ्गिकम् ॥

135. ibid. II.46
पादाहतं यदुत्थाय मूर्धानमधिरोहति ।
स्वस्थादेवापमानेऽपि देहिनस्तद्वरं रजः ॥

136. Śiśu II.48

137. ibid. II.49
तुल्येऽपराधे स्वर्भानुर्भानुमन्तं चिरेण यत् ।
हिमांशुमाशु ग्रसते तन्म्रदिम्नः स्फुटं फलम् ॥

138. Rahgu V.3

Among the three virtues, one is mentioned as *Dāna*'[139] *According to Manu the only aspect of KaliYuga* is *Dāna*.[140]

This virtue was possessed by all the kings in the *Pañcamahāvyas* to a high extent. They collected wealth only for the acts of charity and they honoured the prayers of the supplicants by gifts according to their desires.[141] Their acquired wealth was only for others just like water of a cloud.[142] Not only wealth but their merits also were for the benefit of the subjects.[143] Due to their charity the learned men, who had been extremely poor and hence were supplicants, came to the position of donors on account of their receiving gifts from the kings[144] and the supplicants became non-supplicants for ever.[145]

The great sacrifices performed by the kings were fine opportunities for them to offer gifts to the supplicants. King Raghu donated all his acquired wealth to the *brāhmaṇas* and supplicants, in the performance of the *Viśvajit* sacrifice. Due to the excess of his charity he had to receive the disciple of Varataṇtu only with a clay-pot. King Atithi, in the great sacrifice,offered magnificent presents that his name became identical to

139. Bṛ V.2.3
तस्मादेवदे तत्रयं शिक्षेद् दमं दानं दयामिति ।

140. MS I.86
तपः परं कृतयुगे त्रेतायां ज्ञानमुच्यते ।
व्दापरे यज्ञमेवाहुर्दानमेकं कलौ युगे ॥

141. Rāghu I.6

142. ibid. IV-86
स विश्वजितमाजह्ने यज्ञं सर्वस्वदक्षिणम् ।
आदानं हि विसर्गाय सतां वारिमुचामिव ॥

143. Raghu VIII.31

144. ibid XVII.72
सन्तस्तस्याभिगमनादत्यर्थं महतः कृशाः ।
उदधेरिव जीमूताः प्रापुर्दातृत्वमर्थिनः ॥

145. Nai I.15

that of Kubera.[146] Through the medium of the performance of the sacrifices the kings could exhibit a bright trait of their charity; They praised charity which fulfilled the desires of the supplicants. According to them not only one's wealth but even one's life should be given away like a straw to a supplicant; enjoining of the water with the gifts proves it.[147] The earth is overburdened with the persons who do not fulfill the desires of the supplicants.[148] King Nala supposed himself gratified when he recognized that the Lord of the gods came to him as supplicant.[149] he was attributed as a 'Shower of Wealth'[150] In one place 'Fame' is attributed as a wiie of the King and the four guards in the form of Charity, Kindness, Truth and Hospitality to keep watch over her.[151] Thus by the virtue of Charity the king obtains imperishable fame and welfare of his subjects.

Charity was a prominent virtue which became a part of king's life and the kings were ready to bow down, as if offering their own self for the service of the supplicants, hearing only the word 'supplicant.'[152] They were ceaseless in their charity,[153] and their gifts were offered with due honour to the supplicants.[154]

---

146. Raghu XVII.80
147. Nai V.86 अर्थिने न तृणवद्धनमात्रं किं तु जीवनमपि प्रतिपाद्यम् ।
 अेवमाह कुशवज्जलदापी द्रव्यदानविधिरुक्तिविदग्धः ॥
148. ibid. V.88
149. ibid. V.90
150. ibid. XXI.119
151. ibid, X.28
 चतुःसमुद्रीपरिखे नृमाणामन्तःपुरे वासितकीर्तिदारे ।
 दानं दया सूनृतमातिथेयी न्तुष्टयी रणणसौविदल्ला ॥
152. ibid. V.79
153. Raghu,XVI.3
154. Kirā, I.12
 निरत्यं यं साम न दानवार्जितं न भूरि दानं विरहय्य सत्क्रियाम् ।
 प्रवर्तते तस्य विशेषशालिनी गुणानुरोधेन विना न सत्क्रिया ॥

Thus to acquire merit and to seek a welfare of the subjects, the Kings had shown a creditable aspect of their virtues.

MODESTY : Modesty is a great virtue of the king. Due to the lack of modesty the king gets destruction of the kingdom and himself while he acquires kingdom with the virtue of modesty.[155] A natural modesty of the king is increased and improved by education, as the natural splendour of fire is augmented by the oblations.[156] So possessed of the natural virtue of modesty, the king should learn the principles of *Śāstras* from the authorities.[157]

Other virtues of the king shine brightly by modesty. While the ascetics bestowed praise on Śatrughna for having killed the demon Lavaṇa, he bent down his head with modesty.[158] Prince Raghu though excelled his father in handsomeness, yet he looked lowly on account of his natural modesty.[159] Due to his natural modesty, King Dilpa made his son Raghu the holder of the title *'Yuvarāja'*.[160] Prince Rāma conquered the sage Paraśurāma by his valour, but he showed his natural modesty by touching the feet of the great sage, the repository of asceticism.[161] The merits of King Nala were increased millionfold by his modesty.[162]

---

155. AP 225.21
नश्येदविनयाद्राजा राज्यश्च विनयाल्लभेत् ।
156. Raghu X.79
157. KA I.2.5
नित्यश्च विद्यावृद्धसंयोगो विनयवृद्ध्यर्थं तन्मूलत्वाद्विनयस्य ।
158. Raghu XV.27
159. ibid. III.34
160. ibid. III.35
161. ibid. XI.89
162. Nai XVI.116

Kauṭilya states an importance of *'Vinaya'* for a king. A king modest by the education and engaged in the welfare and well-being of the subjects, enjoys the whole earth.[163]

DISCRIMINATION : Discriminating power means a thinking power or seeing the pros and cons of a thing before taking decision, is very necessary requirement for a king. In Kirātārjuniyam, Yudhiṣṭhira states an importance of discrimination to Bhima who urges for taking a quick action against Duryodhana. He says - one should not do anything without thinking, because want of thinking is a great source of calamities. Fortunes which are attached to merits, choose the person who acts with circumspection. He who nourishes the seeds of the objects by the water of thinking gets the rich harvests in the form of good results.[164] When the discriminative power is confused in the darkness of conflicting opinions the knowledge of *Śāstras* help the person to take the correct decision.[165] A wisdom having the discriminative power is the weapon in the hands of a ruler who is able to gain success against the enemies. Such person does not depend upon only destiny or valour but releasing the situation takes the support of both. According to Manu all actions are dependent on fate and human acts.[166] but which of these to be given prominance is decided by one's discriminative power, Uddhava, the intelligent minister and a wise politician of Kṛṣṇa in *Śiśupālavadha* puts all the pros and cons of the present situation of the decision

---

163. KA I.2.18
विद्याविनीतो राजा हि प्रजानां विनये रतः ।
164. Kirā II.30/31
165. Kirā II.33
166. MS VII. 205
सर्वं कर्मेदमायत्तं विधाने दैवमानुषे ।
तयोर्दैवमचिन्त्यं तु मानुषे विद्यते क्रिया: ॥

of an attack against Siśupāla and by of the coming events due to his deliberation clearly reveal the fact that not a hasty action but action after a discrimination gives success to a ruler.

LOVE FOR FAME : When we analyse the merits of the ideal kings in the *Pañcamahākāvyas,* we find that 'love for fame' is a prominent aspect of the virtues of the kings. Fame was dearer to them compared to their very life and from their dearest possession also. In the very beginning of Raghuvaṁśa the poet depicts the merits of the kings to whom obtaining success in the wars was only to acquire fame.[167] An incident in the second canto of the same poem reveals the value of fame in the life of king Dilīpa. When a lion jumps upon the celestial cow Nandini and wants to eat it, Dilīpa requests him to leave her and take his body and to show kindness to his body in the form of fame.[168]

Defeat in the battlefields was like a death to the warriors. The valorous prince Aja betook only the glory of the kings defeating them and not their lives through mercy.[169] The warriors in the battlefield are always greedy for success to acquire the fame.[170] The famous maxim in *Bhagavadgītā* suggests the same thing that a dishonour to a dignified person is left with surplus than death.[171] A person, who is unable to achieve fame, destroyed by the enemies, through the strength of the arrows, is surely to be called 'dead' or a 'mere grass'.[172] The value of the glory or fame possesses an equal rank of a dignified and loving wife, in the life of high

167. Raghu I.7
168. ibid. II.57
169. Raghu VII.65
170. Kirā XVI.9
171. BG II.34
172. Kirā XI.70

personalities. Arjuna the valorous hero was inflamed by anger seeing the fame being snatched away by his enemies.[173] Though his valour was dimmed by the enemies he has exhibited a great resistance against the powerful enemy, that his glory began to shine like the rays of the sun.[174]

The kings were ready to forsake their best possessions to acquire fame and to avoid ill-repute. King Raghu performed *Viśvajit* sacrifice and distributed all his wealth as the *daksiṇā* to the *brāhmaṇas* and supplicants and he was unable to pay the money which was needed by the supplicant *Kauṭsa.* but it was a thing of reproach for Raghu that a certain suitor went to another doner, not obtaining his object of wish from him.[175] So to avoid the disrepute Raghu decided to attack Kubera who aware of the valour of Raghu, poured wealth in the treasury of Raghu. Raghu satisfied Kauṭsa, offering him the desired wealth.

The second instance is of King Rāma, who forsook his loving wife Sītā to please his subjects. His heart was broken by the unbearable account of the scandle about Sītā contrary to his fame.[176] But when he was convinced that the infamy could not be averted by any other means, he abandoned his wife, his own happiness. It shows that who prize their fame above all were ready to leave their own body where it was in conflict with the claims of their fame.[177]

---

173. Kirā XVII.4

174. ibid. XVII.15
प्रत्याहतौजाः कृतसत्ववेगः पराक्रमं ज्यायसि यस्तनोति ।
तेजांसि भानोरिव निष्पतन्ति यशांसि वीर्यज्वलितानि तस्य ॥

175. Raghu V.24

176. ibid. XIV.33

177. ibid. XIV.35

Not only these kings, but even the dignified queen of *Pāṇḍavas* could not bear the spot to the fame of her husbands who regarded glory as their wealth[178] She could not bear even the praise of the good reign of enemy. Thus the fame was an issue of prestige in the lives of the rulers in the *Pañcamahākāvyas*.

TRUTHFULNESS : Truthfulness was an essential trait in King's life. Janaka, the king of Mithilā was attributed as beholder of a truthful promise.[179] Prince Rāma, not causing his father to deviate from his truthfulness (of conferring boons) entered forest for exile.[180]

Truthfulness was not only a *'dharma'*of a king. Truthfulness is the quality, specially mentioned in the list of the requirements to a king. According to Kauṭilya the king should speak truth and he should never break his promise.[181] The tradition of truthfulness was minutely followed by all the rulers. Lakṣmaṇa the true devotee of his brother, Rāma followed the path of truth only. In the confidential deliberation between *Kāla* and Rāma, Lakṣmaṇa interrupted them, who was aware of the agreement made between them; and with yoga-practice, abandoning his body, made the promise of his elder brother true.[182] For the sake of truth, the kings were ready to abandon their life also. In *Śiśupālavadha* Uddhava emphasizes the merit of keeping the promise.[183]

---

178. Kirā. 1.43
179. Raghu XI.48
180. ibid. XII.9
181. KA VI.1
     सत्यवागविसंवादकः ।
182. Raghu XV.95
     स गत्वा सरयूतीरं देहत्यागेन योगवित् ।
     चकारावितथां भ्रातुः प्रतिज्ञां पूर्वजन्मनः ॥
183. Śiśu II.109

This firm bearing of truth in king's life was recognized by people also. They had a great belief in the unfailing promise of their king. When, King Raghu requested Kauṭsa to wait for two-three days till the accomplishment of his desired object, Kauṭsa who knew the unfailing promise of the king, accepted his request with pleasure.[184] So this virtue of truthfulness has offered the kings a great honour, respect and belief by their subjects, which was a precious achievement for a ruler.

To preserve this virtue it is mentioned that for the sake of truth a king should speak limited speech[185] and he should not speak untruth in humour also.[186] That is why a sensible speech containing very few words is appreciated.[187]

Thus firmly following of the path of truth[188] and true to one's promise was the ideal of these kings. According to thinkers, in the sphere of politics, truth gets different meanings; so truth should not be applied in its normal form. Agnipurāṇa defines truth as the speech which gives the best of the benefits to a being may be called truth.[189] It also adds that one should speak truth and favourable words but one should not speak true but unfavourable words. One should also not speak favourable but untrue and it is the eternal

---

184. Raghu V.26
तथेति तस्यावितथं प्रतीतः प्रत्यग्रहीत्संगरमग्रजन्मा ।
गामात्तसारां रघुरप्यवेक्ष्य निष्क्रष्टुमर्थं चकमे कुबेरात् ॥

185. ibid. I.7

186. ibid. IX.8

187. Śiśu II.13

188. Raghu XVII.42
यदुवाच न तन्मिथ्या.... ।

189. AP 372.7
यद्भूतहितमत्यन्तं वचः सत्यस्य लक्षणम् ।

dharma.[191] In *Śāntiparvan* the definition of truth is - The oration which causes the well being of one's own nation and of the people as a whole, is truth in the political sense of the term.[192]

But a noteworthy point under discussion is that the ideal kings in the *Pañcamahākāvyas* were the firm beholders of truth and to keep the truth they were ready to forsake their lives also and did not accept the categorical idea of truth. They were aware of their duty to follow the *dhrama* which taught the value of truth. They also knew that a king was not only the political head of the state but was a beholder of *dharma* also. So the authors of the *Pañcamahāvyas* strongly advocated a righteous administration by the rulers. According to the kings, the means by which the political ends were to be achieved were as important as the ends themselves. The purity of means and ends should be in conformity with truth, was their principle. Kauṭilya, who sometimes has permitted to use some unlawful means to secure the desired objects also expected from the king not to break his promise.[193] Speaking truth was an eternal *dharma* of the kings. Apart from the idealistic attitude of the righteous rulers, from the political point of view also, a ruler should be ready to bear the truth, though unfavorable to him; because a truth beneficial and pleasing at the same time is rare.[194] and the true well wishers also do not wish to utter an agreeable falsehood.[195] So though disagreeable to him a ruler should face the truth for the benefit of his kingdom.

---

191. AP 372.8
सत्यं ब्रूयात्प्रियं ब्रूयान्नब्रूयात्सत्यमप्रियम् ।
प्रियं च नानृतं ब्रूयादेष धर्म सनातनः ॥
192. ŚP 79.31 Critical Edition by BORI
193. Supra, 181
194. Kirā I.4
195. ibid I.2

According to the opinion of the righteous and truthful kings, the people speak untruth only under the influence of *kali*[196] An intellect even of a ruler, who is fully aware of the dreadfulness of bad policy, also is confused in declining condition and he takes the help of untruth to save himself.[197] So untruth was not the normal tendency of a person. The righteous rulers, on the other hand never spoke untruth;[198] and were true to their words,[199] because truth was not only their great virtue but it was very essence of their life.

IMPARTIALITY : A ruler should be impartial towards his subjects. He should create trust in the minds of the people by his impartial nature. As, among hundreds of rivers there seems no disrespect for any, by the ocean so also there was no partiality from king Aja to any of his subjects and every one of his subjects thought that he was the only favourite of the king,[200] This even course of conduct of the kings was visible in their applications of daṇḍa, towards the subjects. They assumed mildness or severity according to the need of the time and situation, so they were able to control the whole world by their impartiality like the sun by his luster.[201]

RIGHTEOUSNESS AND PURITY IN CONDUCT : By the quality of righteousness, a king is respected and honored by his subjects. Kauṭilya has specially mentioned this quality in the list of king's requiremtns. According to Manu also the importance of righteousness is very great. He states- "No parents, nor wife, nor

196. Nai XVII.171
197. Kirā XIV.19
198. Supra 188
199. Raghu. XVIII.34
200. ibid, VIII.8
201. Kirā II.38

sons will be a man's friend in the next world; but only the righteousness."[201] The kings, though powerful never proceeded by a wrong path For example, the ocean though in its full tide has a way only through the mouth of a river.[202] Arjuna is described as treading the righteous path in his life.[203] the men skilled in state politics, directed the new king both fair and unfair ways but in his case the former were accepted and not the latter.[204]

The righteous kings were very prompt about the purity in their conduct and action. An integrity of character was kept as fore-front by the kings. They were themselves pure in conduct and also ever ready with their bows to wipe out the bad thoughts in the minds of the people.[205] They were the lamps to the families having pure conduct.[206] Their purity in conduct and action is mentioned frequently.[207] King Yudhiṣṭhira was attributed as 'Ācāravān.'[208]

WAKEFULNESS : Wakefulness is one of the important requirements of a king. A king should be wakeful about the minute happenings and incidents in the state and about the information about the internal and external events. The kings were watchful of the enemies who were baffled in their hostile attempts.[209]

---

201. MS, IV.239
नामुत्र हि सहायार्थं पिता माता च तिष्ठतः
न पुत्रदारा न ज्ञातिर्धर्मस्तिष्ठति केवलः ॥
202. Raghu, VII.54
203. Kirā, VI.1
204. Raghu IV.10
205. ibid. VI.39
206. ibid. VI.45
207. ibid. II.13; XII.46
208. Kirā, XI.77
209. Raghu, VIII. 23

Though they had got a central position in the circle of the kings, they were not inactive. A king should be wakeful about a probable danger from an enemy; otherwise he could not conquer his enemy who is surrounded by difficulties.[211] A wakeful king gets an advantage of the situation.

Like the watchfulness in the external policy, it was necessary for a king to be alert in the internal affairs of the state. The messenger of Yudhiṣṭhira in Kirātārjunīyam, described the vigilance of Duryodhana. Duryodhana, who had placed all around trusty guards to watch the doings of his party as well as that of the enemy; outwardly, he dealt with them with an unsuspecting air but inwardly he kept a suspicious look towards them.[212] His skill in the watchfulness lies in the manner that although he know that the servants were ya trustworthy, he did not repose absolute confidence in them. Kāmandakīya nītiāra, and Śātiparvan mention the same principle about the wakefulness of a king.[213] Thus a watchful and vigilant king about the internal and external administration and happenings is able to control the subjects as well as his enemies.

SENSE OF TIME : a quality of the exact apprehension of time for a certain decision or action, is quite essential for a king. A king who accomplishes a work considering its good and bad results and proper time,

211. Śiśu II.80

212. Kirā I.14
विधाय रक्षान्परितः परेतरानशङ्किताकारमुपैति शङ्कितः ॥
क्रियापवर्गेष्वनुजीविसात्कृताः कृतज्ञतामस्य वदन्ति सम्पदः ॥

213. KN V.88/89
अविश्वासी तथा च स्याद्यथा च व्यवहारवान् ।
विश्वासयेदविश्वस्ताविश्तवस्तान्नातिविश्वसेत् ॥
Śp (critical Edition by BORI) 86.32
विश्वासयेत्परांश्चैव विश्वसेन्न तु कस्यचित् ।
पुत्रेष्वपि हि राजेन्द्र विश्वासो न प्रशस्यते ॥

obtains success. If the time factor is duly considered then a great mission also is successfully fulfilled without any force. The king who utilizes the exact opportunity at its proper time, he is surely to get success. Deciding a policy about an enemy, this time-factor is very important for the king. If the time is favourable, he may accept even insults without being disturbed and he may strike the enemy when the proper time comes. So an application of force or mildness depends upon the proper opportunity of time, to the king who has the sense of the proper time.[213] Uddhava, an intelligent politician and minister of Kṛṣṇa explaining the various factors in the decision of the attack on Śiśupāla, urges that before the proper time and opportunity it is not possible for a valorous fighter like Kṛṣṇa to defeat Śiśupāla.[214] So the decision of a quick attack on Śiśupāla will not give them success. Thus the plea of Balarāma for an immediate attack on Śiśupāla without caring for the proper time was not accepted by Uddhava.

In Kirātārjunīyam also, Arjuna revealed this great virtue of recognition of time. After hearing the arrogant speech and a charge of the theft of an arrow by the messenger of Kirātarāja, on Arjuna, he was not perturbed because he was fully aware of the importance and effect of proper time.[215] He knew that valour was not a reply to the haughty speech of the messenger. So steady like a mountain stricken by the waves of ocean, he did not leave his patience and courage.[216]

---

213. Śiśu II.83

214. ibid. II.110

215. Kirā XIV.2

216. ibid. XIV.1
ततः किरातस्य वचोभिरुद्धते पराहता शैल इवार्णवाम्बुभिः ।
जहौ न धैर्यं कुपितोऽपि पाण्डवः सुदुर्ग्रहान्तःकरणा हि साधवः ॥

Thus a king desirous of success, should consider a time factor as very important and he should also count on an authority of time with his own strength and valour.

HOSPITALITY : The kings in the *Pañcamahākāvyas* were famous for their virtue of hospitality. The King Raghu who received kauṭsa is attributed as 'Ātitheyah'.[217] Indra, the king of gods felt a great pleasure in receiving the guests and when there was an absence of guests, he supposes himself to be under some curse.[218] He did not set a high value on his wealth which rendered vile by selfish enjoyment without the reception of guests. When Damayantī receives Nala, she specially mentions the social usage of hospitality.[219] The hospitality of the kings was comprised of gift-giving, mercy and true speech.

DUTIES OF THE KING :

While stressing the duties of a king, it is a convincing point that it is not king's rights but his duties are specially stated in the *Pañcamahākāvyas*. Kingship was not only an opportunity of enjoyment for king but it was burdened with heavy responsibilities. It is mentioned in Raghuvam'sa that the life of the kings, resembling the life of those in bonds, is opposed to the enjoyment of pleasures.[220] but the onerous duties of kingship were accomplished by the kings in an ideal manner. A complete dedication demanded for the duties was gladly offered by the ideal kings. We shall point out here the duties and obligations which were necessary for the kings to discharge.

PROTECTION OF THE SUBJECTS: According to the views of Śāstras, protection of the subjects was the first

---

217. Raghu V.2

218. Nai V.16

219. ibid VIII 20/21/22

220. Raghu XVIII.18

and foremost duty of a king.[221] It is stated before that an intention behind the origin of a king was the need of protection of the people from harassing powers. The kings in the *Pañcamahākāvyas* were fully aware of the significance of the word *'Ksatriya'* and the duties of a *Kṣatriya* king. *A Kṣatriya* is he, who protects the people from destruction.[222] In the third canto of Kirātārjunīyam, while bidding farewell to Arjuna for the performance of penance, Draupadī reminds him that he is truly a *Kṣatriya* who is able to protect the persons needing protection.[223] She also makes him remember that *Brahmā* has created the victorious Kṣatriyahood for the protection of the world.[224]

This duty of protection is comprised of various aspects. A protection was to be done of the weak from the stronger, from the internal calamities, and robbers etc. and from the external attacks of the enemies. The subjects was protected by the dutiful kings from all these sides. Not only the weak but all the living beings were safe and well protected in the reign of these kings' because their bodily strength was to allay tears of the distressed. (Raghu VIII.31) The sense of duty is clearly visible in the event in king Dilīp's life. A lion in the forest catches the celestial cow Nandinī which was guarded by Dilīpa and advises Dilīpa not to forsake his precious life for the sake of a mere cow. But according to king Dilīpa the high standing epithect *Kṣatra* is famous

---

221. MS VII.2; VII.144
ŚP (Critical Edition by BORI) 21.9
राज्यमेके प्रशंसन्ति सर्वेषां परिपालनम् ।
प्रजानां पालनं धर्मो राज्ञां राजीवलोचन ॥32.2

222. Raghu II.53
क्षतात्किल त्रायत इत्युदग्रः क्षत्रस्य शब्दो भुवनेषु रूढः !
राज्येन किं तद्विपरीतवृत्तेः प्राणैरुपक्रोशमलीमसैर्वा ॥

223. Kirā III.48

224. ibid. III.41

in all over the world for the meaning that it protects others from death, so a person who behaves contrary to this, then what is the use of his life and kingdom? According to him an observance of duty for the sake of protection of the needy is itself a lasting reward. So Dilīpa urges the lion to be kind to his body in the form of fame and release the cow. In Naiṣadhīyacarita, King Nala caught the golden swan; at that time the other birds rebuked him by their cries, having left the earth as if saying, "it is not worthwhile to live on this earth whose lord has renounced a customary conduct of a king to protect the beings."[225]

It was the foremost duty of a king to protect his subjects and kingdom from the calamities of two types Divine and Human. The divine calamities were fire flood, epidemics, famine and pestilance, as is mentionsd in Agnipurāna.[226] Drought, attack of grass- hoppers etc. are some more calamities by Nature. King Nala rendered free the earth from all the evils known as 'itis' He even prevented the excessive rains throughout the earth.[227] The subjects of King Dilīpa was experiencing a stable life free from fears and other social calamities because their dutyful king, through the influence of the meritorious act of austerity of the precepter had accomplished the task of the protection of the subjects from the calamities.[228] About the able reign of Daśaratha,

---

225. Nai I.128

226. AP 241.14/15
हुताशनो जलंव्याधिर्दुभिक्ष्यं मरकं तथा।
इति पञ्चविधं दैवं व्यसनं मानुषं परम्।
दैवं पुरुषकारेण शान्त्या च प्रशमन्नयेत्॥

227. Nai I.11

228. Raghu I.63
पुरुषायुषजीविन्यो निरातङ्का निरीतयः।
यन्मदीयाः प्रजास्तस्य हेतुस्त्वद्ब्रह्मवर्चसम्॥

it is described that no disease stepped in. his country; so how can there be ravages by the enemies.[229]

A king should protect his subjects from the thieves and robbers and create a sense of security in the minds of the people. A belief in the protection and security of their life and property of the subjects was created by the kings in full extent. King Duryodhana had warded off all the disturbances by his universal protection.[230] In the reign of King Dilīpa there was not a single crime such as theft etc. So he had no prisoners to whom he could liberate on the happy occasion of the birth of his son.[231] Other kings could not imitate his fame as a guardian of the people and 'theft' was the word remained only in the hearing of men.[232] King Atithī protected asceticism from obstacles and wealth from the robbers.[233]

The king has to protect the people not only from robbers and dacoits but from other anti-social elements. Kauṭilya advises the king to expel the 'Rāṣtropaghātakās' from the cities and villages to the frontiers of the state. Agnipurāṇa stresses the idea mentioning that people should be protected against five dangers. Soldiers, thieves, officers of the king, king's favourites and the ruler's greed. (AP 239.46)

Thus a considerable security and protection was being obtained by the subjects of the dutyful kings. The subjects were fully dependent upon the rulers for their protection. It is mentioned that one should obtain a king and after that wife and wealth because in the absence of king there is no guarantee of wife and

---

229. Raghu IX.4
230. Kirā I.18
231. Raghu III.20
232. ibid. I.27
233. ibid. XVII.65

wealth.[234] While stating this important duty of the king, Agnipurāṇa holds that sacrifice and penance of a king is meaningless if his subjects is not protected.[235] Kauṭilya lays down that the happiness of the king lies in the happiness of the subjects.[236] The king is frequently attributed as *'Goptā*[237] and *'Śaraṇya'*. An efficiency of king's administration lies in making the life and property of the subjects secure. The duty of protection was fulfilled by the kings in the *Pañcamahākāvyas* in an excellent manner that the subjects were supposing them as the protectors even from the god of death.[238] Kauṭsa in Raghuvaṁśa offers a full-fledged credit to the king as how can evil happen to subjects as he is the protector of them [239] Thus the happiness and containment of his subjects was the real receipt for the dutyful kings.

Not only protection of the subjects, but a *Paternal View Of Kingship,* was the salient feature of ancient Indian Polity, which is clearly visible in our *Pañcamahākāvyas.* The kings were the fathers of their subjects, due to protection, education and maintenance and their real fathers were only the generating causes.[240]

---

234. ŚP (Critical Edition by BORI) 57.41
राजानं प्रथमं विन्देत्ततो भार्या ततो धनम् ।
राजन्यसति लोकस्य कुतो भार्या कुतो धनम् ॥

235. AP 223.9
किं यज्ञैस्तपसा तस्य प्रजा यस्य न रक्षिताः ।
सुरक्षिताः प्रजा यस्य स्वर्गस्तस्य गृहोपमः ॥

236. KA I.19
प्रजासुखे सुखं राज्ञः प्रजानां च हिते हितम् ।
नात्मप्रियं हितं राज्ञः प्रजानां तु प्रियं हितम् ॥

237. Ragu II.24/30/60

238. ibid. XV.57

239. ibid. V.13

240. ibid. I.24
प्रजानां विनयाधानाद्रक्षणाद्भरणादपि ।
स पिता पितरस्तासां केवलं जन्महेतवः ॥

In the event, in which the lion reminds the king about his duty, the affection of the king about his subjects is seen. The Lion urges the king, not to lose his valuable life for a single cow because preserving his own life he, the lord of people, can ever protect the subjects, as their father.[241] A climax of the affectionate relation about subjects is seen, when a king is mentioned at the same time a father of his subjects and also a son of the subjects. The king dispelling the fear of obstacles in their religious and other performances was their father and he removing the grief of his subjects was their son.[242] Thus a king can create a belief in the minds of the people that they may rely for protection and security on their king. In Kirātārjunīyam, the messenger of Yudhiṣṭhira narrates the account about Duryodhana. He says - "With his arrogance set aside, with sincerity, he behaves with his servants, as if they were his affectionate friends; his friends as if they commanded the respect due to relatives and his relatives as if they were the possessors of the sovereignty.[243] This account shows that an arrogant king like Duryodhana had to set aside his defects to conquer the minds of his subjects.

The ideal of fatherly affection towards the subjects, which is reflected in the *Pañcamahākāvyas*, is clearly seen in the ancient Indian Polity, as stated before. According to Manu a king should behave like a father towards his subjects.[244] Due to his compassion towards people he is father of the nation.[245] in the advice of *Rājadharma*

241. Raghu II.48

242. ibid. XIV.23

243. Kirā I.10

244. MS VII.80
सांवत्सरिकमाप्तैश्च राष्ट्रादाहारयेद् बलिम् ।
स्याच्चधाम्नायपरो लोके वर्तेत पितृवन्नृषु ॥

245. ŚP (Critical Edition by BORI) 137.100
पिता हि राजा राष्ट्रस्य प्रजानां योऽनुकम्पकः ।

the great sage Vyāsa says -"casting aside the lust anger etc. you have to maintain equalness of mind like a father.[246] Kauṭilya, a true politician also has accepted the paternal attitude of kingship.[247] A king who treads the path of dhrama is expected to show a paternal relation towards his subjects.[248]

But this affection of the people towards their king was not blind. The subjects was wakeful for the duties of the king. The king as a supporter and upholder of law was seen as an ideal and his unimpeachable conduct in every respect was demanded by subjects. The notion[249] that evils and mishaps in the kingdom were caused by the wrongs of the ruler, made them more watchful about their ruler. The *brāhmaṇa* in Raghuvaṁśa dared to charge the premature death of his son to the misrule of Rāma, who being ashamed, at once started for dispelling the cause of unjustice towards the *brāhmaṇa*.[250] So the kings had to consider the emotions of the subjects. The kings strongly dreaded public infamy, and so we may argue that in this connection, the position of the people was somewhat higher than the king, though not from the constitutional point of view. Due to the influence of the public opinion, the kings had to take unfavourable decisions effecting even their personal lives. It can be said that as a lord of the subjects, a king had no such personal life. An event in Rāma's life proves this fact. Though Rāma was confident about the innocence of Sītā, the public

---

246. ŚP (Critical Edition by BORI) 25.13

247. KA IV.3. 43

248. AP 223.32
रक्षेच्च सर्वतस्त्वेनं पिता पुत्रमिवौरसम् ।
संरक्ष्यमाणो राज्ञा यः कुरुते धर्ममन्वहम् ॥

249. ŚP (Critical Edition by BORI) 92.8 to 10
राजैव कर्ता भूतानां राजैव च विनाशकः ।

250. Raghu XV. 42 to 48

reproach weighed higher to his consideration and he had to take the notice of the scandal about Sītā, in subjects,[251] which effected in the decision of her abandonment. In the case of Aja, when his loving wife died, he did not consign his body to flames with his queen, not because he cared for his life but because he apprehended the scandal that the king died after his queen through grief.[252]

Thus considering public opinions, expelling their dangers and griefs, pleasing them, was the chief part of king's duty. The ward rājā though derived from the root *rāj* (to shine) is in Hindu polity generally associated with the root *rañj* (to please). This derivation is clearly seen in our Raghuvaṁśa. While describing king Raghu the poet says- "He became king in the real sense of the word on account of pleasing disposition towards the subjects as the moon on account of its power to please and the sun on account of his brightness.[253] In the sixth canto, the king named 'Paranṭapa' is described as obtaining fame by ever pleasing this subjects.[254] In this primary duty of pleasing the subjects even a complete dedication by the kings, if needed, was expected as an eternal *dharma;*[255] and the demand was fulfilled in excellent manner by the ideal kings.

PROTECTION OF VARṄADHARMA : Upholding of the *varṇadharma* constitutes an important duty of the king. According to Manu the king was created to protect

---

251. Raghu XIV.40
अवैमि चैनामनघेति किंतु लोकापवादो बलवान्मतो मे ।
छाया हि भूमेः शशिनो मलत्वेनारोपिता शुद्धिमतः प्रजाभिः ॥
252. ibid. VIII.72
253. ibid. IV.12
254. Raghu VI.21
255. ŚP (Critical Edition by BORI) 57.11
लोकरञ्जनमेवात्रराज्ञां धर्मः सनातनः ।
सत्यस्य रक्षणं चैव व्यवहारस्य चार्जवम् ॥

the laws of Varnāśrama.[256] It is worthy to be noted that Somadevasūri, a jain writer, accepted the vedic authority and the duty of the king to see whether the rules of *varṇāśramas* are observed by people and no one transgresses the prescribed code of conduct.[257] Protection of *Varṇadharma* an aspect of king's duties was so inevitable that it was equal to the meaning of ruling the kingdom. For instance in Raghuvaṁśa, when the prince Devānīka succeeded the royal throne it is described that king Kṣemadhanvā placed the yoke of the four castes to his son.[258] The rulers were careful about the protection and welfare of the *Varnāśrama* specially of the hermits in the forests. It may further be added that the king's duty to protect was not limited only to the townsmen and and the countrymen but also extended to the hermits living in the forest.

Protection of the religious performances and sacrifices was the important duty of a king. They protected the sacrifices from the disturbances of demons. The sage Viśvāmitra begged for Rāma to protect the sacrificial ceremonies from the obstacles of rākṣasas.[259] A king was not only their protector but was their universal refuge. The ascetics were able to destroy the obstacles through their spiritual power, but they had a profound belief in their protectors so they did not strike the devils with the power of asceticism. The curse-armed sages used their weapon only in the absence of the

---

256. MS VII.35
स्वे स्वे धर्मे निविष्टानां सर्वेषामनुपूर्वशः ।
वर्णानामाश्रमाणां च राजा सृष्टोऽभिरक्षिता ॥

257. NV VII.2
त्रयीतः खलु वर्णाश्रमाणां धर्माधर्मव्यवस्था ।

258. Raghu XVIII.12
पूर्वस्तयोरात्मसमे चिरोढामात्मोदभवे वर्णचतुष्टयस्य ।
धुरं निधायैकनिधिर्गुणानां जगाम मज्वा यजमानलोकम् ॥

259. ibid. XI.1/2

sages used their weapon only in the absence of the protector-king.[260] When the hermits residing on the banks of Yamunā, whose sacrificial rites were being destroyed by the demon named Lavaṇa, came to Rāma, for protection and Rāma promised them to protect them from the distress; because the tendency of the wielder of 'Śārṅga' was for the protection of righteousness.[261] Sītā who was abandoned by Rāma, reminds him through Lakṣmaṇa the duty of a *Kṣtriya-king*. She sends a message to Rāma. "The protection of the different castes and their stages of life, is the duty of a king laid down by Manu. So even though I am banished by you, I deserve to be protected by you in common with other ascetics.[262] In Kirātārjunīyam Arjuna attributes the Kṣatriyas as worthy for the protection of varṇadharma.[263]

A king protects *varṇadharma* punishing the defaulters and transgressors of the rules and regulations, because it affects the whole subjects. Due to a penance performed by a Sūdra, which was a transgression of caste-rules, and untimely death of a *brāhmaṇa* child took place.[264] The dead child resorted to life again when the king punished the *Sūdra* named Śambūka.

Thus in the reign of the kings protecting and regulating the *varṇaśramadharma*, the subjects never

---

260. Raghu XV.3

261. ibid. XV.4
प्रतिशुश्राव काकुत्स्थस्तेभ्यो विघ्नप्रतिक्रियाम् ।
धर्मसंरक्षणामेव प्रवृत्तिर्भुवि शार्ङ्गिणः ॥

262. Raghu XIV.67

263. Kirā XIV. 22
वयं क्व वर्णाश्रमरक्षणोचिताः क्व जातिहीना मृगजीवितच्छिदः ।
सहापकृष्टैर्महतां न संगतं भवन्ति गोमायुसखा न दन्तिनः ॥

264. Raghu XV.51

divated out of the course tiodden from the time of Manu.[265]

WELFARE OF THE STATE : To look after the Welfare of the state and subjects was the second side of king's duty of protection. Protection was only a means to an end viz. welfare. It was expected from the rulers to fulfill the primary requirements of the people. The main stay of national welfare was agriculture, cattle-raring and trade to which, the ruler was keen to supervise. According to Kāmanḍaka, the chief aspects of national-welfare, which should be promoted by the king, are as follows - A king should promote agriculture, trade routes constructions of forts, irrigation-schemes, elephant-catching, Mining, factories and settlement of countryside.[266]

An important aspect of agriculture was sincerely promoted by the kings. The crops in the fields were not parched, but were nourished by the rain resulted by the oblations by the holy priests, offered duly in the sacrificial fires. In spite of these spiritual efforts, the kings, through their human efforts, made a provision of watering the crops, In the reign of Duryodhana, the farmers had not to depend on the rain for fertilization because the lands were well irrigated and the husbandmen were obtaining plentyful crops with ease, even without tillage.[267] King Nala had prevented excessive rains from the entire earth,[268] and by the favour of god Varuṇa, the deserts also were full of water.[269] In the

265. ibid. I.17
रेखामात्रमपि क्षुण्णादा मनोर्वर्त्मनः परम् ।
न व्यतीयुः प्रजास्तस्य नियन्तुर्नेमिवृत्तयः ॥
266. KN V. 77/78
267. Kirā I.17
268. Nai I.11
269. ibid. XIV.83

reign of the kings, careful about the welfare of the subjects, even the earth yielded treasures to them for their universal protection and to the uninterrupted prosperity of the people.[270] King Kuśa and his brothers had successfully undertaken the works of construction of bridges, agriculture trade, cattle-rearing, taming the elephants. etc. To accomplish the interests of the people the kings and also the king of gods were ready with their bows.[271] They were ever vigilant in securing the welfare of the subjects.[272]

An acquisition of the wealth by the kings was only for their subjects. When Kauṭsa was offered a heap of gold obtained from Kubera by the king Raghu, he appreciated the merits of the king, saying, there is no wonder, if the earth be a bringer forth of desires due to the incomprehensible power and the heaven has been made to yield by the king to fulfill the desires of his subjects.[273] Thus the kings with their might were able to fulfill the desires of their subjects, even employing heaven and earth.

JUDICIAL DUTIES OF THE KING AND COURT OF JUSTICE :

Administration of justice was held to be an important and sacred duty of a king. Due punishment to the culprits helped the virtuous, to follow the established rules of the society. The subjects in the kingdom of such a king were assured who could give them justice. Punishing the wrong-doers, for the maintenance of social stability. In order to prevent the

---

270. Kirā I.18
अुदारकीर्तेरुदयं दयावतः प्रशान्तबाधं दिशतोऽभिरक्षया ।
स्वयं प्रदुग्धेऽस्य गुणैरुपस्नुता वसूपमानस्य वसूनि मेदिनी ॥

271. Raghu IV.16

272 ibid. XVIII.9

273. ibid. V.33

law of jungle, it was extremely desirable that there should be a central authority to protect the rights of the weak and poor and to ensure justice for everyone in society.

In ancient India, a king was known to be the supreme judge, a final authority and the head of the judiciary.[274] There was no appelate beyond the king. Though the final judgment or punishment was in the hands of the king, the judges were appointed by him to scrutinize and investigate the cases. The word '*dharmastha-sakhā*' clearly shows that the king consulted with the experts of *Nīti* and learned counsellors as his associates. The king Atithī who was vigilant, personally looked every day into the cases of plaintiff and defendants which owing to their doubtful nature, necessarily deserved a prompt and careful discussion;[275] because in the interest of justice it was necessary that each case should be fully investigated by the experts and that punishment be awarded only when the accused was found guilty. So before taking decisions in the cases of defendants and plaintiffs, the king should collect the opinions of jury and counsellors. The advice of the jury was accepted by the king. According to ancient law-books a king should partake the judicial functions with the learned brāhmaṇas.[276] The king Rāma used to attend the council-hall with his courtiers.[277]

---

274. NS I.307
ग्रामे दृष्टं पुरे याति पुरे दृष्टस्तु राजनि ।
राज्ञा दृष्टः कुदृष्टो वा नास्ति पौनर्भुवो विधिः ॥

275. Raghu XVII.39
स धर्मस्यसखः शश्वदार्थिप्रत्यर्थिनां स्वयम् ।
ददर्श संशयच्छेद्यान्व्यवहारानतन्द्रितः ॥

276. YS II.1व्यवहारानृपः पश्येद्विद्वद्भिर्ब्राह्मणैः सह ।

277. Raghu XV.39
स ददर्श सभामध्ये समासद्भिरुपस्थितम् ।
रामं सीतापरित्यागादसामान्यपतिं भवः ॥

The king was expected to attend the justice-hall daily. That is why, the ancient law makers had included this duty in his daily time-table.[278] The young king Aja occupied the judgment seat in order to look into the cases of his subjects.[279]

A king by his impartial justice, should create a trust about security, in the minds of his subjects. While seated on the seat of justice, a king observing the vow of *Yama,* should be free from malice and be impartial to all. (NS- 1.34) In kirātārjunīyam Duryodhana is depicted as a impartical judge in his court. he checked infringement of duty (crime) by inflicting punishment according to the advice of the judges. He punished defaulters on the part of his son or a foe giving equal justice.[280] King Raghu on account of his just punishments like the southern breeze, nither too not hot too cold, won the hearts of his subjects.[281] For, the effective enforcement of law, means the authority to punish the defaultors, was invested in the King. As *Daṇḍa* was the protector of makind, a king was expected that he should not employ it arbitrarily. If it be used badly it was sure to ruin even the king himself alongwith his family and belongings.[282] Because of impartical justice, a common man in society also dares to step before the king for justice. The Śambūka-incident in Raghuvaṁśa reveals that the king personally punished the transgressor of the rules of *Varṇāśramadharma* and the subjects dared to blame the king who was expected to give justice.

---

278. KA I.19.10, 26
द्वितीये पौरजानापदानां कार्याणि पश्येत् ।
अपस्थानगतः कार्यार्थिनामद्वारासङ्गं कारयेत् ॥
279. Raghu, VIII.18
280. Kirā I.13
281. Raghu IV.8
282. MS VII 19/28

From some scattered references, we can state that there were different kinds of punishments. The punishments were according to the guilts of the persons. Imprisonment was a main feature of Indian punishment. The offenders were imprisoned for the unlawful acts.[283] As mercy was the part of king's justice, the kings released the prisoners from the bondage at the time of happy occasions. Death-penalty,[284] cutting of the organs of the body[285] etc. were included in the punishments.

The punishments, in the judicial administration in ancient India, reveal one important fact. The punishments were caste-ridden. *Brāhmaṇas* were punished lightly in comparison with other castes. It was inevitable effect of the caste-system that the differences in penalties were seen for the same crime, depending on the caste of the offender. From the ancient period of *Brāhmaṇas* the brahmin-caste was considered to be a superior class in the society, so this class was exempted from punishments, According to the legal texts, a *brāhmaṇa* must not be subjected to corporal punishment, he must not be imprisoned, fined or exiled.[286] Manu also mentions that brāhmaṇa might not be killed though guilty.[287] Kauṭilya remarks whatever may be the nature of the crime, no *brāhmaṇa* offender should be tortured; the king should only banish him or send him to the mines of life.[288] King Rāma in Raghuvaṁśa did not

283. Raghu III.20
284. ibid. XVII.19
285. ibid. XII.40
286. Gautama Dharmasūtra VIII.13
287. MS VIII.380
न जातु ब्राह्मणं हन्यात्सर्व पापेष्वपि स्थितम् ।
राष्ट्रादेनं बहिः कुर्यात्समग्रधनमक्षतम् ॥
288. KA IV.8.27 सर्वापराधेष्वपीडनीयो ब्राह्मणः ।
IV.8.29
ब्राह्मणं पापकर्माणमुद्धष्याङ्ककृतव्रणम् ।
कुर्यान्निर्विषयं राजा वासयेदाकरेषु वा ॥

raise his bow to kill the sage Parśurāma the destroyer of Kṣatriyas because he was brāhmaṇa by caste.[289]

According to the law-books, the term *'Vyavahāra'* is applied in the sense of legal dispute, law suit or legal approach towards a transaction. M.M. P.V. Kāne explains this word as 'means of deciding the matter,[290] Raghuvaṁśa mentions the word *Vyavahāra* but the distinction of the legal procedure and punishment between the civil and criminal cases is not distinctly referred in the *Pañcamahākāvyas*. In the legal procedure two types of evidences were used. These were human and divine. Written documents, actual possession and witnesses constitute the first type of evidence while the different types of ordeals come under the second type.

Here the second type of investigation by ordeals is discussed with its specific aspects. Trial by ordeal was considered as an important aspect of judicial procedure. A person, whose guilt or innocence was not proved by means of other evidences he was given an opportunity to prove his innocence by means of ordeals. In a society in which considerable influence of religion was visible, it was natural that ordeals should be considered valid. According to Spellman - "Once, the idea of the personal intercession of the gods for human ends is accepted, then ordeal which is a manifestation of divine truth, becomes the best method of determining guilt.'[291] Yājñyavalkya holds that a person charged with major or serious offence must be tested by means of ordeals.[292]

---

289. Raghu XI.84

290. MM P.V. Kane, History of Dharmaśāstra, (published by BORI Poona 1946 Vol. III, p. 245/248

291. Spellman, Political Theory of Ancient India, Published by Oxford University Press, 1964. p.119

292. YS II.95
तुलाग्न्यापो विषं कोशो दिव्यानीह विशुद्धये ।
महाभियोगेष्वेतानि शीर्षकस्थेऽभियोक्तरि ॥

Different ordeals are stated for different classes of people.[293] From these ordeals, the fire-ordeal is stated in Raghuvaṁśa. The ordeal was not ordered by any judge but the dignified queen Sītā herself experienced it to prove her chastity through the fire. The ideal king knew that people would not accept her with a stain of the stay in enemy's house, without such ordeal. She proved herself to be chaste and pure by the fire-ordeal; but then also the scandal about her purity impelled the king to take the unfavorable decision of her banishment. After some period, on the request of the sage Vālmīki to accept Sītā, the king replied that she had proved her purity in the fire; but people did not believe in it so she may again create confidence in respect of her conduct in the minds of the people.[294] The incident clearly reveals the fact that the rulers, desirous of stainless character and fame and also desirous to place a model before the subjects had to prove their innocence through the ordeals. Naiṣadhīyacarita also mentions the trial by ordeal. When kali, the spirit of sin, makes a pungent attack on the system of religion and intermixture of the castes the gods defend for religious faith. In the argument the gods argued that to preserve class-purity, a murderer of a high chaste man was detected by means of ordeals.[295] The ordeals like an ordeal of water, fire and others are mentioned but not described in details.

An impartial sense of justice was the prime duty of a king on whom the subjects could rely. Not only this. but it was believed that a punishment by the king

---

293. YS II.98
तुलास्त्रीबालवृद्धान्धपङ्गु ब्राह्मण रोगिणाम् ।
अग्निर्जलं वा शूद्रस्य यवाः सप्त विषस्य वा ॥

294. Ragu XV.72/73

295. Nai XVII. 86

to the culprits makes them free from impurity and leads to heaven after death like other virtuous men.[296] The *śūdra* named Śambūka in Raghuvaṁśa, who transgressed the rules of *varṇadharma* was punished by the king Rāma himself, obtained the position of the virtuous, a position he could not secure even by his severe austerity.[297] Though a king was not the creator or a maker of law which was prescribed by scriptures and *dharmaśāstras*, the king was responsible for its enforcement punishing the defaulters and giving justice to the righteous. Performing this duty, the impartial judge viz. the king acquires some secondary benefits. According to Agnipurāṇa- "Piety, wealth, Fame Popularity among the people, Respectability, Firm hold on the people and above all a permanent abode in heaven are the seven benefits, that are obtained by a dutiful judge."[298]

SACRED DUTIES OF THE KING : A king is advised to perform several rites and religious performances to avert national calamities and to promote public welfare. A king should give a prominent place for rituals, not only for his own accord but for his own kingdom. It was believed that the obstacles in the devotion of deserving personages result in fruitlessness. So king Dilīpa, with his queen, served the divine cow with devoted mind.[299]

It is also incumbent on a king to perform the daily rituals. Ancient politicians made it a part of the king's

---

296. MS VIII.318
राजभिः कृतदण्डास्तु कृत्वा पापानि मानवाः ।
निर्मलाः स्वर्गमायान्ति सन्तः सुकृतिनो यथा ॥

297. Raghu XV.53

298. AP 298.83
NP I.26/27

299. Raghu I.79

daily routine.[300] A king should not neglect the daily rituals in any case; because neglecting the rituals was counted as a sin.[301] Nala performed the daily offering of *Agnīhotṛa* oblations to the triad of sacrificial fires. His worship to the sun was so perfect that the deity thought that Karṇa's devotion to him was slight. [302] In *Naiṣadhīyacarita* a whole canto (21) is offered to describe the daily rites performed by Nala.

Thus, by all these functions and duties, performing sincerely, an ideal king makes his kingdom stable and prosperous. Securing his prime duty of protection of all the beings, he obtains success. This foremost duty of protection is equated with the sacrifices, by the ancient lawmakers and politicians also. Kauṭilya compares the functions of the king to sacrifice.[303] Manu states that a king who protects his subjects according to *dharma* and chastises those who deserve punishment, offers as it were the daily oblations performed by the king. [304] Proper performance of duty is an act of religion.[305] These opinions do not make lower the importance of religious rites. But as the duty of protection is the *dharma* of a the ruler, all the other religious obligations are embraced by the concept of protection. As *Agni*

---

300. KA I. 19.17. to 23
प्रतिष्ठितेऽहनि सन्ध्यामुपासीत ।
अष्टमे ऋत्विगाचार्यपुरोहितस्वस्त्ययनानि प्रतिगृह्णीयात्..... ।
MS. VII.145
उत्थाय पश्चिमे यामे कृतशौचः समाहितः ।
हुताग्निर्ब्राह्मणांश्चार्च्य प्रविशेत्स शुभां सभाम् ॥

301. Nai XIX.24

302. ibid. XXI.32

303. KA I.19.38

304. MS VIII.306
रक्षन्धर्मेण भूतानि राजा वध्यांश्च घायतन् ।
यजतेऽहरहर्यज्ञैः सहस्रशतदक्षिणैः ॥

305. MS VIII.11

Purāṇa rightly states what is the use of the sacrifices if the king's subjects is not protected[306] Thus, performance of one's own dharma means duty, is the highest duty of a king. A famous maxim in Bhagvad-Gītā says the principle to perform one's own duty.[307]

ROYAL SUCCESSION :

After considering the merits and duties of a king, we should turn to the rights and his claim to the royal throne. A selection of the eldest son for the royal throne, was the normal mode of disposition, in ancient India. An account of the solar kings, who succeeded the throne, proves that the eldest son succeeded his father as hair to the kingdom. The germ of the law of hereditary succession goes upto vedic period. We come upon the allusions mentioning the kingdom inherited through ten generations.[308] In epic period, the normal method of royal succession was by primogeniture. The central theme of *Mahābhārata*, shows that the law of primogeniture was distinctly the operating principle. The war between karuravas and pāṇḍavas has its origin in a disputed succession. Some scattered references in *Mahābhārata* clearly indicate the royal succession by the rule of seniority. Yudhiṣtira was advised to hold the yoke of kingdom which was acquired by him through hereditary succession.[309] After the end of the great war he was advised to install the brothers and sons and

---

306. AP 223.9

307. BG II.31
स्वधर्ममपि चावेक्ष्य न विकम्पितुमर्हसि ।
धर्म्याद्धि युद्धाच्छ्रेयोऽन्यत्क्षत्रियस्य न विद्यते ॥

308. ŚB VII. 5.3.1 दशपुरुषम् राज्यम् ।

309. ŚP (Critical Edition by BORI) 23.7
पितृपैतामहे राज्ये धुरमुद्वोढुमर्हसि ।
32.3
अनुतिष्ठस्व वै राजन्पितृपैतामहं पदम् ।
ब्राह्मणेषु च यो धर्मः स नित्यो वेदनिश्चितः ॥

gradsons of the dead kings on their throne.[310] A story mentioned in Nirukṭa clearly shows how long before, Yāska the popular belief to suppose a great sin to pass over an elder brother even in marriage and other matters and it results in a serious displeasure of the gods.[311]

The traditional law of succession is clearly seen in the *Pañcamahākāvyas*. In Raghuvaṁśa, we meet the succeeding generations of the solar kings, without any clash for the royal throne. In the case of more than one princes claiming for the right of a throne, the claim goes to the elder brother. The solar princes accepted, not only the right of their elder brother but respectfully obeyed the commands of their brother, the ruling king, This excellent brotherly feeling was a hereditary virtue of their dynasty.[312] The princes in the solar race were not greedy for the royal throne, on the contrary, they accepted the royal throne as their inevitable duty. Rāma and Bharata the princes exihibited an ideal brotherly feeling in the matter of the right of succession.

When Bharata came to know the account of snatching away the right of the proper claimant, the devoted brother was aversed to the desire for the thirst of the kingdom.[313] He protected the kingdom as if he

---

310. ibid. 34.31

311. Nirukṭa II.10
देवापिश्चार्ष्टिषेणः शन्तनुश्च कौरव्यौ भ्रातरो बभूवतुः।
स शन्तनुः क नी या न भिद्येचयाञ्चक्रे।
देवापिस्तपः प्रतिपेदे। ततः शन्तनोः
राज्ये द्वादश वर्षाणि देवो नववर्ष।
तमूचुर्ब्राह्मणाः अधर्मस्त्वयाचरितो ज्येष्ठं भ्रातरमन्तरित्याभिषेचितम्,
तस्मात्ते देवो न वर्षतीति।
स शन्तनुर्देवापिं शिक्षित राज्येन तमुवाच देवापिः
पुरोहितस्तेऽस्मानि याजयानि च त्वे ति।

312. Raghu XVI.1

313. ibid. XII.19

was trustee of his brother's kingdom.[314] Rāma who was aware of the devotion of Bharata to him, says that Bharata kept the promise of father and protected the kingdom not polluted by enjoyment. He in his youth also did not enjoy the fortune, transmitted to him by his father and he had followed as it were a practice of *Asidhārāvrata* for fourteen years.[315] This whole account is admirable, when the elder brother leaves the claim to the throne and the younger brother protects the kingdom, as a trustee. Not only this, but, Bharata considers himself to be a 'parivettā' by accepting the earth when his elder brother had not accepted the royal Fortune (Raghu XII.16), In Rāmāyaṇa also Bharata seems to be urgefully denying the wish of the people, to accept the royal throne.[316] It was the tradition of the Ikṣvāku family that a younger brother was not crowned when the elder existed.[317]

The successor of the kingdom was expected to be meritorious. Kuśa succeeded the royal throne because he was the eldest due to both aspects, by birth and by personal virtues also. According to Kāmanḍaka a disciplined son should be installed on a throne by a king.[318] The princes succeeding the throne in the solar dynasty were well disciplined.[319]

A succession of the eldest son, to the royal throne was inevitable, as the society was situated in the

---

314. Raghu XII.18
315. ibid. XIII.65/67
316. R II. 73.7
ज्येष्ठस्य राजता नित्यमुचिता हि कुलस्य नः ।
नैवं भवन्तौ मां वक्तुमर्हन्ति कुशला जनाः ॥
317. R II.110.36
औक्ष्वाकूणां हि सर्वेषां राजा भवति पूर्वजः ।
पूर्वजे नावरः पुत्रो ज्येष्ठो राजाभिषिच्यते ॥
318. KN VII.6 विनीतमौरसं पुत्रं यौवराज्येऽभिषेचयेत् ।
319. Raghu III. 35; XVIII.18

framework of *Varṇaśrama*. Alongwith the common people, the kings observed the rules and regulations of the four life-stages viz. the *āśramas*. In the third stage of life, they accepted the ascetic-life setting the yoke of the kingdom upon their young sons.[320] It was the family-vow of the Iksvākū-kings to entrust the royal insignia to their youthful sons and to accept the forest-life suitable for a sage.[321] Naturally, there seems to be no problem of snatching away of the royal throne by the princes as feared by ancient politicans. Kāmandaka has mentioned the probable perils, when there are more claimants for the royal throne.[322] According to Kauṭilya a king who protects himself from his sons, relatives and even queen is able to protect his kingdom.[323] The prudent poet of Raghuvaṁśa was aware of this red-signal indicated by the politicians. While depicting the modest prince Aja, he says —"The kingdom, which the sons of the kings strive to come by even foul means, was accepted by 'Aja, not out of thirst for enjoyment but out of regard to the command of his father.[324] Not only this, but the newly installed king Aja desired that his father, who was desirous to accept the ascetic stage, should not leave him.[325] Thus observing the regulations of life-stages the ideal kings

320. Raghu VIII.11
321. ibid. III.70
322. KN VII.2
राजपुत्रा मदोद्वृत्ता गजा इव निरङ्कुशाः
भ्रातरं कापि निध्नन्ति पितरं वाभिमानिनः ॥
323. KA I.17.1
रक्षितो राजा राज्यं रक्षत्यासन्नेभ्य परेभ्यश्च ।
पूर्व दारेभ्यः पुत्रेभ्यश्च ।
324. Raghu VII.2
दुरितैरपि कर्तृमात्मसात्प्रयतन्ते नृपसूनवो हि यत् ।
तदुपस्थितमग्रहीदजः पितुराज्ञेति न भोगतृष्णया ॥
325. ibid. VIII.12

bestowed the royal throne to their sons and the modest sons, who aversed from the desire of royal power, accepted the throne, only to obey their father.

Ancient politicians have not permitted the women as the successors of the throne. According to them, the rights of women were restricted by their natural limitations. According to them, women cannot give protection to the subjects, because they themselves need protection from others.[326] Kauṭilya seems to be of the similar opinion. According to him, if a king does not get modest and humble son, then he should endeavour to get a son from his daughter.[327] A suggestion of this remedy shows that he did not permit to install the daughter of the king as a heir. While supporting these opinions Prof. A.S. Altekar mentions. - a Hindu law did not permit an only daughter to succeed her father as a ruling queen and suggests that the majority of constitutional writers opposed the succession of women to the throne, because their natural limitations prohibit them from being efficient administrators.[328]

But it was not a rigid rule. For instance, after the end of the Great war, Bhīṣma advised Yudhiṣṭhara to install the sons and brothers of the dead kings and to install on the throne, the daughters of those, who have no sons.[329] An installation of the widow of the dead king Agnīvarṇa in Raghuvaṁśa is the shining instance to prove the point under discussion. King Agnivarṇa died due to the incurable disease viz. consumption and left no issue. The queen, who was bearing the auspicious signs of pregnancy, was installed on the royal throne

326. MS IX.9

327. KA I.17.49 पुत्रिकापुत्रानुत्पादयेद्वा ।

328. A.S. Altekar, State and Government in Ancient India, (Published by Motilal Banarasidas 1962) p.87/88

329. ŚP (Critical Edition by BORI) 34-33
कुमारो नास्ति येषां च कन्यास्तत्राभिषेचय ।

by the ministers. This decision of the watchful ministers was quite correct to keep the kingdom stable where no scope was kept for the seditious powers, internal as well as external due to the absence of the king. The queen who was seated on the golden throne, efficiently ruled the kingdom according to the rules laid down by *śāstras,* with her commands never disputed.[330] *She proved to be an able administrator, an exceptional case, inspite of her womanhood* This shows that incidentally the queens in the royal dynasty ruled the kingdom very efficiently.

POSITION OF THE LADIES IN ROYAL DYNASTY :

In connection with the topic of the royal succession, the incident of the installation of King Agnīvarṇa's widow, on the royal throne and her able administration, are enough to prove that the women in royal dynasty were capable for the dignity and right in the royal succession; and inspite of the constitutional restrictions of the ancient politicians the ministers and the subjects willingly accepted their queen as their real administration.

Apart from the question of the constitutional rights, the ladies in the royal dynasties mentioned in *Pañcamahākāvyas* revealed a considerable influence in the political field. It will not be out of place to state the position of the women viz. the queens in the *Pañcamahākāvyas,* their impression and knowledge of polity.

Generally, in the Hindu society having the patriarchal pattern of family-life, 'man' had got more privileged position than a woman. it was not surprising that the performance of vows, penances and sacrifices were for the sake of son[331] and not for a daughter; because son was the perpetuator of the family-line who delivered

330. Raghu XIX.57

331. ibid. I.34/35; X.4

his father from hell.[332] But the daughters also were brought up with fond care and love with all comforts in the house of their father.[333] Alongwith other arts they acquired the knowledge of *śāstras* and *smṛtis*. They were conversant with *Rājadharma*.[334] Though, they did not take an active part in the administrative functions, they were efficient counsellors of the kings.[335] The sweet and courteous manner of a wife's counsel has become proverbial in sanskrit literature.[336] In this connection, Draupadī in Kirātārjuniyam shines prominently. She was aware of the fact that an advice given by a woman to a person like Yudhiṣṭhira, is like an insult to him, but the mental pains she had suffered, dared her to overstep the bounds of conduct proper for women.[337] She could not bear the peace policy of Yudhiṣṭhira towards the wicked enemies. So the spiritual queen of Pāndavas performed her duty as a dutiful wife to advise the king. Considering the straightforward policy of Yudhiṣṭhira against the crooked policy of Duryodhana, she dares to say Yudhiṣṭhira that the persons of dull intellect meet with defeat, who do not use fraud against fraud.[338] She was bold enough to charge that he was the only king who had let not only the kingdom but his own wife wrested by the enemy.[339] As a chaste wife, the miserable condition of her husbands occasioned by the enemies, tears her heart but as a spiritual queen, her anger is roused by Yudhiṣṭhira's

---

332. Raghu I.66/67/68/69
333. Ku I.27
334. Raghu XIV.67
335. ibid, VIII.67
336. Kāvya- Prakāśa I.2
     कान्तासंमिततया उपदेशयुजे ।
337. kirā I.28
338. Kirā I.30
339. ibid. I.31

inactiveness. As a dutiful counsellor and not only as a wife, she wants to stimulate his self-respect and enterprise because she knows that people do not show respect to the person devoid of self-respect.[340] According to her opinion peace policy behoves to sages free from worldly desires and not fit for the kings desirous of conquest.[341] She taunts him that if he supposes forbearance as the means of happiness, he should give up the bow, the emblem of Royalty and give oblations to the sacred fire, wearing matted hair.[342] She urges him to give up the inactiveness and to display his valour to regain his lost kingdom.

As a wife, she expected to be protected by her husbands; because protection of wife was the prime duty of a husband; not only because she belonged to the weaker sex, but also because, she was a symbol of his personal and family honour. The word 'Pati' comprises the same meaning.[343] The same expectation of protection, not due to the relation of a wife, but as an ascetic in common, is expressed by Sītā in Raghuvamśa. When she came to know about her abandonment, from Laksmaṇa, she sent a message to Rāma her husband that though she has been banished, she deserved to be looked upon by him as a hermit in common as the duty of a king laid down by Manu.[344] Here Sītā also reveals the same spirit as that of Draupadī to remind the king his duty prescribed by *Smṛti*. A wounded heart of Sītā is seen in her message that the king has abandoned her who was purified in the fire

---

340. Kirā I.33
अवन्ध्य कोपस्य विहन्तुरापदां भवन्ति वश्याः स्वयमेव देहिनः ।
अमर्षशून्येन जन्तुना न जातहार्देन न विद्विषादरः ॥

341. ibid. I.42

342. ibid. I.44

343. Kirā XI.52

344. Supra Ref. No. 334

in his presence. After listening to the malicious report of the people, she did not utter any harsh word to her husband,[345] but wished him to be her husband again, without separation, in the coming births.

Thus the spirited ladies in the royal dynasty had shown a great courage and boldness to guide their husbands, viz. the king reminding their duty as a ruler. The queens were partners of their husbands not only in the sacrificial performances but in the duties like the protection of the subjects.[346] Though the queens never disregarded their husbands[347] and considered them as a veritable deity,[348] their love was not blind but it stimulated them to keep the dignity of their family. With a true chivaorous spirit of *Kṣatriya* wife, Draupadī asks Arjuna not to feel disconsolate on account of the separation but reminds him their insults by enemies and also reminds the concealed valour of Pāṇḍavas to make Arjuna enthusiastic for the penance. She also reminds him the duty of a Kṣatriya King[349] and to be watchful against the internal enemies also.[350]

A dignified spirit of Pārvatī shines forth in Kumārasaṁbhava; though not with political aspects. She was a loving daughter of Himālaya and Menā. All the earth was pleased by her birth. She desired Lord Śiva to be her consort, but Śiva the self restrained ascetic burnt the cupid who through the help of the extra ordinary beauty of Pārvatī tried to tempt him. It was the insult of her beauty, but the resolute Pāravtī determined to conquer Śiva by a severe penance. her

345. Raghu XIV.57
346. ibid. XIV.64
347. ibid. VIII.48
348. ibid. IX.22; XIV.74
349. Kirā III.38/41
350. ibid. III.53

penance was so formidable that the other ascetics offered her pre-eminent place among all. A tender princess, due to her firm spirit successfully trade the path of penance through which she acquired her desired consort. Like Pārvati, Damayantī in Naiṣadhīyacarita, acquired her consort Nala, passing through all the deceitful means of the four gods by her devotion.

FOUR VIDYĀS AND EDUCATION OF THE KING :

In *Nītivākyāmṛta,* it is stated that anarchy is preferable in comparison to the rule of an illiterate king.[351] In order to prepare the prince to eminently shoulder his responsibilities of administration, a great attention was paid to his education and training. Almost all the Indian writers on *Dharmaśāstra* and *Arthaśāstra* emphasize, not only an education of a prince but also his moral discipline. Though a great divergence of views in connection with the number of the *vidyās* prevailed,[352] Kauṭilya and others[353] had accepted the four main *Vidyās* viz. *Ānvīkṣikī Trayī, Vārtā* and *Daṇḍanīti,* in the education of a prince. Somadevasūri mentions them as 'Rājavidyā[354]

---

351. NV V.37
वरमराजकं भुवनं न तु मूर्खो राजा ।

352. KA I.1.2/3
त्रयीवार्तादण्डनीतिश्चेति मानवाः ।
वार्तादण्डनीतिश्चेति बार्हस्पत्याः ।
दण्डनीतिरेका विद्येत्यौज्ञनसाः ।

353. KA I.2.8
चतस्त्र अेव विद्याऽति कौटिल्यः ।
MS VII.43
त्रयी विद्येभ्यस्त्रयीं विद्यां दण्डनीतिश्च शाश्वतीम् ।
आन्वीक्षिकीं चात्मविद्यां वार्तारम्भांश्च लोकताम् ।
KN II.2, ŚN I.152, AP 238.8

354. NV V.55
आन्वीक्षिकी त्रयीवार्तादण्डनीतिरिति चतस्त्रो राजविद्याः ।

The kings in the *Pañcamahākāvyas,* were aware of acquiring the essential education, from their childhood, Prince Raghu after his tonsure ceremony, learnt his letters and entered into the great ocean of learning;' and by his sublime genius he acquired the four lores resembling the four oceans.[355] In Kirātārjunīyam, Bhīma mentions specially *Ānvīkṣikī* by which one is able to discriminate wrong and right.[356] These four *vidyās* are hereditary learning, the instructions of which is essential for an administrator.[357] They work as an eye of the three worlds.[358]

We have to explain here in details, what is meant by these four *vidyās,* and how they help the administrator. The first is *Ānvīkṣikī* means logic or the lore of reasoning. *Ānvīkṣikī* examines the relative strength of the other three *vidyās* with reasoning and thereby benefits the world, gives quietitude to the mind in calamity as well as in prosperity and imparts excellence in ntellect, speech and action. According to Kauṭilya *Ānvīkṣikī* is not only a science of reasoning, but it comprehends *Sāñkhya, Yoga* and *lokāyata.* It looks strange that the word *lokāyata* which means 'atheist or materialist' in later literature is included in *Ānvīkṣikī,* but Kauṭilya uses it only in the sense of logic based on premises desired from ordinary experience. So *Anvīkṣikī* is the torch of all the vidyās.[359] Kāmanḍaka explains it as metaphysics. In śukranīti, we see a combination of the above two meanings.[360]

---

355. Raghu III.30
356. Kirā II.6
357. Ragu XVII.3
358. Nai XVII.5
359. KA I.2.12
प्रदीपः सर्वविद्यानामुपायः सर्वकर्मणाम् ।
आश्रयः सर्वधर्माणां शश्वदान्वीक्षिकी मता ॥
360. ŚN I.152

A prudent administrator, on the ground of reasoning, takes into account, the pros and cons of the problem and solves it relying on *Ānvīkṣikī*. in Kirātārjunīyam, Bhīma is surprised to see the inactiveness of *Yudhiṣṭhira*, because the intellect of Yudhiṣṭhira which was grounded by the four *vidyās* now reversed itself and unable to discriminate wrong and right.

'Trayī' or the study of three *vedas* is the second essential *Vidya* included in the curriculum of the king's education. The knowledge of the three vedas is like the eyes of the three world,[361] or it is the third eye of the king.[362] The work of this eye was to show subtle purposes to be achieved by the king.[363] *Dharma* and its opposite were learnt by the kings through the three vedas. The framework of Hindu society was moulded by the for urcastes and four life-stages and king's duty was to make the people observe the rules and regulations of the varṇāśramas, so the king had to rely on the vedas, and he was required to be well-versed in the *vedas* to know the sacred code of conduct.

Trayī means not only the three vedas, but it comprehends other sciences also. Śukranīti and Manusmṛti mention fourteen *vidyās* that comprehend *Trayī*[364] *In* Raghuvaṁśa also fourteen traditional branches of learning are referred.[365] In Nasadhīyacarita eighteen branches are mentioned which comprehend Medicine, Military Art, Music and Polity.[366] it is

361. Nai XVII.85
362. ibid. I.6
363. Raghu IV.13
364. ŚN I.154
अडगानि वेदाश्चत्वारो मीमांसान्यायविस्तरः
धर्मशास्त्रपुराणानि त्रयीदं सर्वमुच्यते ॥
365. Raghu V.21
366. Nai VII.63

described about King Nala that learning, a dancer on the tip of his tongue became eighteenfold, like the three vedas multiplied by six Vedāñgas as if out of a desire to conquer the sovereignty of each of the eighteen islands.[367]

Vārtā, the third important vidyā comprehends cattle-rearing, Agriculture and Trade. It benefits the state by acquiring grain, cattle, gold, metals etc. *Vārtā* is not specifically mentioned in the *pañcamahākāvyas,* but the prosperous agriculture, surplus grains, mines in the reign of the ideal kings were the results of the full-fledged knowledge of *Vārtā-śāstra* acquired by the kings. In the kingdom of Duryodhna, the farmers had not to depend on rain for fertilization because the provinces were well irrigated and the fields were smiling with plentyful crop obtained by the husbandmen.[368] The king Atithī in Raghuvṁśa, obtained surplus elephants from the forests.[369] A specific mentioning of Vārtā is seen in the successful undertaking fulfilled by Kuśa and his brothers.[370] Thus the main stay of national welfare was agriculture, cattle-rearing and trade and the ruler was expected to keenly supervise it only So the knowledge of the science of *Vārtā* was necessary for a king.

The knowledge of the fourth vidyā viz. *Daṇḍanīti* was an inevitable part of king's education. King's prime duty consisted in protection of the subjects from the strong powers. The knowledge of Daṇḍanīti helps the king in protecting the virtuous and punishing the

367. ibid I.5

368. Kirā I.17

369. Raghu XVII.66

370. Raghu XVI.2

wicked.[371] By the power of *daṇḍa,* the world is led on to right path. Without *daṇḍanīti,* the whole world would break all bounds, for it is a support of this world.[372] *Daṇḍa,* used in a proper manner controls the wicked and protects the subjects but if it be used in an improper manner it destroys the king himself.[373] The kings well-trained in *Daṇḍanīti* employed d*aṇḍa* in a proper manner, like the southern breeze neither too hot not too cold[374] They were aware of the fact that a harsh employment of daṇḍa harasses the people and the mild use of *daṇḍa* defeates the king.[375] They punished the criminals for the preservation of the society.[376] They knew where to use *daṇḍa* and where not.[377] It controls the four *varṇas,* as to lead them to the performance of their duties, and its proper use makes them desist from '*adharma*'.[378]

Daṇḍa is the means of stability and welfare of the first three vidyās viz. *Ānvīkṣikī, Trayī* and *Vārtā* and the rules to employ *daṇḍa* are called *daṇḍanīti,* it is a means of acquiring which is not acquired, It safeguards what

---

371. NV V.60 दण्डनीतिः साधुपालनानिग्रहः ।
372. ŚP (Critical Edition by BORI) 121.23
373. MS VII.19/28
374. Raghu IV.8
     स हि सर्वस्य लोकस्य युक्तदण्डतया मनः ।
     आददे नातिशीतोष्णो नभस्वानिव दक्षिणः ॥
375. KN II.37
     उद्वेजयते तीक्ष्णेन मृदुना परिभूयते ।
     दण्डेन नृपतिस्तस्माद् युक्तदण्डः प्रशस्यते ॥
376. Raghu I.25
377. Śiśu II.83
378. ŚP (Critical Edition by BORI) 70.3
     दण्डनीतिः स्वधर्मेभ्यश्चातुर्वर्ण्यं नियच्छति ।
     प्रयुक्ता स्वामिना सम्यगधर्मेभ्यश्च यच्छति ॥

is acquired; It increases which is guarded and it distributes among the deserving.[379]

Daṇḍa is the chief support of king. The word *daṇḍa* is used also in the sense of 'Army!' The vast army of the king Atithi, which was constantly increased by his father, had a perfect training in the art of missiles and which was living upon war.[380] As expeditions of the conquest, was an important aspect of the king's life in ancient India, it was natural that every king was careful in preparing a standing Army.

Thus, all these *Vidyās* were an essential part of king's education. To prepare the prince, of bearing the responsibility of the kingdom efficiently, much stress was given upon the education of the king. The princes acquired the education from the experts and in association with old men in the field of knowledge.[381] Discipline was the chief aim of this education, which was clearly visible in the princes in the *Pañcamahākāvyas*. The ideal princes in the Raghu-race were gentle by nature and had increased their modesty by education.[382] Kauṭilya had mentioned two-fold classification of *Vinaya*, Natural and acquired.[383] The learned preceptors of the kings were very eager to train such naturally modest princes because their attempts were not unsuccessful in such cases.[384] Modesty was the essential trait of the

---

379. KA I.4.4./5/6.
आन्विक्षिकी त्रयीवार्तानां योगक्षेमसाधनो दण्डः।
तस्य नीतिर्दण्डनीतिः। अलब्धलाभार्था लब्धपरिरक्षणी।
रक्षितविवर्धनी वृद्धस्य तीर्थेषु प्रतिपादनी च।

380. Raghu XVII.62

381. ibid. XVIII.46

382. ibid. X.79

383. KA I.5.3
कृतकः स्वाभाविकश्च विनयः।

384. Raghu III.29

administrator, as states, Manu, many kings perished with their empire through want of modesty and discipline while others who residing in forest also gained kingdom only through *'Vinaya'*[385]

The knowledge of these four vidyās directs a person or a king towards the three aims.[386]

I) Inculcating in him a sense of high respect towards dharma, the animating force of the entire social and political life of those times.

II) Invigorating him with a strong urge for public welfare.

III) Fashioning him into an efficient and strong administrator.

THE VICES AND CONTROL OVER THE SENSES :

As a protector of the subjects, king was expected to be free from the vices and other personal weaknesses. While mentioning the virtues of the kings, the ancient politicians had indicated a red signal of the vices to save the rulers from the annihilation of themselves and their kingdom.

The political thinkers had classified the vices into two groups. The vices springing from lust (Kāma) and others arising from Wrath. ie. Krodha Kauṭilya mentions the first group as hunting, gambling, women and drinking.[387] The vices springing from wrath are verbal injury, violation of property and physical injury.[388] In

385. MS VII. 40.41.42

386. Ramashraya Sharma, A Socio-Political Study of Vālmīki Rāmāyana
(Published by Motilal Banarasidas) p.305 Delhi-1971

387. KA VIII.3.38
कामजस्तु । मृगया द्यूतं स्त्रियः पानमिति चतुर्वर्गः ।

388. ibid. VIII.3.23
वाक्पारुष्यमर्थदूषणं दण्डपारुष्यमिति ।

the first group Manu adds untimely sleep, purposeless wondering, dancing singing, playing on the instruments and reviling.[389] He also mentions eight vices springing from anger malignity, rashness, treachery, jealousy envy, financial corruption, verbal and physical injury.[390] A ruler should avoid all these vices which result in his total destruction.

The ideal rulers in the *Pañcamahākāvyas* were watchful about their virtues and were guarding themselves against the six inner enemies and the vices springing from them. The kings of the solar-race, in their youth also were destitute of vices producing evil effects.[391] Kuśa tells the woman who entered his palace in the midnight that the minds of the self-restraining Raghus possess a propensity totally turned away from the attraction towards the wives of other men.[392] In the case of Daśaratha, neither pleasure in hunting nor gambling nor yet wine ornamented with the reflection of moon, nor his beloved in the bloom of her youth diverted him from striving for the prosperity of his kingdom.[393] the vices springing from anger, which could very easily dethrone the king, were totally absent in King Daśaratha. He never uttered abusive language even to his enemies because his nature was far from being angry.[394] Duryodhana had subdued his six internal foes i.e. the passions.[395] The envoy of yudhiṣṭhira states that

---

389. MS VII.47
390. ibid. VII.48
391. Raghu XVIII.14
392. ibid. XVI.8
393. ibid. IX.7
394. ibid. IX.8
395. Kirā I.9
कृतारिषड्वर्गजयेन मानवीमगम्यरुपां पदवीं प्रपित्सुना ।
विभज्य नवतंदिवमस्ततन्द्रिणा वितन्यते तेन नयेन पौरुषम् ॥

haughtiness, an annihilating obstacle in the path of virtue is totally forsaken by Duryodhana.[396] Thus all the dutiful rulers were watchfully observing the destructive results of the vices and tried to avoid them as far as possible.

Even a single vice also annihilates a successful reign of the king. For instance, the king Dhṛvasandhi, whose peaceful policy towards the enemies was successful was killed by a lion at the time of hunting.[397] In Kirātārjunīyam, Arjuna admitted that in the deceitful gambling, Yudhiṣṭhira lay on bet all his dearest possessions, his kingdom, his brothers, wife and himself; Arjuna wanted to hide his elder brother's weakness of gambling under the guise of destiny.[398] This vice of gambling of Yudhiṣṭhira is mentioned by Kauṭilya also.[399] Drinking is counted as the dangerous obstacle for a king; for a drunkard in the intoxicated condition cannot preserve secrecy.[400] An intoxication resulting from the consumption of wine affects the mental capacity.

It appears strange indeed in this context that in some places the weaknesses of the kings are placed before us under the guise of virtue. For instance, hunting is not prohibited for the king. It is stated through the mouth of the golden-swan to whom the king Nala sets free. While praising the merciful spirit of the king he says— Even the kings well-versed in the law-books do not condemn hunting, yet thou didst set me free.[401]

396. ibid. I.21

397. Raghu XVIII.35/36

398. Kirā XI.47

399. KA VIII. 3.41/43
द्यूते तु जितमेवाक्षविदुषा यथा जयत्सेन
दुर्योधनाभ्याम्....इति नलयुधिष्ठिराभ्यां व्याख्यातम् ।

400. Kirā IX.68

401. Nai II.9/10

Even the merits of hunting are mentioned in Raghuvaṁśa. "Hunting makes one intimate with the art of throwing down the moving target, it gives an understanding of their signs of fear and ferocity and it makes the body endowed with excellent qualities on account of a conquest over fatigue.[402] According to Draupadī, anger, which is counted in the list of the vices, is not always destructive, but a very helpful virtue for a king to encourage him for action. She thinks that people yield to a person, whose anger does not prove futile. Secondly, when a person is void of anger, people are quite regardless as to his being friendly or inimically disposed towards them.[403] Draupadī is astonished to see that making him exited also the anger of Yudhiṣṭhira did not inflame him.[404] Thus she wanted to stimulate the anger of Yudhiṣṭhira, by which he could think of some active policy against the enemy.

It may be indicated that the vices which are enlisted by the ancient politicians are destructive when a king is subdued by them. When a limit is transgressed, the person is captured by the jaws of destruction, and it becomes difficult for him to emancipate himself. King Agnivarṇa is an illustration of the downfall due to the excessive passions and lust. He seems to be an exceptional case among the solar-kings who were far away from the vices. Agnivarṇa in his prime of youth had solely devoted to the service of young women.[405] He was completely fascinated by the passions that he was unable to bear an interval of even a moment, destitute of enjoyment of the object of senses and he did not pay a regard to his subjects who were anxious to have an interview with him He was shameless enough

402. Ragu IX.60

403. Kirā I.33

404. ibid.I.32

405. Raghu XIX.4

to show only his feet through the window to the subjects awaiting for him[406] This excessive enjoyment of lust was resulted in his decay caused by consumption[407] and he could not escape from the fate brought by the formidable disease, as a flame of a lamp cannot outlive the wind.[408]

Thus, Agnivarṇa, proves to be a clear picture of the victim of excessive passions. In Naiṣadhīyacarita, we come across a graphic depiction of the vices viz. lust, wrath, greed and delusion, which are mentioned as the panegyrists of Kali, the spirit of sin, whc was anxious to attack the righteous king Nala and his subjects but remained unsuccessful.[409]

While considering the virtues of the kings, we have seen that control over the senses is a prominent merit to be acquired by a king. Here we discuss the topic of control over the senses, with special reference to the speeches of Draupadī and Yudhiṣṭhira in Kirātārjunīyam. When Draupadī got the information about the ideal reign of Duryodhana, she was provoked by anger and her mind again recorded the insults despised by Duryodhana; and she could not bear the inactivity of Yudhiṣṭhira. According to her opinion, controlling wrath and other passions behove the sages and ascetics, because the sages free from worldly desires and having subdued to inner enemies attain their objects by means of quietude. But it is not proper for a ruler, specially for a high- spirited person to swallow the insults by the enemies. She was astonished to see the king, the lover of truth, bearing silently the adverse condition of his brothers.[410] Controlling the passions

406. Raghu XIX.6/7

407. ibid. XIX.50

408. ibid. XIX.53

409. Nai XVII.th Canto

410. Kirā I.34

may be a qualification of the ascetics but it does not behove to a king who is desirous to conquer the whole world. Anger, which is counted among the six inner enemies, is more useful than forbearance and anger may turn into virtue if it be utilized on the right occasion. Even the world fears a man having irresistible wrath but the extreme tolerance invites dangers.

On the wrathful speech of enraged Draupadī, Yudhiṣṭhira replies that control over the passions is a virtue to be acquired by not only sages striving for emancipation, but it is an essential virtue to be acquired by a 'ruler', who is desirous of conquest of the world, Calmness or subduation of anger is an ornament of a valorous person. A command over the passions, which is an essence of *śāstras,*[411] is inevitable for a king. When one's mind is disturbed by the controvertial opinions, the knowledge of *śāstras* shows a right path. Subduation of the senses, which is motivated by training by the *śāstras,* should be acquired by a *'Vijigīṣu'* Such persons overcome the force of anger and get their desired objects.[412] Before conquering the external enemies they get command over the impulse of passions and wait for a favourable opportunity. It is not proper to leap in the dark through the force of passions; but one should calculate the time when one can obtain a success. A person desiring to wipe out the darkness of anger, must first dispel it by the light of his intellect; Even the sun does not rise, without having dispersed by his rays the darkness caused by night.[413] Wrath is a dangerous

---

411. KA I.6.3
कृत्स्नं हि शास्त्रमिदमिन्द्रियजयः ।

412. Kirā II.35
शिवमौपायिकं गरीयसीं फलनिष्पत्तिमदूषितायतीम् ।
विगणय्य नयन्ति पौरुषं विजितक्रोधरया जिगीषवः ॥

413. ibid. II.36

enemy of an ambitious person, if he works under the influence of anger, his downfall cannot be avoided. He loses all his extravagant powers like the dark fortnights devoid of digits of the moon.[414]

It is very difficult for a person possessing a regal power, to control the senses and the fickle wealth cannot be retained by those, whose senses are unsteady.[415] So the subduation of senses is most essential for a king. According to Yudhiṣṭhira, fickleness attached to the godess of wealth is due to the nature of a person who after acquiring the knowledge of *śāstras* also can not check his passions.[416] Anger makes one to transgress proper time and means and it inflames one's body and other senses.[417] So a person specially possessing a royal power, like an ordinary person, may not lose his gains by the force of passions. Instead of taking a hasty action, it is proper for a ruler to wait and catch an opportunity at proper moment.

Yudhiṣṭhira also mentions the importance of forbearance. He states that endurance is highly conducive to future prosperity, a great source of success and an unfailing destroyer of enemies.[418] So a ruler should avoid excessive passions and should maintain an even course of conduct like the sun, not always severe neither too mild. Such a king presides over the whole world.[419]

414. Kirāa II.37
बलवानपि कोपजन्मनस्तमसो नामिभवं रुणद्धि यः।
क्षयपक्ष इवैन्दवीः कलाः सकला हन्ति स शक्तिसम्पदः॥

415. ibid. II.39

416. ibid. II.41

417. Kirā II.42

418. ibid. II.43
उपकारकमायतेर्भृशं प्रसवः कर्मफलस्य भूरिणः।
अनपायि निबर्हणं द्विषां न तितिक्षासममस्ति साधनम्।

419. ibid. II.38

Yudhiṣṭhira, a prudent politician, while deciding a policy, thinks about the drawbacks of his enemies also. He was well acquainted with the haughtiness of Duryodhana. Yudhiṣṭhira was sure that inflated with vanity, Duryodhana would surely insult his friendly kings and the kings would not tolerate the contempts; for, even an ordinary person cannot bear in insult by others[420] So it is the proper opportunity to conquer an enemy. Secondly a king who is puffed up with arrogance and conceit and accompanied by imprudence, falls away from the path of right policy.[421] Such a ruler is disliked by his subjects also; and he who is tossed by the wind of disaffection is easy to be uprooted by one having patience.[422] So, in avoiding an excess of passions the watchful policy of Yudhiṣṭhira notes the vices of the enemies also. A prudent politician always takes an advantage of a proper opportunity and the root of all these, is subduation of excessive passions.

These passions are the treacherous enemies of a man, so they should be avoided by a thoughtful person.[423] In the political field also the concept of control over the senses is highly respected by the ancient politicians. They had emphasized the importance of control over the passions in a whole chapter. Kauṭilya, Manu etc. had illustrated the names of the kings who were doomed to the position of total destruction by the force of passions.[424] A ruler is specially instructed to practise constantly to control the senses, because a self-restrained king can control his subjects and

---

420. Kirā II.47
421 ibid. II.49
422. ibid. II.50
अपरागसमीरणेरितः क्रमशीर्णाकुलमूलसन्ततिः ।
सुकरस्तरुवत्सहिष्णुता रिपुरुन्मूलयितुं महानपि ॥
423. ibid. XI.35
424. KA I.6.5 to 10

command respect from them.[425] It would be worthwhile here to mention the verse in Aśvaghoṣa's Buddhacarita in which the king Śuddhoḍana is depicted as controlling his own self and strengthening the seven constituents of the state. The poet describes- "He controlled one i.e. his own self, maintained the seven (constituents), one i.e. his own self, maintained the seven (constituents), abandoned seven (vices) and secured five (political expedients), obtained 'Trivarga' and recognized the three powers; He knew the two (good and bad policy) and renounced the two (desire and anger).[426]

SECURITY OF THE KING :

After stating an importance of safeguarding the king from the inner enemies viz. the passions, it is proper here to state the means of the security of king's person from the external dangers. The king protects the kingdom when he himself is protected.

We come across some allusions, declaring that the able rulers had no need of outward arrangement of protection; and the princes born in the line of Manu were protected by the power of their own. For instance the king Dilīpa who proceeded to visit his preceptor in the forests to perform some religious austerities, dismissed the rest of the band of his followers, as he was rested for the protection upon his own valour and might.[427] But these quotations do not suggest that the kings did not need any arrangement for their security. These allusions only reveal a profound belief in the valour of their own arms. But then also a provision for the security of the king was not neglected. In

425. MS VII. 44

426. Buddhacarita II.41
अेकं विनिन्ये स जुगोप सप्त सप्तैव तत्याज ररक्ष पञ्च ।
प्राप त्रिवर्ग बुबुधे त्रिवर्ग जज्ञे द्विवर्ग प्रजहौ द्विवर्गम् ॥

427. Raghu II.4

Kirātārjuñiyam, Arjuna was specially instructed by the honourable sage Vyāsa, when Arjuna started for the forest for securing a penance. He suggested Arjuna to take his weapons and not to allow anyone to approach him while leading the life of an ascetic, when there was an increase of his power by yoga.[428] So Arjuna bore his weapons due to the instructions of sage Vyāsa to face the obstacles, in the path of obtaining the desired objects.[429] Draupadī and the yakṣa also advised Arjuna to take care of himself. (Kirātā 3.53; 5.49) So a king should not lose patience in danger and should not be careless about his own security.

A special provision for the safety and security of the king is described in Raghuvaṁśa. The swimming tanks and rivers were safe as the alligators were retracted out by the fishermen. The lake was protected by the soldiers placing the tents around, during the watersports of the king.[430] Kauṭilya and Kāmanḍaka have mentioned the safety of the lakes for the kings.[431]

King is the root of the state and he bears the responsibility of the protection of his subjects, so he should be protected first.[432] According to Somadevasūri also everything is protected if the king is protected;[433] A protection from his own people is prominently hinted

---

428. Kirā III.28
429. Kirā V.49
430. Raghu XVI.55
431. KA I.21.39
मत्स्यग्राहविशुद्धमवगाहेत । KN. VII.34.
परितापिषु वासरेषु पश्यंस्तटलेखान्तिकमाप्तसैन्यचक्रम् ।
सुविशोधित मीननक्रजालं व्यवगाहेत जलं सुहृत्समेतः ॥
432. AP 225.12
मूलं स्वामी स वै रक्ष्यस्तस्माद्राज्यं विशेषतः ।
राज्याङ्गद्रोहिणं हन्यात्काले तीक्ष्णो मृदुर्भवेत् ।
433. NV XXIV.1

by all the ancient politicians. King should protect himself from his own sons and wives because the princes resemble to crab in nature who eat their own father.[434] The princes in the *Pañcamahākāvyas* are an exception to the red- signal showed by the ancient politicians. The princes were modest, obedient and affectionate to their fathers and accepted kingdom only to obey their command and not through greed to acquire the kingdom.[435] While mentioning an obedience of the princes, the poet was aware of the fact in the political history mentioned by the politicians for he says- Aja accepted the kingdom to obey the command of his father; the kingdom, which the sons of the kings indeed tried to snatch by even foul means. Thus a watchful king should make a provision of his personal safety from every possible side of danger; because, if he protects himself then the kingdom is protected, The ideal kings protected their self not only for enjoyment of worldly objects but for the protection of their subjects and to acquire the goals of life.[436]

DAILY ROUTINE OF THE KING :

The dutyful rulers in the *Pañcamahākāvyas* were aware of the fact that kingship was not only for their enjoyment. To discharge the various duties successfully the kings had to observe a strict time-table of their daily-routine. From some scattered allusions and the mentioning of the daily programme of King Nala in Naiśadhacarita (19th canto) we can sketch out a picture of the daily routine of the kings in the *Pañcamahākāvyas*.

---

434. KA I.17.1/5
रक्षितो राजा राज्यं रक्षत्यासन्नेभ्यः परेभ्यश्च । पूर्वं दारेभ्यः पुत्रेभ्यश्च ।
कर्कटकसधर्माणो हि जनकभक्ष्याः राजपुत्राः ।

435. Raghu VIII.2

436. Ragu I.21

The kings were roused from the sleep by the auspicious eulogistic songs of the bards.[437] These songs were called *Bhogāvalī,* containing the description of king's particular work at that time. By this song of the bards people could know, in which work the king was busy.[438] At the dawn of the day, the king finished the rites enjoined by the *śāstras* and the morning ablutions.[439] Then he visited the feudatory kings bowing down to his feet and offering marvelous jewels to him.[440] He asked the kings about their welfare. Then the valorous king trained the students to practice weapons, hurling and striking,[441] and also the art of wielding weapons. He finished his bath with fragrant paste and perfumed water.[442] After the bath he uttered vedic incantations holding a crystal rosary.[443] He offered oblations to gods and manes.[444] In the household temple, in the chamber of worship, he prayed the gods with great devotion.[445] After the midday-rites he accompanied with the queen took his meals.[446] The king himself looked into the intricate sides of plaintiffs and defendants for the prompt decision[447] and everyday he had a consultation with his ministers.[448] After finishing his evening rites etc. in

437. Kirā I.38
438. Śiśu V.67
439. Raghu V.76 Nai XIX.66
440. Nai XXI.2/3
441. ibid. XXI.5/6
442. ibid. XXI.7
443. ibid. XXI.19
    सम्यगस्य जपतः श्रुतिमन्त्राः संनिधानमभजन्त कराब्जे ।
    शुद्धबीजविशदस्फुटवर्णाः स्फटिकाक्षवलयच्छलभाजः ॥
444. Nai XXI.20
445. ibid. XXI.32
446. ibid. XXI.121/122
447. Raghu XVII.39
448. ibid. XVII.50

the second part of the night also he thought about the administration of the kingdom.[449] Consultation with the spies contained a chief part of king's daily time-table, though the exact time for it, is not mentioned.[450]

The general attitude of the king's daily programme reveals the thing that it was influenced by the traditional model of daily routine prescribed in the works on polity. For instance, King Duryodhana to reach the line of conduct laid down by Manu, had apportioned the days and nights to secure the different functions.[451] A division of the day and night into eight even portions, which are named as *'Nalikās'* and the functions to be secured in these various *nalikās,* are stated in details by Kauṭilya. The duties allotted in these portions are as follows. At the day division - Hearing report regarding income and expenditure; adjudication of law-suits; bath and meal; collection of revenue; consultation with ministers; amusement and conversation, inspection of the army and consultation with commander-in-chief regarding military matters. At the night division the functions are : Evening worship and interviewing secret agents; taking of meal and study of scriptures; going to bed with the sound of trumpets; consultation with and deputation of spies with priest and other *brāhmaṇas.*[452]

This programme is not followed in a rigid manner by the kings in the *Pañcamahākāvyas.* Kauṭilya himself mentions it as subject to modification if necessity demanded.[453] An information about the daily

---

449. Śiśu XI.6

450. Kirā I.1

451. ibid I.9

452. KA I.19.9 to 29
तस्माद्देवताश्रम.....च क्रमेण कार्याणि पश्येत् कार्यगौरवात् आत्ययिकवशेन वा ।

453. KA I.19

programme of the kings, does not create an impression that the daily routine of the king was rigid and strenuous. But it also should be noted that kings definitely relied on the model timetable as their ideal. In the seventeenth canto of Raghuvaṁśa the poet himself states that whatever is ordained in the law-books to be done to the rulers of the earth, in different divisions of the day and hight he (Atithī) averse to hesitation, observed with a rigid resolve.[454]

In this verse in Raghuvaṃśa the words 'Niyoga' and 'Vikalpa' are purposefully approved which are used by Kauṭilya to impress that a work to be done acquires success only by such a manner, when there is no escape due to other alternative.[455] In order to carry out his duties, the king was expected to be punctual and methodical, and he should not find any escape from his duties.

The King was expected to perform many other duties which are not mentioned in the daily programme of the king. In his busy routine he was expected to show his person to the subjects anxiously awaiting for the king.[456] The king was enjoined to make himself easily accessible to the petitioners and to attend personally to the subjects of their application and complaints. King Rāma punctually attended to the affairs of the citizens.[457] The king personally heard the injustice if happened in anybody's case.[458] Thus a personal contact of the ruler, with his subjects was an

---

454. Raghu XVII.49
455. KA XV. 1.63/65/67
कार्याणां नियोगविकल्पसमुच्चया भवन्ति । अनेनैवोपायेन नान्येनेति नियोगः । अनेन वान्येन वेति विकल्पः । अनेन चेति समुच्चयः ॥
456. Raghu XIX.6
457. ibid. XIV.24
458. ibid. XV.25

essential part of king's daily routine. Much stress in given by the ancient thinkers, on the daily timetable of the duties of the king.[459]

CONSECRATION CEREMONY OF THE KING :

A person was not entitled to be called a king unless he was duly consecrated by the priests. To carry out his duties effectively the king was expected to be backed by religious sanctions. In the Brāhmaṇa texts Rājasūya, Vājapeya, Sarvamedha, sacrifices are mentioned to be related to king's coronation. Rājasūya sacrifice was the normal ceremony of coronation of the king and the Vajapeya, Sarvamedha sacrifices also were connected to king's coronation.

Due to the rule of primogeniture, the elder prince succeeded the throne. It was the outcome of the pattern of the four *Āśramas* which glorifies the kings. The kings in their old age handed over the office to the crown-prince and retired to the forest for the ascetic-life.[460] So the kings themselves conferred the kingdom to their sons and performed a coronation-ceremony before retiring to acquire emancipation. In the account of the solar-race in Raghuvaṁśa the princes succeed the royal throne after their father. So the details of the coronation ceremony were not always described, but probably the whole coronation rituals were to be gone through.

Some popular rites are referred in some scattered references. In these rites coronation-bath was an important rite which was performed through preceptors and the ministers. King Aja was coronated with holy waters poured by Vasiṣṭha.[461] At the consecration-

---

459. MS VII.145/146/222/ to 225
AP Adhāya 235
460. Raghu III.25/70; VIII.1; XVIII.12/26
461. ibid. VIII.3

ceremony of Rāma, the waters from the sacred water places, rivers, lakes and seas were fetched by the chief of the demons and monkey-chiefs and was brought in the golden jars.[462] The ceremony was performed by the old ministers, which was already commenced by the tears of the joy of the mothers.[463] Rāma appeared exceedingly handsome, wearing the royal suit and he was fanned by the chowries by his younger brothers and with an umbrella held up by Bharata over his head.[464]

In the seventeenth canto of Raghuvaṁśa we come across the consecration-ceremony of king Atithi, with some details. the artists erected a new pavilion supported on four pillars with a raised platform for the ceremony.[465] The ministers attended on the king, who had occupied his seat on the splendid throne, with holy waters filled in golden jars.[466] Trumpets were blown making a deep and agreeable sound.[467] He enjoined the nirājana rites consisting chiefly of young sprouts, barks of banian-trees, sprouts of *yava-grass* and *durvā* shoots offered to him by his old kinsmen.[468] The brāhmaṇa headed by the family-priest sprinkled him with holy waters of Ganges and the victorious chants in *Atharvaveda* were recited at that time.[469] The panegyrists praised his greatness.[470] The king offered ablutions with

---

462. Raghu XIV.7
अथाभिषेकं रघुवंशकेतोः प्रारब्धमानन्दजलैर्जनन्योः ।
निर्वर्तयामासुरमात्यवृद्धास्तीर्थाहृतैः काञ्चनकुम्भतोयैः ॥
463. Raghu XIV.8
464. ibid. XIV.11
465. ibid. XVII.9
466. ibid. XVII.10
467. ibid. XVII.11
468. ibid. XVII.12
469. Raghu XVII.13/14
470. Raghu XVII.15

waters purified by excellent *mantras*. He offered the *snāṭakas* as much wealth as would enable them to complete their own sacrificial ceremonies. He received blessings from the highly pleased *brāhmaṇas*.[471]

At the auspicious occasion of coronation, the king ordered to release the prisoners from jails. It was an old practice recommended by Kauṭilya (KA 2.36). A king even released the yoke of the beasts, and the pet-birds were set at liberty from the cages.[472]

A conronation of the crown-prince slightly differs from the regular coronation of a king; for it was performed for a prince when his father was still ruling the kingdom. Moreover, its object was only to declare the prince as heir -apparent. So we do not come across a detail account of the ceremony. In the event of king's death also a provision of consecration of the heir-apparent was done by the ministers and it was done according to the rules but it was short and emergent.[473] It was done after observing a deplorable condition of the people without a king. Secondly it was done to set at rest all possible confusion consequent upon the death of the king. In the nineteenth canto of Raghuvaṁśa, the ministers consecrated the queen of Agnīvarṇa after his death.[474] The account[475] reminds Kauṭilya's advice to the ministers to guard the secret of king's death till the accession of the successor to the throne.[476]

---

471. Raghu XVII.17/18
472. ibid. XVII.19/20
473. ibid. XVIII.36
474. ibiḍ. XIX.56
475. ibid. XIX.54
तं गृहोपवन अेव संगताः पश्विचमक्रतुविदा पुरोधसा
रोगशान्तिमपदिश्य मन्त्रिणः संभृते शिखिनि गूढमादधुः ॥
476. KA V.6.1/2
राजव्यसनमेवममात्यः प्रतिकुर्वीत ।
प्रागेव मरणबाधभयात् राज्ञः प्रियहितोपग्रहेण
मासद्विमासान्तरं दर्शनं स्थापयेद्....इत्यपदेशेन ।

A CAPITAL OF THE KINGDOM :

A capital of the state was an important seat of the goverment and it was well protected directly under the eye of the king. It was the centre of eminent activities, transaction, and of political administration. Ancient authorities in politics and stated that the king living in a capital city should discharge his daily duties.[477] In the capital, the royal court of justice was held everyday, where the hard working sovereign dispatched the business of the citizens of his state.[478]

As a centre of administration and residing place of the king,[479] The capital was well protected and guarded. The city had huge gates which were closed with huge doors with strong bolts.[480] The city marked with a circle in the shape of its circular moat, was not accessible to the enemies, and was difficult to tackle.[481] The ramparts of the city were encircled by a broad and deep ditch.[482] The ramparts of the capital named Oṣdhiprastha, described in Kumārasaṁbhava, were comprised of the herbs dropping light by which the capital was guarded and proctected by Nature[483] and the stream of Ganges encircling the capital was, as if, a ditch to protect the capital so it was free from the attacks of enemies.[484] When the king left the capital for expedition of conquest, he caused it to be protected by suitable garrisons.[485] King Raghu started for expedition having his metropolis

477. ŚN I.274
478. Raghu VIII.18
479. Āpa. Dharmasūtra II.9.25.1; Nai II.82
480. Raghu XVIII.4
481. Nai II.95
482. Raghu XII.66
483. Ku VI.38
484. ibid. VII.50
485. Raghu IV.28

and the frontier fortresses well guarded. For the safety, the capital was situated inside a fort or independent of it. Manu specifically mentions that king should situate the capital and his residence inside the forts and should store all types of materials inside of it.[486] Thus the kings were very watchful for the protection of their capital cities.

A capital mirrored the prosperity of the country, so it was always full with all kinds of rich decorations. The administrator was meant to reside in his hereditary capital. King Kuśa was residing in a newly situated capital named Kuśāvatī. So one day, the presiding deity of Ayodhyā, which was the hereditary capital of Raghus, informed Kuśa the ruined condition of Ayodhyāa, devoid of king, after the departure of Rāma. Ayodhyā which eclipsed the city of gods by its prosperity had reduced to a pitiable condition without the king.[487] But the ruined remnants were the witness of the lost prosperity of Ayodhyā. When the king was residing in the royal palace of Ayodhyā it was shining with grandeur. The city was situated on the banks of Sarayu. The lakes were full with water and the gardens were blown wish fragrant flowers and creepers, and were decorated on the skirts of the capital.[488] The royal palace was in the midst of the city and was decorated with pictures of the ancestors[489] and paintings.[490] Beautiful images were engraved on the posts.[491] The sandy banks of Sarayu were bereft of the rites of bali-offerings and the water was always perfumed obtaining a contact of

486. MS VII.70/76

487. Raghu XVI.10

488. ibid. XVI.13

489. ibid. XIV.15

490. ibid. XVI.16

491. ibid. XVI.17

the powders in the ablutions. The royal street was decorated with rich shops.[492]

Kuśa transferred his capital to Ayodhyā again to obey the order of the presiding deity. He made the capital renew by new constructions. He employed a multitude of artists and made the city altogether a new one by reason of their being furnishing with necessary materials.[493] The city was with wares arranged in its shops, with the horses resting in its stables, with the elephants fastened to the posts fixed in the stables according to the rule, was appearing like a young lady with ornaments, arranged in their proper place on her limbs[494]

Another capital named Mathurā was situated by Śatrughna on the banks of Kālindī. On account of the prosperity of the citizens caused by the benign rule of the king, it looked like a colony planted with the surplus population of heaven. The capital Oṣadhiprastha of Himālaya had surpassed the prosperity of the city of gods.[495] In the second canto of Niṣadhīyacarita, we come across a graphic description of the well situated capital of king Bhīma. The houses in the city had frames of crystal and they contain walls pure like a digit of moon.[496] The building were so high that the flags flying over them appeared like rods to drive the horses of the sun.[497] The royal palace was so high that it had got a

---

492. Raghu XIV.30
ऋद्धापणं राजपथं स पश्यन्विगाहयमानां सरयूं च नौमिः ।
विलासिमिश्चाध्युषितानि पौरैः पुरोपकण्ठोपवनानि रेभे ॥

493. Raghu XVI.38

494. ibid. XVI. 41

495. Ku VI.37
अलकामतिवाहयेव वसतिं वसुसम्पदाम् ।
स्वर्गमिष्यन्दवमनं कृत्वेवोपनिवेशितम् ॥

496. Nai II.74

497. ibid. II.80

border of the blue clouds.[498] The city was so prosperous that it surpassed the beauty of heaven and nether world. It was marvellous with the choicest gifts of the three worlds. The city gates were thickly studded with jewels. The highways were pleasant to the people in all the seasons.[499] The city was decorated with pleasure-hills and gardens.[500] The great market, in the city, with shops was appearing like an ocean which was roaring with conches, gems, camphor etc. It was full with perfume shops and stalls of saffron.[501]

The prosperous and well planned capitals were not only the centres of administration and dignity of the king but the kings had an affectionate feeling for the cities also. They had a great love and affection for their land and rivers. This feeling is revealed through the words of Rāma who describes the lands in the returning journey towards Ayodhyā. He says- "The river Sarayu, is flowing near the capital Ayodhyā and the lands of Uṭṭarkosalas who are familiar with the pleasure of moving on the lap of the sandy banks and who are nourished by the milk-like waters.".[502]

---

498. Ku VI.40 Nai II.82

499. Nai II.93/94

500. ibid. II.105/106

501. ibid. II.90

502. Raghu XIII.62/63

CHAPTER II

A SYSTEM OF SOCIAL POLITY - VARNĀŚRAMADHARMA

A glance at the administration of the kings in *Pañcamahākāvyas* reveals a fact that the administration of the kings was not a mere ruling machinery. When the ancient Indian society was formed, the codes and regulations which were binding to the members of society, were established; because without some rules and regulations it was not possible for the people to work and make progress for themselves and for the society. So the social order of the Hindu Society was based on the double division of four castes and four life-stages, which was known by the term *Varṇāśramadharma*. This system of *Varṇāśramadharma* was based on some valid principles. Different works and professions and the different stages of life were duly arranged in the frame-work of *varṇās* and *Āśramas;* and it was observed that every member of the society should conduct his life according to the established laws. The kings, the beholders of *daṇḍa* were to regulate the people on the path of rules and regulations. The kings could regulate the life of an individual, as well as of the society through the strict observance of the rules and regulations prescribed by *Varṇāśramadharma*.

The duties of the *Varṇās* and Āśramas are specifically stated in the ancient law-books. While mentioning the four *vidyās* and an importance of *Trayī*, Kauṭilya says - The law laid down in this vedic lore is beneficial as it prescribes the respective duties of the four *varṇās* and *Āśramas*.[1] The special duties of the brāhmanas are; studying teaching; performing sacrifies for self, officiating at other people's sacrifices, making gifts and receiving gifts. Those of the *Kṣatriyas* are - studying, performing sacrifices for self, making gifts, living by the profession of arms and protecting the beings. Those of vaiśya are studying, performing sacrifices for self, making gifts, agriculture, cattle-rearing and trade and those of the *śūdras* are, a service of the three *varṇas*, engaging in economic calling and the profession of the artisan and the actor.[2]

The duties of the four *Āśramas* are as follows: In the first life-stage of *brahmacarya*, the duties are, studying the *Veda*, keeping sacred fire, acquiring knowledge residing with the preceptor in his hermitage. The duty of a householder is having a married life, worshipping gods, manes and guests. Those of the forest-anchorite are observing celibacy, growing matted locks and wearing antelope-skin, worshipping the gods and guests and living on forest-produce only. The duties of an ascetic are having a full control over the senses, retiring from the active life.[3]

The four *varṇās*, in which the society was divided, were *Brāhmaṇa*, *Kṣatriya*, *Vaiśya* and *Śūdra*. The prescribed duties mentioned above, were particularly followed by the *varṇās*. The learned preceptors from the

---

1. KA I.3.4
   एष त्रयीधर्मश्चतुर्णां वर्णानामाश्रमाणां च
   स्वधर्मस्थापनादौपकारिकः।
2. KA. I.3.5 to 8
   स्वधर्मो ब्राह्मणस्य.....कारुकुशीलव कर्म च ।
3. KA I.3.9 to 12
   गृहस्थस्य स्वधर्माजीव.....च शौचम् ।

brāhmaṇa caste, skilled in *vedas* and other sciences offered the knowledge to the students and princes.[4] The kings performed the sacrifices under the guidance and direction of the learned priests. The spiritual power of the *brāhmaṇa* class in making the sacrifices for the king was complementary to the rulers not only from the religious point of view but mainly from the political point of view. It was believed that the oblations offered by the priests to the fires in due form were converted into rain for the crops.[5] Thus the prescribed class-duties were helpful to increase national welfare. Their spiritual service was desired by the rulers for liberating people from their fears and calamities.[6] Even the chants recited by the learned priests were able to protect the kingdom by counteracting the invisible charms of the enemies.[7]

The second class was of the *Ksatriyas*. The word *kṣatriya* itself means 'one who protects the people from dangers.[8] So a prime duty of *Kṣatriyas* was to depend upon arms and to protect the living beings. The *kṣatriya* kings of the solar-race fulfilled their duties viz. the protection of the subjects. In the reign of king Dilīpa, there was no fear of theft and it remained merely as a term to be heard.[9] Due to the absence of theft and other offences, Dilīpa had no prisoner to release on the happy occasion of the birth of his son. In Kirātārjunīyam Draupadī reminds Arjuna of the duty of a *kṣatriya* king.[10] She also reminds of the maxim of Manu about the duty

4. Raghu XVIII.47
5. ibid. I.62
6. ibid. I.63
7. ibid. I.61
8. ibid. II.53
9. ibid. I.27
10. Kirā III.48
स क्षत्रियस्त्राणसहः सतां यस्तत्कार्मुकं कर्मसु यस्य शक्तिः ।
वहन् द्वयीं यद्यफलेऽर्थजाते करोत्यसंस्कारहतामिवोक्तिम् ॥

of a *kṣatriya.*[11] *Kṣatriyas* were considered as *'Āśramagurus'* It was their duty to protect or to control all the remaining *'dvijas'* and other castes. (Śiśu - XIV.38) Alongwith the duty of protection, fighting for the acquirement of one's lost kingdom and not retreating from the battle field, were the duties of a true *kṣatriya.*[12] To turn back from the battlefield was deemed as a sin for the *kṣatriya.*[13]

As depending upon arms was an important duty of *kṣatriyas,* they were called a warrior-caste. *Kṣatriya* caste was attributed a title *'Bāhuja'* s being born from the arms of the Creator. Due to their natural valour and bodily strength the duty of protection was assigned to them so naturally they were considered competent to become rulers, and were preferred for the post of a king. The arrangement of the caste-system was so deep-rooted in the ancient *Hindu society that kṣatriyas* alone were considered fit to become rulers.

It is singnificant to point out that though tradition preferred kṣatriyas for the post of a king, it does not debar members of other castes from being the rulers.[14] Though, a good lineage was necessary to become a king, there was no insistence on cast qualification. Lord Kṛṣṇa in Śiśupālavadha is the shining example to prove this point under discussion. Kṛṣṇa was not known as a *kṣatriya-king.* But by his valour and other kingly qualities, he proved to be an able administrator. he was not a mere king to bind himself in the limit of caste system but a deity who had taken birth as a human administrator, for the protection of the good and

---

11. MS VII.2
12. ibid VII.87
    समोत्तमाधमै राजा त्वाहूतः पालयन्प्रजाः ।
    न निवर्तेत संग्रामात्क्षात्रं धर्ममनुस्मरन् ॥
13. Kirā III.51
14. Tanṭravārtika (by Kumārila) p.580
    तथा राज्यमविशेषेण चत्वारोऽपि वर्णाः कुर्वाणा दृश्यन्ते ।

destruction of the wicked, viz. the distressing forces like Śiśupāla.[15]

The third *varṇa* was *Vaiśya varṇa,* which was important for the welfare of the society and from the point of economics. Along with the duties of studying and performing the sacrifices, the special duties of the *vaiśyās* were agriculture, cattle-rearing and trade. They were engaged in agriculture, purchase and sale of goods. They used to travel to far off regions for the sake of trade. (Śiśu-III.76). In the *Nītiśara* of Kāmanḍaka, while stating the undertaking of the king,[16] an importance is given to the promotion of agriculture and an increase of irrigation- schemes. Frequent references of the prosperous reign of the kings in the *pañcamahāvyas* reveal that the kings were giving an able guidance and kept a watch on the duties of the third class of the society. King Kuśa and his brothers in Raghuvaṁśa, were successful in the work of construction of bridges, encouragement to agriculture and others.[17] Daśaratha was wakeful about the prosperity in agriculture, the result of which, the earth was fruitful towards him[18] King Duryodhana was aware of the fact that encouragement to agriculture gives a prosperous life to the subjects. His land was smiling with surplus crops grown easily by the irrigational facilities[19] and the earth was as if pleased by his merits showered abundant wealth on him.[20] thus though we do not get any direct reference

---

15. Śiśu I.69/73
16. KN V.77/78
    कृषिर्वणिक्पथो दुर्ग सेतुः कुञ्जरबन्धनम् ।
    खन्याकरो वनादानं शून्यानां च निवेशनम् ।
    अष्टवर्गमिमं साधु स्वस्थवृत्तं विवर्धयेत् ॥
17. Raghu XVI.2
18. ibid. IX.4
19. Kirā I.17
20. ibid. I.18

of the *vaiśya* society, we can guess from the prosperous reigns of the kings that they were watchful about the duties performed by the *vaiśya* class.

The duty of the *Sūdras* was to serve the three classes. *Śudras* were prohibited to perform sacrifices study of vedas etc. The Śambūka incident in Raghuvaṁśa proves this fact. A Śūdra named Śambūka practised a penance and by its result an untimely death of a brāhmin-child occurred. In Naiṣadhīyacarita, we come across some scattered allusions about the duties of *śūdras*.

The kings in the *Pañcamahākāvyas.* were strictly regulated by the four stages which were named *Āśramas.* The rules and regulations of the four life-stages as mentioned before, were properly followed by the kings. In the commencing lines of the first canto of Raghuvaṁśa, the poet describes the kings, who spent their boyhood in the study of *vidyās,* enjoyed pleasures in their youth, who led anchorite's life in their old age and who finally resigned their bodies by means of Yoga i.e. fixing their minds upon the supreme spirit.[21] In the first stage of life the kings learnt vedas with their ancillary texts and aṅgas. Kālidāsa had described the studentship of prince Raghu with due details. "When his (Raghu's) tonsure-ceremony was performed, he accompanied by the minister's sons of the same age and with waving locks of hair, mastered properly the alphabet and thereby entered the vast field of learning. Learned preceptors educated him and found that their labours were not wasted upon him. Gifted with an excellent capacity to understand, he, by the force of all the powers of intellect got the knowledge of four lores. Clad in the holy skin of *'Ruru'* he learnt the art of using missiles together with their incantations.[22]

21. Raghu I.8
22. ibid. III.28 to 31

After the completion of the studies, living at the residence of the preceptor, the student becomes worthy to enter the second stage of householdership. Ancient thinkers had permitted a student to step in the second stage of life after the completion of studies.[23] It is stated in Raghuvaṁśa that King Dilīpa seeing prince Raghu, whose childhood was gradually supplanted by youth, gave him the oath of marriage, after the ceremony of the cutting of hair had been performed.[24] When Raghu received an invitation of the *swayaṁvara* of Indumatī, the king thought that his son had arrived at the marriage-age and he sent prince Aja with an army to the wealthy capital of Vidarbhas.[25]

The kings enjoyed the sexual pleasures in their youth; but they were not drowned in them passionately. On the contrary, it is stated that they consorted with their wives solely for the sake of offspring,[26] who could continue the practice of domestic duties and rituals and who could replace the king as a heir of the kingdom. This stage of householdership was important from another viewpoint also, In Naiṣadhīyacarita, the householdership is mentioned as valuable in comparison to other stages, because it provides nourishment to other stages. A religious - student, forest dweller and ascetics are dependent on the householder for their subsistence.[27] In the sixth canto Damayantī praises this second stage of life. She says "I am desirous of attaining that

---

23. Raghu III.2
वेदानधीत्य वेदौ वा वेदं वापि यथाक्रमम् ।
अविप्लुतब्रह्मचर्यो गृहस्थाश्रममावसेत् ॥
KA I.5.9/10
ब्रह्मचर्यं आ षोडशाद् वर्षात् । अतो गोदानं दारकर्म च ।
24. Raghu III.32/33
25. ibid. V.39/40
26. Raghu I.7 प्रजायै गृहमेधिनाम् ।
27. Nai XVII.32

religious virtue, by serving my husband in this *Bhārata* country which is the greatest among lands as is the family stage among the other stages of life.[28] Manu has laid down an importance of householdership As the living beings live depending upon their so also the other three *āśramas* live by the shelter of a householder.[29] King Himālaya was grateful to his householdership being fruitful as the honorable sages came to him as supplicants on behalf of Lord Śiva.[30]

There is one more advantage of the householdership. Through the medium of householdership a man releases himself from the obligations of the gods, parents and manes. King Dilīpa wanted the fruit of householdership viz. the son, to become free from the debts of the ancestors.[31] The king Aja, by performing sacrifices and by begetting a son was free from the debts of preceptors, gods and manes.[32] This second stage of life is important not only to acquire the personal ends of life but also to acquire the social good. "*Gṛhastāśrama* gives sample scope for development of powers and potentialities to build up family economics and to discharge number of obligations to the society and community where secular ends have not been totally ignored and it is the well established directive of the *Śāstra* that one should not take resort to life of asceticism or renunciation without passing through the *Gṛhasthāśrama* of life."[33]

---

28. ibid. VI. 97
29. MS III.77
30. Ku VI.88
    अेहि विश्वात्मने वत्से । भिक्षाऽसि परिकल्पिता ।
    अर्थिनो मुनयः प्राप्तं गृहमेधिफलं मया ॥
31. Raghu I.71
32. ibid. VIII.31
33. Geeta Upadhyaya, Glimpses of Political Thought in Sanakrit Kāvya, Published by Chaukhambha Orientilia 1979 p.239

The third stage of life is of the residence in forest, The ideal kings had wishfully accepted this ascetic stage. It was the family-vow of the Ikṣvākūs to retire from the worldly objects, offering all the responsibility of the kingdom to their sons.[34] The kings were so firm-minded that they did not hesitate in doing their duty. "When the father (Raghu) prepared to leave for his forest-life, his son with his head adorned by a coronet, bowed down to his feet and prayed him not to forsake him; Raghu, for the love of his son, granted the boon to him whose face was tear-stained but he did not take up his royal state, as a snake resumes not the slough once cast away.[35] Thus, the kings were not ready to transgress the due order of the *āśramas* and were not tempted even by the affectionate request by their sons also. It was a practice of the family of Dilīpa to make over in their old age the kingly state to their virtuous sons and being self-controlled, would treat the bark-clad hermit's path.[36] The kings never clung to the household when there was one capable of bearing the yoke of the family. [37] So King Raghu seeing that his son was now established among his subjects turned away from the perishable objects of senses. The kings passed their old age very peacefully in the hermitages.[38]

In the fourth stage of life the kings revert from even worldly desires and leave their lives by the way of yoga.[39]

---

34. Raghu III.70
35. ibid. VIII.12/13
36. Raghu VIII.10/11
37. ibid. VII.71
38. ibid. XVIII.7/9/26
39. ibid. I.8
    शैशवेऽभ्यस्तविद्यानां यौवने विषयैषिणाम् ।
    वार्धक्ये मुनिवृत्तीनां योगेनान्ते तनुत्यजाम् ॥

Thus the rules and regulations and the prescribed order of the four *āśramas* was strictly observed by the ideal kings. The rulers, strictly observing the codes of *āśramadharma,* had placed an ideal before their subjects. In Naiṣadhīyacarita it is described that *Kali,* the spirit of sin, did not find a rest for his foot because the houses were full of householders, the woods were full of anchorites and the habitations were full with ascetics.[40]

Thus an establishment of the fourfold classification of the *varṇas* and the four life-stages was very essential to preserve the stability of the society. The codes and laws prescribed for the particular classes were enjoined to follow their duties. The duties situated in the four life-stages were not only to acquire personal interest, but each and every person was made to realize his responsibility and duty for his family, society and state also.

The fourfold classification of the society was based on the well grounded principle of division of labour; and by the strict observance of the class rules every member of the society was able to behave according to the established law. According to some thinkers the rules, prescribed duties and the privileges for the higher castes, do not offer a justice to the principle of division of labour, in the real sense of term. "The duties, set the seal of inferiority and servitude on a large proportion of the population. It is the inevitable result of the *Varṇāśramic* ideal. We can never maintain, as some of our modern writers try to do, that the Indian polity was founded upon the true principles of division of labour and social harmony.[41] The charge, that some

40. Nai XVII.175

41. Pratapagiri Rāmamūrti, The Problem of the Indian-Polity, Published by Longmans ocean Co. Ltd. Calcutta, 1935; p.223

classes, as *brāhmaṇa* class, got many advantages, as exemption from taxes, death punishments etc. and the *śūdra* caste had only to serve the three classes, instead of any facilities, is true to some extent. We are neither interested to enter deep in the pros and cons of the problem nor are we pleading that the differential treatments were justified and balanced or not; One can however argue that whatever may be the suitability or otherwise of the class system in ancient period, it served its purpose of strengthening the society. The class system was based upon the division of *'guṇa'* and *'karma'*. So every member of the society was able to exhibit his merits through his *karma*. An observation of the strict rules of the duties, kept the society on the path of order and stability. As the sacred law made the rules of *varṇas* and *āśramas*, it also offered the power of daṇḍa and the rights to the ruler.[42] So the kings were able to control the rules and regulations of *varṇāśramas* by their daṇḍa power. As the transgressors of the rules were severely punished by the kings; the intermixture of the castes was not there[43] and a social equilibrium was preserved. A violation of the class rules was supposed as a serious offence which could create bad effects in the society. We have seen before that King Rāma a regulator of the *varṇas*, killed the śūdra and the dead child got his life again. So a transgression of the class rules by an individual affects the whole machinery of the polity and society.

Thus, whatever may be the drawbacks of the class system, from the modern point of view, in the ancient period it was a part and parcel of the ancient Hindu society and polity. The duties of varṇāśramas were thus a social adjustment which was situated in the framework of *varṇāśramadharma*.

---

42. MS VII.17

43. Nai XVII.86

THE BRĀHMA-KSĀTRA RELATIONSHIP :

It will be interesting to peep into the mutual interdependence and affectionate relation between the two higher classes of the society reflected in the *Pañcamahākāvyas*. The might of the *Kṣtriyas* and the spiritual power of the *brāhmaṇas* were complementary to eachother. These two powers successfully held the society in a prosperous condition. According to Manu *Kṣatriya* without *Brāhmaṇa* or a force without intellect and a *brāhmaṇa* without *kṣatriya* can never thrive, By their mutual co-operation they prosper in this world.[44] *Brāhmaṇa* protects a king and the kingdom by the sacrificial and propitiatary rites and spiritual power; *Kṣatriya* protects the *brāhmaṇas*. and their sacrifices by his might. The power of *Kṣatriya* becomes glorious when it is augmented by that of *brāhmaṇa*. The co-operation of these two powers is well stressed by the poets of the *Pañcamahākāvyas*. It is described in Raghuvaṁśa that King Aja, whose coronation ceremony was guided and performed by his preceptor, versed in knowledge of *Atharvaveda*, became unassailable to his enemies because it was like the union of fire and wind that the *brāhmanical* power was associated with the *kṣātra* power of missiles.[45] Unfailing arrows of the mighty bowman Atithī were associated with the counsel of his preceptor. So there was nothing unattainable to the king.[46] The ascetics were able to destroy the dangers and obstacles from the demons, through their spiritual power; and 'curse' was the weapon in the arms of the *brāhmaṇas* which

44. MS IX.322
45. Raghu VIII.4
    स बभूव दुरासदः परैर्गुरुणाऽथर्वविदा कृतक्रियः ।
    पवनाग्निसमागमो ह्ययं सहितं ब्रह्म यदस्त्रतेजसा ॥
46. ibid. XVII.38

was very powerful against their enemies; but they relied on the ruler as the protector of *varṇas* and *āśramas* so they did not utilize their ascetic power and the weapon in the form of curse for the destruction of demons which was believed to be done by the rulers.[47]

A 'might' of a *kṣatriya* and an 'ascetic virtue' of the '*brāhmaṇa*' were the power points of these classes in their own provinces. But it is notable that these discriminating merits of these two classes were complementary to eachother. In Kirātarjunīyam the great sage Vyāsa advised Arjuna to apply his weapons if necessary at the time of the performance of penance also; because his propitiation was for the obtainment of the divine missiles. So his temporary ascetic stage and the employment of weapons was not controversial to the rules of the ascetism, as replies Arjuna in the 11th canto of Kirātārjunīyam. The distinguishing virtue of the sages viz. the *Śama* was essential for a *kṣatriya* also. According to Yudhiṣṭhira, a clever politician, quietude was a virtue not only of sages, but it is important for a politician, a ruler, in his 'wait and see' policy. Thus not only the duties of *Brāhmaṇa* and *Kṣatriya* were complementary to eachother but their distinguising means also were inevitable to eachother to acquire their aims.

These two powers, with their mutual co-operation contribute to the prosperity of the kingdom and welfare of the state. But in some exceptional cases one meets with their controversial relations also. The sage Paraśurāma, who was united with both the *brāhma* and *kṣātra* power as bearing father's portion characterized by sacred thread and mother's portion, mighty and powerful on account of the bow,[48] had a hostile attitude

47. Raghu XV.3
48. ibid. XI.64

towards *kṣatriyas.* He had as if taken a vow for the destruction of the *kṣatriyas*[49] So his eyes were shining like a flame of the fire of anger against *kṣatriyas.*[50] The sage wanted to subdue Rāma with his might; but Rāma, the descendent of Raghu accepted his challenge and defeated him stringing his mighty bow. Rāma, the real devotee of *brāhma*-power did not aim at Paraśurāma. Paraśurāma praised Rāma in eulogistic words. He confessed that his defeat had given an irreproachable fruit as the influence of *'rajas'* viz. action and passion inherited from mother, disapperared and peacefulness, the proper quality of ascetism from his paternal descent is obtained by him[51] Here, the occasional controversy between *brāhmaṇa* and kṣatriya resulted in happy ending.

The preceptors pleased with the righteous spirit of the rulers, showered on them, the fruit of their religious and spiritual merit, sometimes setting aside their spirit of equanimity towards all[52] The rulers also, fully believing and entrusting in their spiritual virtue, offered the entire credit of the prosperous kingdom, free from the calamities to the preceptors.[53] The religious merit acquired by the brāhmaṇas procures the king long life, wealth and increase of his territory.[54] The means of brāhmaṇa and *kṣatriya* viz. the study of *Śāstras* and the might relied on the bow were complementary to both and were capable to bestow prosperity, wealth on the kingdom.[55]

---

49. Raghu XI.67
50. ibid. XI.69
51. ibid XI.90
52. Kirā III.11/12
53. Raghu I.63
54. MS VII.134/136
55. Raghu I.19

THE AIMS OF HUMAN LIFE-REFLECTED IN THE PAÑCAMAHĀKĀVYAS :

The aims of human life were duly set in the system of four life- stages, with their particular functions. An achievement of the four goals viz. *Dharma, Aratha, Kāma* including *Mokṣa* was an ideal before every person in the Hindu society. An attainment of the three goals was essential, not only for the personal satisfaction of the needs of life but for the society in which the individual lived.

One should pursue equally all the three elements of the triad *dharma, Artha* and *kāma;* because all these are equally important in the life of an individual as well of the society and state also: With the importance of *Dharma* an obtainment of *Artha* is necessary, but the continuous running after the wealth is condemned by the *Śāstras*. Kāma, the third aim of life, which is situated in the second stage of life viz. house-holdership is also important as it gives scope for the development of powers to build up family undertakings and to fulfill the obligations of the society.

This equal practice of these goals is very important for an administrator. Because the breach of the equanimity in the practice of the three goals affects not only the king's personal life but mostly it affects his administration and his subjects. So he should obtain the three aims of life without being attached only to one of them. The ideal rulers in the *Paṇcamahākāvyas* offered an equal justice to the obtainment of the three goals.[56] The three aims of life were not in conflict in their life.[57] it was supposed to be a great offence to enjoy only Kāma keeping aside the acquisition of *dharma* and *Artha*.[58] So a ruler should not enter in the jaws of

56. Raghu I.21, X.84, XIV.21, XVII.57
57. Kirā I.11
58. Śiśu XVI. 49

only one of the goals.[59] In the circumstances, where all these three goals are in conflict with one another and a person has to make choice of one among the three, the ideal rulers voted for dharma over and above the other two. Representing the ideals prescribed by *dharmaśāstra,* the kings ruled the kingdom. Here *dharma* means not only the religion, but it comprises mainly one's own pious duty prescribed by the system of *varṇas* and *āśramas* as mentioned before. The *'dharma'* also comprises a righteous conduct of a person which is able to offer all the three goals of life to the person. It gives merit to the ascetics, Wealth to the desirous of pleasure and emancipation to the desirous of salvation.[60] The righteous kings were the firm observers of *'swadharma'* viz. their prescribed duties. It was the very reason that Arjuna, in Kirātārjunīyam, who was securing penance to obtain the divine missiles, as a duty of a kṣatriya, could not accept the advice of Indra who strongly supported salvation as the highest goal of human life. Indra tried to convince Arjuna the merits of salvation and demerits of *Artha* and *Kāma*. According to him *Artha* and *Kāma* were the hindrances to the obtainment of spiritual knowledge.[61] A person who gets the transient wealth by harmin others, becomes full with calamities as the sea is full with rivers. Wealth is a source of danger and the enjoyment of wealth also is dangerous like a hood of a serpent. Wealth is fickle in the case of saintly persons also.[62] Like wealth the *kāma* etc. also are the dreadful enemies, of a person as

---

59. Nai XVIII.2

60. Kirā XIII.44
तिष्ठतां तपसि पुण्यमासजन् संपदोऽनुगुणयन् सुखैषिणाम् ।
योगिनां परिणमन् विमुक्तये केननास्तु विनयः सतां प्रियः ॥

61. ibid. XI. 20.

62. ibid. XI.21 to 25.

they capture the person in their jaws.[63] So one should drive away these enemies from the path of salvation. The righteous persons knowing the fragile nature of wealth and life make efforts to get salvation.[64]

But this praise of salvation could not affect Arjuna. He explained Indra that his ascetic life was to obtain the divine missiles from Indra and Śiva and it was not for an obtainment of emancipation. He was in the second stage of life and was not desirous of transgressing the prescribed course of *varṇas* and *āśramās. As a Kṣatriya* it was his duty to fight with the enemies and increase his might; so salvation also was a hindrance in his path to acquire the wealth in the form of success over the enemies.[65] As a dutiful Kṣatriya he was afraid of the fragility of human life and thus was not anxious for salvation, before taking revenge of his deceitful enemy.[66]

Thus, the righteous kings, after duly securing the duties and enjoying the objects of senses, placing the responsibility of the kingdom on their able sons, acquired salvation renouncing the worldly life. [67] In the last stage of life they got an absolute peace of mind practising Yoga, restraining the mind from the external objects.[68] The righteous kings with their discriminative wisdom revealed an equal practice of the four aims of

---

63. Kirā XI.35
श्रद्धेया विप्रलब्धारः प्रिया विप्रियकारिणः ।
सुदुस्त्यजास्त्यजन्तोऽपि कामाः कष्टा हि शत्रवः ॥
64. Ibid. XI.13
65. Ibid.XI.69
वंशलक्ष्मीमनुद्धृत्य समुच्छेदेन विद्विषाम् ।
निर्वाणमपि मन्येऽहमन्तरायं जयश्रियः ॥
66. Ibid. XI.67
67. Nai XI.118 Ragu XVIII.3/33
68. Raghu X.23

life.[69] In the picture gallery of Nala, some sages were depicted in the pictures, who without crossing the ocean of austcrities were captured in the network of the nymphs.[70] Thus the prescribed order and equal justice to the four goals of human life leads the individual and also the society to prosperity.

It would be out of place to stress the opinion of Cārvāka, which is mentioned in the 17th canto of Naiṣadhīyacarita. Through the speech of Kali, the leader of vices, the views of *lokāyatikas* are represented. The exponents of the sensual pleasure regard an enjoyment of the worldly objects to be the only aim of human life. They do not believe in the purity of the caste-system[71] nor in the system of rules built by scriptures which teach that one enjoys happiness by religious merit.[72] According to them a man should do what tends to increase his happiness, should freely indulge in the desired pleasure[73] and should not think of the sin which is laid down to be suffered in the next birth because once the body is burnt, there remains nothing.[74] So one should try to gratify one's mistress, instead of quietude, because a creature once reduced to ashes never returns.[75] In this connection perception only is the strongest means.[76] Smiling upon the religious vows and virtues, they assert that abstention from stealing etc.

---

69. Nai XVIII. I, 1/2
70. ibid. XVIII.26
71. ibid. XVII. 40
72. ibid. XVII.39
73. ibid. XVII.48/50
74. ibid. XVII.52
75. ibid. XVII.69
    कः शमः क्रियतां प्राज्ञाः प्रियाप्रीतौ परिश्रमः ।
    भस्मीभूतस्य भूतस्य पुनरागमनं कुतः ॥
76. ibid XVII.45

means a long lease of life to poverty.[77] The command of cupid is obeyed even by gods, so it is worthy of greater respect than the scripturs, which is a command of gods. So according to them, one should try to satisfy one's senses, the treasury of joy. Thus enjoyment and indulgence in the passions is the chief motto of this life. The poet had condemned such heretics through the speech of Indra and other gods.[78]

Apart from the incidentally quoted views of the exponents of Kāma, the ideal kings placed an ideal of the equanimous achievement of the goals, before the subjects. An inportance of the equal practice of the the three aims is stated by the politicians and thinkers. Kauṭilya states that one should enjoy *Kāma* not making any conflict with *dharma* and *Artha*. These three elements are mutually connected. An excessive enjoyment of only one of them oppresses oneself and also others.[79] In Raghuvaṁśa, an exceptional case of king Agnivarna who destroy himself by the excessive force of passions is enough to stress the need of equanimous attitude towards the achievement of four goals of human life.

The principle of divine creation is applied to the four goals of human life also.[80] It serves the purpose to make the people follow the order of the human ends.

THE POSITION OF THE PRIEST :

An institution of the priest was very prominent and influential in ancient Indian polity. Though a priest was the head of the religious institution he had to secure

---

77. Nai XVII.83

78. ibid. XVII.85 to 106

79. KA I.7.5
एको हि अत्यासेवितो धर्मार्थकामानामात्मानमितरौ च पीडयति ।

80. Raghu X.22
चतुर्वर्गफलं ज्ञानं कालावस्थाश्चतुर्युगाः ।
चतुर्वर्णमयो लोकस्त्वतः सर्वं चतुर्मुखात् ॥

public and political matters along with the religious duties. It should be noted that the priest was to be distinguished from the sacrificial priest[81] though the priest performed the sacrificial duties. Due to his prominent influence upon polity and religious performances, he was the foremost maintainer of the kingdom.[82]

Like the king, the priest was the guardian of the realm. He had a prominent share in the king's duty of protection of the kingdom against the natural calamities and the external dangers of invasions. He was to protect that nation by diverting human and divine calamities.[83] He spiritual power of the priest liberated the subjects from all types of dangers. King Dilīpa in Raghuvaṁśa offered a full credit of the fearless and prosperous condition of the state, free from calamities, to the meritorious act of austerity of the preceptor.[84] The king was aware of the fact that, his fortunes were progressing towards prosperity due to the special care taken by his preceptor Vaśiṣṭha.[85] It was believed that the oblations offered by the priest to the fires in due form were converted into rain for the crops.[86]

The spiritual and religious power of the priest was able to drive away the dangerous external attacks from the enemies. By the influence of the *mantras* uttered by the holy priest, the king was invincible by his enemies. He was the *brahman* placed like a shield before the king averting the dangerous powers. It is described that the

---

81. MS VII.78
82. ŚN II.74
    पुरोधाः प्रथमं श्रेष्ठः सर्वेभ्योराजराष्ट्रभृत् ।
83. Raghu I.60
84. ibid. I.63
85. ibid. I.64
86. ibid. I.62

demons could not enter the city protected by the inchantations of the priests of King Bhīma.[87] Sometimes, the spiritual strength of the priest was deemed to be more powerful than king's might. King's arrows could pierce only visible objects, but the priest was able to protect the kingdom by counteracting the invisible magical charms of the enemies.

These functions of the priest are mentioned by Kauṭilya. According to him *Purohita* should belong to a distinguished and good family, highly learned, versed in all the sacred lores, as well as the science of astronomy and the theory of polity, skilled in propitiating gods by the various rites prescribed in the *Atharva Veda* to ward of calamities providential or otherwise occurring in the kingdom.[88] In the commentary on Kāmandakīya Nītisāra, the meaning of the term *Purohita* is explained as one who is employed to search out the means for the seen and unseen.[89]

From these qualifications of the *purohita* is seems that he was the master of not only the spiritual virtues but he was expected to be well-versed in *Trayī* and *Daṇḍanīti*. He was expected also to perform the propitiary rites prescribed by *Atharva manṭras*. He is frequently mentioned as '*Atharvanidhi*'[90] Thus he was skilled in both *Śāstra* and *śastra*. As well-versed in *Daṇḍanīti*, the kings could place the responsibility of the kingdom and administration on the royal priest, when needed. For instance, Kuśa marched towards the city of Ayodhyā, consigning the capital Kuśāvatī to the

87. Nai X.11

88. KA I.9.9
पुरोहितमुदितोदित कुलशीलं साङ्गे वेदे देवे निमिते
दण्डनीत्यां चाभिविनीतमापदां दैवमानुषीणामथर्वभिरुपायैश्च प्रतिकतीरं कुर्वीत ।

89. Commentary on KN IV.30/31
पुरो धीयते नियुज्यते दृष्टादृष्टेषु इति पुरोहितः।

90. Raghu I.59; VII.4

brāhmaṇas,, well-versed in *Vedas.*[91] When a king was busy in performing a long sacrificial session, the responsibility of the administration was shouldered by the royal priests.[92]

The priests, though masters of the spiritual virtues, were fully aware of the fact that a victory in the battle field should be gained by might and powerful arms. In Kirātārjunīyam, the great preceptor Vyāsa properly advised Yudhiṣṭhira to obtain powerful missiles from Lord Śiva.[93] Dhaumya, the family priest of the Pāṇḍavas offered weapons to Arjuna, which were invested with the *'abhicāramanṭras'*.[94] With the consultation and co-operation in the administration, the *purobita* sometimes took an active part in the operation in the battlefield also. In the *Rg-Veda*, there is an evidence to indicate this point. Prof. Hopkins in his journal of American Oriental Society (Vol.XV, page 260) states that Viśvāmitra was the purohita of king Sudās and took part in the operations of war against him by the allied forces of ten tribes well known as the 'battle of the ten kings'.[95] So occasionally but not frequently they used their military capacities,[96] for the success of the kings. In Arthaśāstra in the chapter of encampment of the war, four divisions of the camp are mentioned in which

---

91. ibid. XVI.25
92. Āpasṭamba Dharmasūtra XX.2.12.3
93. Kirā III.17
94. ibid III.56
    अथाभिपश्यन्निव विद्विषः पुरः पुरोधसाऽऽरोपितहेतिसंहतिः ।
    अभार रम्योऽपि वपुः स भीषणं गतः क्रियां मन्त्र इवाभिचारिकीम् ॥
95. Prof. Hopkins, journal of American Oriental Society, Vol. XV, p.260- Quoted by VRR Dikahitar 'Hindu Administrative Institutions' Published by university of Madras 1924, P.115.
96. ŚN II.78 षडङ्गवित्सांधनुर्वेदविच्चार्थधर्मवित् ।
    II.78 नीतिशास्त्रास्थव्यूहादिकुशलस्तु पुरोहितः ।

in the first are purohita and the primeminister (KA X.1). Thus from the earliest known literature, down to the treatises on polity and classical literature, the *purohita* maintained a high position in the state polity.

The sacrificial sessions were guided and performed under the supervision of the royal priest. Duryodhana, the supreme ruler of the earth, propitiated the oblations in sacrifices by the approval of his family priest.[97] The priest was entrusted with the supervision of religious as well as politico- religious ceremonies for the royal family or the state. General attention to the strict conduct towards the whole ceremonial was his lookout. The saṁskāra-rites of the princes were performed by the royal priests. Vaśiṣṭha the royal priest conducted the *saṁskāra* rites of Rahgu[98] and Vālmīki to that of the sons of Sītā.[99] The marriage rites, prescribed by the scriptures were performed by the priests. It is stated in Naiṣadhīyacarita that Bṛhaspati the preceptor of gods also had conducted the marriage-rites of Indra and Śachī[100] The revered priest of the Bhojas after the religious rites, tied the bride and the bride groom in wedlock.[101] A king was coronated by the royal preceptor. Even the *Anṭyeṣṭi* rite of the king was performed under the guidance of the royal priest.[102]

Proper guidance in the field of astrology, in seeking the omens and their prophesis, the effects of heavenly bodies was being consulted by the priests. While changing the capital, Kuśa narrated a dream to the

97. Kirā I.22
98. Raghu III.18
99. ibid. XV.31
100. Nai XVI. 45
101. Raghu VII.20
102. ibid. XIX.54

priests in the assembly and obeyed their consultation.[103] It was believed that success was sure if backed by good luck. So the kings used to commence the expeditions of conquests after performing the auspicious rites.[104] Relying on the science of astrology the priests could predict the effects of the heavenly bodies. An epithet (Kṛtyavid) is applied to the preceptor Vaśiṣṭha, who knew what was proper to be done regarding the pacification of the illomens. (Raghu XI.62)

The Purohita was appointed sometimes to carry on the negotiations between the king and other parties for various purposes, political and otherwise. King Janaka sent his priest Śaṭānanda to King Daśaratha, to accept his daughter for prince Rāma in marriage.[105] In Kumārasaṁbhava also, by the request of Pārvatī, Śiva sent the seven luminous sages to king Himālaya to ask for his daughter in marriage.[106] Due to their fatherly authority the preceptors could console the kings in their sorrows.[107]

One of the reasons for this affectionate fatherly relation of the preceptors towards the kings, was the hereditary appointment of the preceptors. Sometimes there seems to be only one *purohita* for more than one families of kings. In the race of Raghu kings, Vaśsiṣṭha was the *purohita* of the kings viz. Dilīpa, Raghu, Aja, Daśaratha, Rāma etc. He was the spiritual-head of the *Ikṣvākū* family.[108] The same fatherly relation is seen in

---

103. ibid. XVI.24
तदद्‌भुतं संसदि रात्रिवृत्तं प्रापर्द्विजेभ्यो नृपतिः राक्षस।
श्रुत्वा त अेनं कुलराजधान्या साक्षात्पतित्वे वृतमभ्यनन्दन्।

104. Raghu IV.26

105. ibid. XI.49

106. Ku VI.29

107. Raghu VIII.76/77

108. ibid XIII.70

the case of Vālmīki, when he consoles Sītā, abandoned by her husband importuning her to regard his hermitage to be the house of her father, situated in a different country.[109]

Vālmīkī was the friend and also had taken the responsibility of the education of the princes.[110] All this account reveals the fact that the preceptors guided many generations of the kings.

The spiritual power of the priests was able to give his desired object to the king. King Dilīpa, anxious for the progeny praised his preceptor to the effect that the objects difficult to be achieved by the kings born in the line of *Ikṣvāku,* were entirely in their successful disposal.[111] When the king stayed at the hermitage of the preceptor, he, to observe the regulations of the hermitage did not arrange for any special royal facilities though he was able to do it.[112] The animals which were nourished by the preceptor were not hurt by even the god of death.[113]

A great reverence and respect was accorded by the rulers to their priests and preceptors. When Bharata started with a large army to receive Rāma, he placed Vaśiṣtha, the family priest in the front.[114] In the

---

109. Raghu XIV. 72
जाने विसृष्टां प्रणिधानतस्त्वां मिथ्यापवादक्षुभितेन भर्त्रा:
तन्मा व्यथिष्ठा विषयान्तरस्थं प्राप्तासि वैदेहि ! पितुर्निकेतम् ।

110. ibid XV.33

111. Raghu I.72
तस्मान्मुच्ये यथा तात । संविधातुं तथार्हसि ।
ईक्ष्वाकूणां दुरापेऽर्थे त्वदधीना हि सिद्धय: ॥

112. ibid. I.94

113. ibid. II.62
तं विस्मितं धेनुरुवाच साधो ! मायां मयोद्भाव्य परीक्षितोऽसि ।
ऋषिप्रभावान्मयि नान्तकोऽपि प्रभु: प्रहर्तुं किमुतान्यहिंस्रा: ॥

114. ibid. XIII.66

marriage-procession towards the capital of King Bhīma, the royal priest was in the front. (Nai-XVI.1). Rāma bowed down at the feet of Vaśiṣṭha and then met his brothers.[115] In Śiśupālavadha, Śrīkṛṣṇa left his seat to receive Nārada, when he saw him from a long distance.[116]

Thus, the *purohita* had to attend several functions in the political, religious and social field of the kingdom. From the earliest literature down to our Pañcamahāvyas, the *purohita* has enjoyed a high position in the state polity. According to Bhīṣma in Śāti-Parvan, a king should appoint a *purohita* who would help him in protecting the righteous and putting down the unrighteous.[117] Both the king and the priest by their power and by their mutual cooperation equally tend towards the good of the common people.[118] Arthaśāstra also states the importance of *purohita* in the political field. There is no doubt that the energy of a *kṣatriya* backed by that of *purohita* and assisted by the deliberation of the ministers following the precedents laid down in the *śāstras* doubtlessly leads to success.[119] The *purobita* is counted among the eighteen *Tīrthas* of the state administration. Due to his special function of supporting of the king by his spiritual power he is

115. ibid. XIII.70

116. Śiśu I.12/14

117. ŚP (Critical Edition by BORI 73.1
य अेव तु सतो रक्षेदसतश्च निबर्हयेत् ।
स अेव राजा कर्तव्यो राजन्राजपुरोहितः ॥

118. ŚP (Critical Edition by BORI) 74.4
परस्परस्य सुहृदौ संमतौ समचेतसौ ।
ब्रह्मक्षत्रस्य संमानात्प्रजाः सुखमवाप्नुयुः ॥

119. KA. I.9.11
ब्राह्मणेनैधितं क्षत्रं मन्त्रिमन्त्राभिमन्त्रितम् ।
जयत्यजितमत्यन्तं शास्त्रानुगमशस्त्रितम् ॥

attributed as *'Viśeṣa-Amātya'*[120] Because of his spiritual excellence and knowledge of *daṇḍanīti*, a great respect was shown by the ruler. According to Kauṭilya, a king should follow his *purohita*, as a student his teacher; a son his father and servant his master,[121]

Thus *purohita*, the spiritual head, was a directing force in the administration also. His advice, consultation and cooperation were essential for the welfare of the state. It should be noted here with reference to the *Pañcamahākavyas* that he was not designated in the administration directly but the situation of the Hindu society in the framework of religion inevitably offered him a prominent place in the state-polity. No office of chieftaincy existed even in very early times without this office of *purohita*. Both appear to have been twins of the same mother, the state; Every state had a chieftain or king and every king had invariably a *purohita*..[122] So we cannot depict and evaluate king's administration and power properly without the mentioning of purohita.

INFLUENCE OF DHARMA :

It is a peculiarity of the ancient Indian Polity that the idea of *'Dharma'* has been immensely imbeded in it. The concept of religion was invariably connected with the concept of polity. Here it is intended to see the scope of the concept of Dharma with reference to the *Pañcamahākāvyas* and decide the place of dharma in the political thoughts expressed in them.

The word 'dharma' comprises not only a single idea but it had number of connotation and most of them are of an ethical nature. It has religious, political and

---

120. Commentary on KA IV. 30/31
पुरोहितस्याप्यमात्यविशेषत्वात् । वैशेषिकममात्यकार्यमित्याह ।

121. KA I.9.10
तमाचार्यं शिष्यः पितरं पुत्रो भृत्यः स्वामिनमिव चानुवर्तेत ।

122. VRR Dikshitar, Hindu Administrative Institutions, Published by University of Madras, 1929, p.119

social implications. Dharma means virtue, piety, right action, law of nature, code of customs or traditions, righteousness, nature of the farme-work of the society and its rules. So we have to discuss her the concept of *dharma* with all its aspects.

From the very ancient period of the vedas, the concept of *dharma* stands supreme in the life of a Hindu in general and of the King in particular. An importance of the concept of '*dharma*' is frequently stated in the vedic literature. In the very beginning of this world there was *brahman*. It did not flourish because it was single, it created *kṣātra-* power. Still it did not flourish, So it created *dharma*. So *dharma* influenced as the ruling power of *kṣatriya* class and there was nothing higher than *dharma*.[123] *Mahābhārata emphasizes the superiority of dharma* over other ends of human life.[124] According to Manu, *dharma* should be preferred if *Artha* and Kāma are in conflict with it[125]

It is stated before that the rulers in the *Pañcamahākāvyas* seem to make a creditable balance in the achievement of the four goals. [126] The four aims were not in conflict in the life of the kings.[127] But even though the four goals had an equal value in their life, it is notable than *dharma* was always uppermost in their minds. A dominance of Dharmaśāstra canons is clearly visible here. The kings gained wealth and gratified their desires but never transgressed the limits of *dharma*.[128]

123. Bṛhadāraṇyakopaniṣad I 4.14
स वै नैव व्यभवत् तच्छ्रेयोरुपमत्यसृजत् धर्म
तदेतत् क्षत्रं यद्धर्मस्तस्माद्धर्मात्परं नास्ति ॥

124. ŚP (Critical Edition by BORI) 69.68
धर्मश्चार्थश्च कामश्च सेवितव्योऽथ कालतः ।
धर्मेण हि महीपालश्चिरं पालयते महीम् ॥

125. MS IV. 176 परित्यजेदर्थकामौ यौ स्यातां धर्मवर्जितौ ।

126. Raghu I.21; X. 84; XIV.21

127. Kirā I.11

128. Raghu I.21

In one place in Raghuvamśa the preceptor Viśvāmitra is described as 'dharma-incarnate' and Rāma and Lakṣmaṇa the *artha* and *kāma* respectively.[129] Not only the human ends of life but the duties of the kings were viewed as an aspect of *dharma* and the requirements of *artha* and *kāma* were subordinate to the claims of *dharma*. The three goals stand in the hands of a person who beholds *dharma* as the basis of *artha* and *kāma*.[130] Thus the kings, the protagonists of *dharma* were *'Iśvara-incarnate.[131] and were inseparybly attached to dharma.[132] Thus a prominence was given to dharma* over and above *artha* and *kāma*. In the Mahābhārata also, stating an importance of *dharma*, Bhīṣma asserts that a king is for the sake of *dharma* and not for the sake of only pleasure.[133]

It is essential for the king to acquire *dharma;* but not for his personal interests. As a ruler of the subjects he has to follow and protect *dharma*. A king is not only a head of the administration but is a prominent power in preserving the rituals and religious activities. He himself accepts the code of *dharma* and following it, places a model before his subjects that they should follow the religious orders. The king maintains the established order so he should compel his subjects to follow their respective *dharma*.[134] It is his duty to protect

---

129. ibid. XI.35
राघवान्वितमुपस्थितं मुनिं तं निशम्य जनको जनेश्वरः।
अर्थकामसहितं सपर्यया देहबद्धमिव धर्ममभ्यगात् ॥

130. Nai XIV.81

131. Kirā XVIII.83

132. Rahgu I.23

133. ŚP (Critical Edition by BORI) 91.3
धर्माय राजा भवति न कामकारणाय तु।
मान्धातरेवं जानीहि राजा लोकस्य रक्षिता ॥

134. Sp (Critical Edition by BORI) 60.19
स्वेषु धर्मेष्ववस्थाप्य प्रजा सर्वा महीपतिः।
धर्मेण सर्वकृत्यानि समनिष्ठानि कारयेत् ॥

dharma.[135] he, who does not perform this duty is called a destroyer of *dharma.*[136] The rites and rituals constituted an important aspect of *dharma*. It was believed that the failure in the devotion of deserving personages results in fruitlessness. So king Dilīpa with his wife served the divine cow with devoted mind, obeying strictly the orders of the preceptor. The inner grief of king Dilīpa which he reveals before his preceptor, indicates the influence of religious conceptions over the mind of the ruler. The early Hindu scriptures provide emancipation from this world only for those who beget sons. This was more important for the king for the continuance of the royal dynasty and for the smooth succession to the throne. An anxiety of the king for the son is hinted many times in Raghuvaṁśa. The king pleads himself guilty being unable to offer the *swadhā*- offering after his death due to the absence of progeny.[137]He thinks that the ancestors have to drink the libations of water offered by him made tapid by their sighs. A merit arising from an offspring, born of a pure family is for happiness, both here and hereafter.[138] Thus the kings were not free from the religious conceptions of acquiring the freedom from the three debts.

It was also incumbent on a king to perform some daily rituals. Kauṭilya and some other thinkers make it a part of king's daily routine to perform certain rites befores entering the public hall of justice in the

---

135. KA I.3.16
तस्मात्स्वधर्मं भूतानां राजा न व्यभिचारयेत् ।
स्वधर्मं संदधानो हि प्रेत्यश्चेह च नन्दति ॥

136. ŚP (Critical Edition by BORI) 32.7
धर्मं विनश्यमानं हि यो न रक्षेत्स धर्महा ।

137. Raghu I.67

138. ibid. I.69

morning.[139] Neglecting the rituals was counted as a sin.[140] In Naiṣadhīyacarita, we come across many allusions showing the religious nature of the king performing the daily rituals. The gods were pleased with Nala, so it was his duty to offer them oblations in return. he performed the daily offering of Agnihotṛa oblations to the triad of the sacrifical fires. His worship to the sun was so intense that the deity thought that Karṇa's devotion to him was insignificant in comparison to that.[141]

Not only the human kings but the gods also were strictly on the path of *dharma*. The divinities obeyed the injunctions given by Vedic texts. In Naiṣadhīyacarita Brahmadeva, the Creator is attributed as a grandfather and no marriage with grandfather was permitted by vedic texts; that is why the Creator, conversant with law-books, did not go the the *swayaṁvara* of Damyantī.[142] Indra and other gods desirous of being Damayantī's consorts, invoked Nala on the basis of *dharma*, knowing his religious nature. They prayed that man is not everlasting but the fame and charity last for ever, so Nala's words should be true like *śruti*, so he should favour them by accepting the messengership of the gods.[143] Damayantī's father decided to perform the marriage-ceremony according to the injunctions of scriptures and law-books.[144] Lord Śiva in Kumārasaṁbhava did not miss the daily rituals, while

---

139. KA I.19 MS VII.145
उत्थाय पश्चिमे यामे कृतशौचः समाहितः।
हुताग्निर्ब्राह्मणांश्चार्च्य प्रविशेत्स शुभां सभाम् ॥
140. Nai XIX.24
141. ibid. XXI.32
142. ibid. X.16
143. ibid. V.135
144. ibdi. XV.7

enjoying the pleasures in the company of Pārvatī.[145] These instances clearly indicate the influence of the injections of the scriptures and law-books not only on the rulers but also upon the divinities. In Naiṣadhīyacarita, Kali censured the scriptures and the gods in reply pleaded for scriptures. They mentioned the illustrations of the people performing the religious activities through the power of *dharma* prescribed by the scriptures. Indra pleaded further that there should not be any doubt about the religion while it gives visible results as a birth of a child, destruction of the enemies, showering of rain etc.[146] Indra added that the vedic religion and the ancillary texts are well established and one must rely on it.[147] Thus, the rites and rituals, which was a part of *dharma,* were strictly followed by the ruler.

Though the rituals comprise an important aspect of *dharma,* dharma does not mean only performing the rituals and sacrifices. It will not be out of place to quote here the opinion of M.M. P.V. Kane about the position of *dharma.* He says '*Dharma* was a far-reaching concept; the writers on Dharmaśāstra meant by *dharma* not a creed. It was not a code of conduct but a mode of life which regulated a man's works and activities as a member of society and as an individual, and was intended to bring about the gradual development of a man and enable him to reach what was deemed to be the goal of human life.[148] Each member of the society has his duties and obligations to perform. These duties and obligations form an important aspect of *dharma.* If

---

145. Ku VIII.48
146. Nai XVII.93/94
147. ibid. XVII.101
148. MM P.V. Kane, History of Dharmaśāstra published by BORI, Poona, 1941 Vol. II, Part I. p.2

each person promotes his own *dharma* then he himself promotes the dharma of his caste and ultimately that of the society. So here *dharma* means the duties of a person prescribed for the framework of the society viz. the *Varṇadharma* and *Āśramadharma*. As a protector of *dharma* the ruler had to act in accordance with the rules of *varṇas* and *āśramas*, placing a model before his subjects. He should protect the religion, should punish the transgressor and should compel his subjects to follow their respective *dharma;* if the people cut the boundary lines of the caste-rules and *āśrama* rules then they affect the security of the whole society. The doctrine of *dharma* helps in his function to secure the society from chaos. As a controller of the caste-rules, the power of *Daṇḍa* is given to the king by the Creater himself. To keep the people on the right path of their duties, the Creator produced *daṇḍa* in the form of *dharma.*[149] By the fear of *daṇḍa* all the beings do not deviate from the path of dharma.[150] The king indeed is *dharma* roaming on the earth in a visible form with thousand eyes; if the people transgress his orders than they can not sustain at all.[151]

The rules and regulations of the *varṇāśramas* were very rigid. Breach of the rules was counted as a sin not only by the performer but also by the ruler himself. It was believed that the breach of the rules results in some bad augury. When king Rāma searched the reason of the untimely death of a *brāhmin* child, he found that this mishap resulted by a penance performed by a *śūdra* named Śambūka which was prohibited for a Śūtra Rāma punished *śūdra* cutting his head to remove the

149. MS VII.14
150. ibid. VII.15
151. NS XVII, 20
राजेति संचरत्येष भूमौ साक्षात् सहस्रदृक् ।
न तस्याज्ञामतिक्रम्य संतिष्ठेरन् प्रजाः क्वचित् ।

impurity in the *varṇsa*[152] and consequently the dead child was brought to life again.[153] Thus the strict observance of the rules and regulations of the *varṇas* by the ruler and the subjects was the very essence of *dharma*.

To insist the people for the strict observance of the caste rules a provision of the various ordeals to detect the tranagressor was prescribed by *dharma*. In Naiṣadhīyacarita it is stated that if a class-purity did not exist, the murderer of a highly chaste man would not be detected through ordeals.[154] A person committing adultery with a *brāhamin* woman does not win in an ordeal.[155] These ordeals are stated in religious-books and relying on them a ruler can check the impurities in the *varṇas*. Indra, the lord of the of the gods asks to Kali that when he himself, governs the three worlds, how can there be any impurity in the *varṇas?*[156] Thus the judicature in ancient India was partly relied on the system of ordeals to detect the defaulter and to preserve the class-purity. The caste system had a great influence upon the laws in the field of justice. There were distinctions and dissimilarities in penalties for the same crime, depending upon the caste of the offender. *Brāhmaṇas* were considered to be the superior class due to their spiritual power, so they enjoyed many privileges and exemptions from the punishments prescribed by law-books. In *Śāntiparvan* it is stated that a *brāhmaṇa* should not be given any capital punishment for any

---

152. Raghu XV.51
तपस्यनधिकारित्वात्प्रजानां तमघावहम् ।
शीर्षच्छेद्यं परिच्छिद्य नियन्ता शस्त्रमाददे ॥

153. Raghu XV.56

154. Nai XVII.86

155. ibid. XVII.87

156. ibid. XVII.85

offence.[157] A staunch politician like Kauṭilya also remarks, whatever may be the nature of the crime, no *brāhmaṇa* offender should be tortured. A king should either banish him or send him to the mines, for a life.[158] Due to superiority of the *brāhmaṇa-class*, the kings were bound by the laws to exempt the *brāhmaṇa* offenders from the punishments. In Raghuvaṁśa, King Rāma did not strike Paraśurāma who was brāhmin by caste, though he was the aggressor towards Rāma,[159] but the same king cut the head of the *śūdra* the transgressor of the caste-rules. Here, an equnimous nature of the king towards all, should not be suspected, because the king was only a controller of the rules to enforce with strictness and impartiality of the dharma which was neither of his making nor of his choice. It should be stated that, it was the responsibility of the brāmaṇa class to keep the laws which offered them superior position and an exemption from the punishments. Whatever may be the case, it was an inevitable effect of the caste-system which affected to some extent the judicature in ancient India.

Along with the system of the four *varṇas*, the arrangement of the four life-stages, was an important aspect of *dharma*. while stating the duties prescribed for the four *āśramas* it is stated before that the righteous kings duly followed the conduct of the life stages. It was the Kuladharma of the Raghu-race ie. handing over the responsibility of the kingdom to the virtuous sons, and the self-controlled kings, then trade the hermit's path.[160] The duties of the respective āśramas was the dharma of each person in the society. The leaders of

157. ŚP (Critical Edition by BORI) 56.31/32/33.

158. KA IV. 8.29

159. Raghu XI.84

160. Raghu VII.11

the people also were meticulously observing the duties of *āśramas* and were not ready to transgress the order of the *āśramas.*[161]

Dharma means righteous conduct which affects not only the king's personal life but his whole kingdom. The subjects always follow their leader.[162] So a righteous king leads his subjects to righteousness. Duryodhana, ruling the kingdom, which was snatched from Paṇdavas, was aware of the fact that he should win the people by his righteous conduct and administration.[163] A king represents four ages, according to righteous or unright conduct. If the king behaves unrighteously, the age of *Kali,* which earns great sin, increases. In Naiṣadhīyacarita, we come across a graphic description of *kali,* the spirit of sin and his colleagues viz. *Kāma,* Wrath Delusion etc., could not step in the kingdom of the righteous king Nala and his righteous subjects, following the code of conduct as that of their king. Kalī, the spirit of sin, lost his balance of mind and was filled with despair, at the sight of rites and observances pertaining to religion, followed by the people in Nala's kingdom.[164] Thus the king and the subjects both were religious and righteous who believed in the maxim prescribed by the law books. No parents, nor wife, nor sons will be a man's friend in the next world, but only righeousness.[165] Here it is clear that the word *'dharma'*

---

161. Kirā XI.76

162. BG III.21
यद्यदाचरति श्रेष्ठस्ततदेवेतरो जनः।
स यत्प्रमाणं कुरुते लोकस्तदनुवर्तते ॥

163. Kirā I.17
विशङ्कमानो भवतः पराभवं नृपासनस्थोऽपि वनाधिवासिनः।
दुरोदरच्छद्मजितां समीहते नयेन जेतुं जगतीं सुयोधनः ॥

164. Nai XVII.163 to 204

165. MS IV.239

is used showing mainly its one aspect, the righteousness.

The influence of religion, exercised a moral pressure upon the rulers. The unseen controlling power of *dharma* could keep the ruler on the path of virtue and rectitude. By the fear of sin and curse of *brāhmaṇas* the king and the subjects obeyed the commands of religion.[166]

In Raghuvaṁśa in the second canto the lion asks Dilīpa if he is afraid of the power of austerity and lustre of the precepter like a fire.[167] In another place, Lakṣamaṇa also breaks the agreement between Kāla and Rāma and disturbs their confidential deliberation, only by the fear of the curse of the sage Durvāsas.[168]

One is, however, struck by one more noteworthy point in this connection. The priest, the head of the religious institutions had a great influence over the king and the society, but he was never the head of the administration in ancient India and the king; the administrator also was not a chief of *dharma*, like the pope of the Vatican Kingdom. In Europe during the 8th and 9th centuries A.D. the pope and the bishops claimed the right to punish the king, but in ancient India one does not see any priest ruling the kingdom. In Raghuvaṁśa, the priests like Vaśṣṭha had a profound influence over the royal court. The king Daśaratha could not tranagress the command of sage Viśvāmitra to send the two young princes with him to protect the sacrifices. Though the priests had a deep knowledge of polity, they were not taking active part in administration. Their

---

166. ŚN II.78
     यत्कोपभीत्या राजाऽपि धर्मनीतिरतो भवेत् ।
167. Raghu II.49
168. ibid. XV.94
     विद्वानपि तयोर्द्वाः स्थः समयं लक्ष्मणोऽभिनत् ।
     भीतो दुर्वाससः शापाद्रामसंदर्शनार्थिनः ॥

guidance and advice were always sought for by the kings. But the preceptors were not greedy to acquire the royal power. If the brāhmaṇas and the priests would have been really avaricious or ambitious they could have easily aspired to occupy the royal offices. If they had only wished, they could have easily adorned the thrones of many a state; buy instead of it, they sought voluntarily hard and strenuous life of fasting and penance. They expected only dignity and reverence from the kings and were satisfied by the due respect offered by the kings to them.

The king, also was not the head of the religious institutions, He was only an agent of the state to enforce the *dharma* strictly and evenly. So the rulers were ruling according to the commands of *dharma*. The kings by their own strict and disciplinary conduct of following the rules of *dharma* directed a right path to his subjects; and the subjects also particularly obeyed the orders of their rulers which were prescribed by *dharma*.

Thus, *dharma* comprised of all these aspects, was significant part of kingship. Kingship was rooted in *dharma*, which upholds the person or the society. By the influence of *dharma* a person observes his code of conduct prescribed by the law-books and the duties observing the rules of *varṇas* and *āśramas* in the frame work of which the person resides. Sustaining his own dharma and acquiring the aims of life through the path of *dharma* in the society and state, he establishes *dharma* in the society and state. N.N. Law remarks "Government like all other concerns of life, is associated in the eye of a Hindu, with an ultimate spiritual purpose. A well conducted government forms the basis, without which the aggregate spiritual progress of the people in an orderly and effective way is not possible[169] The

169. N.N. Law, Aspects of Ancient Indian Polity, Published by Orient Longmans 1960, p.148

ideal of the state, set forth in the epics and later Sanskrit literature is the attainment of the spiritual purpose.

Thus the concept of government, was not complete without the concept of dharma, both were mutually interrelated.

SACRIFICES IN THE PANCAMAHĀKĀVYAS : A POLITICAL MOTIVE BEHIND THEM

In the *Pañcamahākāvyas,* we come across a large number of references to the various sacrifices performed by the kings. But the sacrifices are mentioned with the motive to depict the character of kings, their powers and their inclination towards the expeditions of conquest. So the minute details about the sacrificial rites are not expected here at all. The sacrifices viz. *Aśvamedha, Rājasūya, Viśvajit,* which are mentioned in the *Pañcamahākāvyas* contain only the popular elements of the sacrifices and the very few of the religious rites are referred to in the midst of other poetic descriptions.

The purpose of discussion in this topic is not to step deep into the system of religious rites performed in the sacrifices but to investigate the political motive behind them.

From the remote ancient Vedic period, there appears a clear tendency of displaying the valour by the king and that is the chief motive behind the performance of two great sacrifices viz. *Aśvameha* and Rājasūya. An inclination to acquire the dignity of the title *'Cakravartin'* was a general tendency among the ancient kings. *Aśvamedha* sacrifice is mentioned to be a kṣatriya's sacrifice,[170] which is to be performed by a king who covets to be the sovereign of the entire earth. Another quotation from the same text says— By performing the *Rājasūya* sacrifice, one becomes a king.[171] The perfor-

170. ŚB XII 4.1.2

171. ŚB IX. 3.4.8
राजा वै राजसूयेनेष्ट्वा भवति ।

mance of these sacrifices establishes the supremacy of the king. Rather it was a religious symbol or seal upon his overlordship. The idea is expressed in Śiśupālavadha, where *Rājasūya* sacrifice is mentioned as a symbol of kingship.[172] It was the right of an able sovereign to prove his influence by performing these sacrifices. As J. Gonda states. "The horse-sacrifice which no doubt was one of the ancient and important religious ceremonies by which the monarch ratified his claim to suzerainty over his neighbours was only performed by those rulers whose strength, power and wealth justified such an ambitious undertaking.[173] This tendency and intention of declaring sovereignty over the other kings is clearly visible in the kings of *Raghu*-race. The kings were ambitious and were desirous of the royal designation - 'Cakravartin'. They were eager to bring the whole earth under one '*chaṭra*' So king Raghu conquered ten directions and his son Aja gained a wealth excelling that.[174] In the very beginning of Raghuvaṁśa, the poet declares that he is describing the kings of Raghu-race, who held the sway over the whole earth bounded by ocean and the wheel-marks of whose cars lay as far as the celestial regions.[175] King Daśaratha had got the position of the chief of the circle of twelve kings.[176] All these kings of Raghu-race had performed a horse-sacrifice, due to the natural intention, tradition and to have a seal on their sovereignty. An incident of the horse-sacrifice performed by King Dilīpa, is depicted by the poet to impress on reader's minds the valour of

---

172. Śiśu XIV.14
तत्सुराज्ञि भवति स्थिते पुनः कः क्रतुं यजतु राजलक्षणम् ।
अदधृ भवतिकस्य वा भुवः श्रीवराहमपहाय योग्यता ॥

173. J. Gonda, Ancient Indian Kingship from the Religious Point of View, Published by E.J. Brill, 1966, p.110

174. Raghu IX.5

175. ibid. I.5

176. ibid. IX.15

prince Raghu. The sacrificial horse, which was set free by Dilīpa, to wander through the territories of the other kings, was not obstructed by any other king, which was an indication of supremacy of the monarch. The lord of the gods, Indra, stole the sacrificial horse through jealousy. Prince Raghu, who guarded the horse, valiantly opposed Indra, who was very much pleased by the valour of Raghu and he promised him to bestow the merit of sacrifice to his father.[177] The event proves that horse-sacrifice, a symbol of supreme power, was an essential requirement for a monarch. After the reign of Dilīpa, his son Raghu arranged an expedition of conquest in all directions and conquered the entire earth. He performed the '*Viśvajit*' sacrifice, the name of which is expressive of the universal supremacy of the monarch. There are many allusions to the horse-sacrifices performed by King Daśaratha[178] Rāma, Atithi.[179] etc. From all these illustrations we recollect the fact that the kings of the solar-race were desirous of obtaining sovereignty and therefore of performing the horse-sacrifice.

It is already stated that a depiction of the rituals in the sacrifices is not a subject matter of the *Pañcamahākāvyas,* but in the conventional description, one obtains an information about some of the sacrificial rites. From the references of the sacrificial ceremonies in Raghuvaṁśa and Śiśupālavadha, one is acquainted with the rites in the horse-sacrifice and Rājasūya-sacrifice respectively. These sacrifices were not a single ceremonial, but a series of rituals, several of which had an independent existence. It was a combination of a

---

177. ibid. III.65
अमोच्यमश्वं यदि मन्यसे प्रभो ! ततः समाप्ते विधिनैव कर्मणि
अजस्रदीक्षाप्रयतः स मद्गुरुः क्रतोरशेषेण फलेन युज्यताम् ॥

178. Raghu IX.20

179. ibid, XVII.76
पराभिसंधानपरं यदयप्यस्य विचेष्टितम् ।
जिगीषोरश्वमेधाय धर्म्यमेव बभूव तत् ॥

number of 'Iṣtis'. The period of completion of the whole ceremony of Rājasūya was spread over about two years and three months. *Aśvamedha* occupies a period of one year. The sacrificial horse was allowed to roam at its will for a whole year. A direct mentioning about the period of the sacrifice is not found but from some suggestive references in Raghuvaṁśa one can guess about the lengthy duration of the great sacrifices. At the completion of the sacrifice, the king permitted the princes to return to their capitals whose wives of the harem were anxiously waiting for them due to the pangs of along separation.[180]

It would be in the fitness of things if we discuss some rites which are accomplished in these sacrifices. At the commencement of the sacrifice the host binds himself by an oath. In the Rājasūya of Yudhiṣṭira, he uttered an oath by the permission of Śrīkṛṣṇa.[181] The holy bath of the host is mentioned in the same verse. The holy bath and the oath ceremony of Daśaratha are described in Raghuvaṁśa : "with his speech restrained, holding the antelope hide and a staff, wearing a waist-band of *kuśa-* grass and furnished with the horn of a dear, he got the position of a consecrated host of the sacrifice.[182] A presence of the crown-queen was essential for the oath-ceremony. In the *Aśvamedha-* sacrifice, performed by Rāma, a golden statue of the crown-queen Sītā was placed as she was abandoned by the king.[183] In a particular rite, the wife of the host

---

180. Raghu XIV.87

181. Śiśu XIV.18
आननेन शशिनः कलां दधर्शनक्षयितकामविग्रहः ।
आप्लुतः स विमलैर्जलैरभूदष्टमूर्तिधरमूर्तिरष्टमी ॥

182. Raghu IX.17
अजिनदण्डभृतं कुशमेखलां यतगिरं मृगशृङ्गपरिग्रहाम् ।
अधिवसंस्तनुमध्वरदीक्षितामसमभासमभासयदीश्वरः ॥

183. ibid. XV.61

was respectfully honoured because it was believed that the oblations were sanctified when they were seen by the wife of the host and such holy oblations were offered to the sacrificial fire.[184] The oblations were offered by the priests with the recitations of *Yājyā* and *Anuvākyā*.[185] A correct recitation of the *mantras* was essential. A recitation without any fault gives the proper meaning of the *mantra*. It was believed that the faulty utterance of the *mantras* badly affect the sacrifice and also the performer of the sacrifice. In the *Rājasūya* sacrifice performed by Yudhiṣṭhira, the sacred fire got brightness by accepting the oblations which were purified by the chants having very clear syllables.[186] Even the perfume of the duly offered oblations was worthy of destroying the sins of the living beings who smelt it.[187]

The priests, under whose guidance and direction, the sacrifices were performed, were learned in the vedic-lore and were qualified in their sphere. The *Hotṛ* whose speech was true, favourable and agreeable was reciting the chants in *Rgveda* and the *Udgātṛ* was singing the *sāma* without *faltering*.[188] The King Yudhiṣṭhira was sensitive and conscious about the righteous conduct, high birth and the knowledge of the *brāhmaṇas*. He heard them reciting the chants of *Swasṭyayana*, who were pure in conduct and born in noble families without any intermixture of castes and who were learned in the *sāstras* which were agreeable to Vedas.[189]

---

184. Śiśu XIV.22
185. ibid. XIV.20
186. Śiśu XIV.26
तत्र मन्त्रपवितं हविः क्रतावश्नतो न वपुरेव केवलम् ।
वर्णसम्पदमतिस्फुटां दधन्नाम चौज्ज्वलमभूद्धविर्भुजः ॥
187. ibid. XIV.27
188. ibid. XIV.21
189. ibid. IV.37
शुद्धमश्रुतिविरोधि बिभ्रतं शास्त्रमुज्ज्वलमवर्णसङ्करैः ।
पुस्तकैः सममसौ गणं मुहुर्वाच्यमानमश्रृणोदिद्वजन्मनाम् ॥

It would be worthwhile to turn to an important aspect of the sacrifices. That is the donation of the gifts to the *brāhmaṇas* and the petitioners. The contribution of the gifts may be considered here from different view points.

As a religious aspect, charity is the essence of *dharma*. So it was a notable virtue of the pious kings, who were treading the path of *dharma*. The *Viśvajit* sacrifice performed by King Raghu is a fine instance to reveal the aspect of charity. He donated all the acquired wealth to the priests and petitioners.[190] It was a natural instinct of the pious rulers to distribute all the wealth to the petitioners as the clouds shower the water. The treasury of king Raghu was thus emptied so much, that he could receive the disciple Kautsa, who was in need of wealth, with an earthen-pot.[191] he appreciated even the poverty of a paramount emperor, resulting from the sacrificial fee paid in the sacrifice.[192]

The donations in the sacrifice had a significance from another point of view also. It was a duty of the protector of the subjects to seek welfare of people. A ruler should allow his subjects to share his acquired wealth through the pretext of the sacrifices. After the conquest of the four directions, the emperor performed the great sacrifice and showered gifts to his subjects. In this context a view stated by M.R. Kale is noteworthy. While appreciating the charity of king Raghu he says - "It was natural that Raghu should perform a sacrifice at the termination of his successful campaign to please the *brāhmaṇa*-class. He had advanced and honoured the chief *kṣatriya* warriors by his conquest; opened facility

190. Raghu. V.186

191. ibid. V.2

192. ibid. V.16

स्थाने भवानेक नराधिपः सन्नकिंचनत्वं मखजं व्यनक्तिः ।
पर्यायपीतस्य सुरैर्हिमांशोः कलाक्षयः श्लाघ्यतरो हि वृद्धेः ।।

for trade and so pleased the *Vaiśyas* and by acquiring new lands for cultivation gratified the *Śūdras;* and it now remained for him to please to *brāhmaṇas,* whose blessings he must have received at the beginning.[193]

The King Atithī also, after the performance of the great sacrifice, honoured the priests with bountiful presents, so much, so that his name and that of Kubera have got identical position.[194] In the *Dharmakośa,* it is mentioned that a king should perform the sacrifices with sumptuous gifts and should give the brāhmaṇas wealth for the sake of *dharma.*[195]

So while stabilizing political supremacy over the other kings the dutiful kings like Raghu and others were careful about the welfare and contentment of their subjects. Liberal distribution of wealth among the poor and needy was an important part of such performances. These sacrifices were important not only as religious performances but at the same time they possessed a great economic and cultural significance. As Rāmāshraya Sharma quotes - The *Kṣatriyas* were a prosperous community and in order to prevent accumulation of wealth at one place, the performance of periodical sacrifices was enjoined upon them as a religious obligation.[196] A large part of the depiction of the sacrifices viz. Rājasūya and Aśvamedha in the *Pañcamahākāvyas,* is occupied by the offering of the

193. M.R. Kale, Raghuvaṁśa, of Kālidāsa (Contos I-V) Motilal Banarasidass, Delhi 1972

194. Raghu XVII.80

195. Dharmakośa (MS VII.79)
यजेत राजा क्रतुभिर्विधैराप्तदक्षिणैः
धर्मार्थं चैव विप्रेभ्यो दद्याद्भोगान्धनानि च ॥

196. Ramashraya Sharma, A Socio Political Study of the Vālmiki-Rāmāyaṇa published by Motilalal Banarasidass 1971 p.119

gifts.[197] At the commencement of the sacrifice, Yudhiṣṭhira asked Śrīkṛṣṇa, how to utilize the wealth acquired in the conquest of the four directions.[198] He donated even the lands, impressing a seal on the documents.[199]

In the sacrificial ceremony the friends and feudatory kings offered presents to the emperor. In the Horse-sacrifice performed by Rāma, all the *rākṣasas* and monkey-kings offered valuable gifts to Rāma.[200] Yudhiṣṭhira obtained precious gems, which were difficult to be obtained at any other place.[201]

The sacrificial ceremony was, as it were, a get together of the invitees and it was noteworthy that all the kings and friends were cooperating the host in various functions. The people who were participating in the various duties were seen by others with eyes full of respect.[202] Even lord Kṛṣṇa requested Yudhiṣṭhira to employ him in some sacrificial activity.[203] The *rākṣāsas,* who were the destroyers of the sacrifices, were now the protectors of the sacrifice performed by Rāma.[204] There was no deficiency of any object and prosperity and affluence were visible in every function.[205]

After considering the religious rites and ceremonials, a peep into the symbol of *Aśvamedha* i.e.

---

197. Śiśu XIV.33/35/40
198. ibid. XIV.11
199. Śiśu XIV.36
200. Raghu XV.58
     तमध्वराय मुक्ताश्वं रक्षः कपिनरेश्वराः ।
     मेधा सस्यमिवाम्मोभिरभ्यवर्षन्नुपायनैः ॥
201. Śiśu XIV.39
202. ibid. XIV.42
203. ibid. XIV.15
204. Raghu XV.62
205. Śiśu XIV.32

the 'Horse' and its significance will indeed help the elucidation of the topic under discussion. At the commencement of the sacrifice a horse was set free to roam at its will in the desired direction. In the *Aitereya brāhmaṇa* it is mentioned that the horse, when set free is to wander into the north-east direction, which is suggestive of 'invincibility' i.e. victory, where the door of heaven is visible and where the victory is obtained.[206] Wherever the horse wanders unobstructed, the over-lordship of the king is supposed to be established there. In the Vedic texts the horse is mentioned as a symbol of regal power.[207] A wish is pronounced that through the horse, the king may kill his enemies, be irresistible and be a sovereign ruling, a wealthy and prosperous people and attain old age.[208]

The sacrificial horse, while roaming, was guided and protected by the royal princes. In the horse-sacrifice performed by Dilīpa, the horse was guarded by prince Raghu accompanied with hundred other princes.[209] The conversation between Raghu and Indra proves the significance of a horse in the sacrifice. Raghu requests Indra, the restrictive of enemies, not to hamper the sacrifice undertaken by a righteous king, by stealing the horse.[210] he prays Indra to set free the horse, the most essential factor of the sacrifice.[211] Indra, pleased by the

---

206. AB I.14
207. ŚB XIII.2.3.16
अथो क्षत्रं वाऽश्वः। क्षत्रस्यैतद्रूपं यद्धिरण्यं क्षत्रमेव तत्क्षत्रेण समर्धयति।
208. Taiṭṭirīya Brāhmaṇa III.8.5
अनेनाश्वेन मेध्येनेष्ट्वा। अयं राजा वृत्रं वध्यादिति।
अयं राजाऽप्रतिधृष्योऽस्त्विति। अनेनाश्वेन
मेध्येन इष्ट्वा....अयं राजा सर्वमायुरेत्वेति।
209. Raghu III.38
210. ibid. III.45
211. ibid III.46

valour of Raghu was ready to offer any other favorable object instead of the sacrificial steed.

Thus, through the sacrificial symbol i.e. the horse, the sovereigns used to establish their supremacy over the other kings. There are also some subordinate motives behind the performance of horse-sacrifices. In the abovementioned instance, Indra was not ready to return the horse; so Raghu asked for his father, the entire fruit of the sacrifice.[212] In the *Aśvamedhika Parvan* it is stated that the horse- sacrifice is the sanctifier of all sins; so to get rid of the sins, one may perform the horse sacrifice.[213] In *Jaiminīya Brāhmaṇa*, the meaning of this sacrifice. is expressed as follows It was in the beginning mystically 'seen' by *Prajāpatī*, when he was desirous of offspring and cattle and when he wished to extend the world and to gain exclusive ownership of the heroic power specially belongs to Indra. So anyone, who wished to obtain the same results, should perform this sacrifice.[214]

Thus the intentions behind the performance of the sacrifices were extension of kingdom and power, establishment of overlordship and general acquisition of strength. Besides these expensive sacrifices comprising lengthy rituals and having a strong political motive behind them, some other sacrifices are also alluded to in the *Pañcamahākāvyas*. In *Naiṣadhīyacarita*, *Sauṭrāmaṇi* sacrifice is mentioned. In the depiction of the ideal reign

---

212. Raghu III.65

213. Āśvamedhika Parvan (Critical Edition by BORI) 70.16
अश्वमेधो हि राजेन्द्र पावनः सर्वपाप्मनाम् ।
तेनेष्ट्वा त्वं विपाप्मा वै भविता नात्र संशयः ॥

214. Jaiminīya Brāhmaṇa II.266
अथैषोऽश्वमेधः । प्रजननकामो हेतेन यजेत ।
प्रजापतिर वा अकामयत—बहु प्रजया पशुभिः प्रजायेय
वीमान् लोकान् आप्नुयाम्, अथेन्द्रियं वीर्यं रुन्धीयेति ।
स अेतत् यज्ञम् तम् आहरत् । तेनायजत ।

of King Nala, it is stated that, Kali, the spirit of sin, was seeking some drawbacks to destroy him. The *brāhmaṇas* were performing the *Sautrāmaṇi Yāga* in which they offered and drank wine, so kali felt that the *brāhmaṇas* transgressed the restrictions of *dharma* and then he could catch the *brāhmaṇas* red-handed. *Sautrāmani* is not a separate sacrifice, but a portion of *Rājasūya* sacrifice and is performed in the accomplishing rites of Rājasūya. Another sacrifice named *'Puṭrakāmeṣṭi'* is mentioned in Raghuvaṁśa. A divine birth of the sons of Daśaratha took place as the desired fruit of the sacrifice.

In short, while considering the sacrifices in *Pañcamahākāvyas,* specially from the political motive behind them with a veil of *'dharma'* one may significantly note that they had occupied an essential and unavoidable position in the reign of each emperor. The objects obtained through the performance of these sacrifices are an external development of the kingdom and the internal welfare of the subjects by an ideal ruler. The sacrifices offered opportunity to the princes to indulge in royal magnanimity.

PENANCES : FROM THE POLITICAL POINT OF VIEW :

Observance of penance influenced prominently the lives of the kings in the *Pañcamahākāvyas.* Observance of penances was supposed by them as the means to increase their kṣātra-power. The main theme of Kirātarjunīyam is the acquirement of the *Pāśupata* missile by Arjuna by Propiciating hard penance for the favour of Indra and Śiva. The great sage Vyāsa came to impart the knowledge of the mystic lore by which Arjuna practiced very hard austerities and acquired thereby the means for the Pāśupata missile and extraordinary valour to uproot the enemies.[215]

---

215. Kirā III.22

To test the sincerity of Arjuna in the observance of penance, Indra argues that Arjuna's dress of a warrior equipped with arms is contradictory to ascetism. Arms and armour are not necessary for keeping peace.[216] Bearing of the weapons is not fit for a person desirous of salvation which is acquired by the penances.[217] According to Indra a person who violates the action of acquiring salvation by violence, he spoils the holy water of Ganges.[218] Penance is a direct means to salvation which is contradictory to the way of violence, viz. war.

But Arjuna is not ready to accept this mode of thinking. According to him, as directed by Vyāsa, the divine weapons are to be acquired by observing severe penance only. Performance of penances, through ascetism is accepted by Arjuna but he is not ready to receive salvation, as the result of observing ascetism. He is performing his duty as a valiant *Kṣatriya* and as a householder, so he supposes salvation a hindrance in the path of his 'swadharma.[219] He chooses only the sādhana viz. ascetism and not sādhya viz. the salvation as his target. There is no confusion in his thoughts and he supposes no contradicion in bearing weapons while performing penance because the weapons are useful to avert the obstructing elements.[220]

Thus to face the enemies stronger in valour, missiles and army, one must gain superiority, on which depends success in battlefield. Arjuna tried successfully to gain superiority in missiles and weapons which he obtained by the means of severe penances only.

---

216. Kirā XI.17
217. ibid XI.18
218. ibid. XI.19
219. ibid XI.69
220. ibid. XIII.13

Thus observance of penances was not a special province of only the ascetics but it was an accepted way of the rulers to increase their kṣātra-power to employ against their enemies.

SIGNIFICANCE OF DAIVA IN THE POLITICAL FIELD :

It is very interesting to examine the concept of *Daiva* or Destiny and a relative superiority of fate and exertion in the political field.

Much importance is offered to manly efforts to acquire success. But sometimes we experience that *daiva* dominates human exertions. The highest position of human efforts seems to be molested by destiny; but in such circumstances the defeat is not credited to the person and his fame is not affected by the failure. In Raghuvaṁśa King Dilīpa, who had a great belief in his velour of arms, tried his best to save the divine cow from the attack of the lion but became unsuccessful as his fingers stuck to the arrow remained fixed like one drawn in a picture. The lion replied that the thing which was beyond protection through arms did not impair reputation of those who hold weapons.[221] But the king was intact in his decision to protect the cow. Here the king's devotion about his preceptor was tested by the divine cow for which the illusive situation was created. But in other cases also when creatures know that their weal and woe are dependent on destiny and not on their exertion, they should not grieve and leave the efforts remembering the effect of destiny. Where the power of valour is restricted, there stands the influence of destiny. When *daiva* is against the person his exertion becomes fruitless. In Kirātārjunīyam, in the tussle between Arjuna and the Kirātaraja, Arjuna the expert warrior employed various missiles, but lord Śiva

221. Raghu II.40

in the guise of Kirātarāja made all the missiles effectless. But Arjuna, a sincere follower of *kṣātradharma*, did not accept the defeat by destiny[222] and after the futility of missiles was prepared for the fight.

When fate stands in the way, even efforts stern with endeavour assume not the character of causes.[223] The utterly uncontrolled heart of man follows the creator's will in the direction in which it moves.[224] Everyone being subordinate to fate for ever, a man who acts knowingly not deserves any censure.[225]

There is one point worthy to be noted here. These heroic characters, though they take recourse to the idea of fate in their argument, in actual practice they do not cease from their attempts. In Kirātārjunīyam we see that when Yudhiṣṭhira accepted the challenge of playing dice, he was fully aware of the evil consequences of gambling but then also as a dignified *kṣatriya* he thought it as below his dignity to refuse the challenge. Arjuna, a true devotee of brotherhood and who stood always in the commands of his elder brothers, did not blame Yudhiṣṭhira, who accepted the challenge of gambling which resulted in the loss of kingdom, brothers and wife; but he attributed the bad results in the name of destiny.[226] The high personalities, though accept the effect of destiny, do not devote much attention to it but rely on human activity which is in the range of thinking. According to Manu, all undertaking is dependent upon the order of destiny and of human efforts, of these two, destiny is incomprehensible and action is

---

222. Kirā XVI.63
223. Nai XI.55
224. ibid I.20
225. ibid VI.103
226. Kirā XI.47

possible only in regard to human exertion.[227] It is remarkable that the kings though aware of the influence of destiny never remained inactive to wait upon the effects of destiny but relied on the superiority of human efforts. It is clear that aided by good policy and not frustrated by destiny an undertaking gets success.

Ancient thinkers and politicians had advocated the superiority of human efforts in political undertakings, but they had accepted the fatalistic influence on human efforts, had exhibited faith in astrology and possibility of averting the influence of fate by performing propitiatory rites. We come across the mentioning of some visitations named *'Itis'* which are human as well as providential. The dangers like fire, flood, diseases etc. are providential and they are averted through the worship of gods, performing propitiatory rites prescribed in *Atharvaveda* and those undertaken by preceptors. It is alluded that King Dilīpa offers full credit of his prosperous kingdom without dangers, either human or divine, to his preceptor who averts the dangers. His subjects lives in the full extent of man's life, free from miseries due to the meritorious act of austerity of the preceptor. Not only the providential distress but to avert the dangers caused by human-make like attacks by enemies, the preceptors' *mantras* are effected along with the piercing bows of the king.[228] Thus the valour and the exertion of the king was strongly backed by the power of the preceptor to check the destiny. King Dilīpa was fully confident that his preceptor would change his destiny the of his issueless condition.[229]

---

227. MS VII.205
सर्वं कर्मेदमागतं विधाने दैवमानुषे ।
तयोर्दैवमचिन्त्यं तु मानुषे विद्यते क्रिया ॥

228. Raghu I.61

229. ibid. I.72

Though the kings were not inactive fatalists, they believed in the power of fate. So the relative influence of the divine and human action is pointedly stated by Indian thinkers in the political fields.[230] In the case of the persons who follow the path of creditable virtues, even the fall caused by adverse fate does not give ground for blame,[231] because it is the fate that controls the activities of man. While pursuing the right path, if a man meets failure on account of his adverse fate, that failure too is creditable. According to Kāmanḍaka, one should not be condemned if he could not attain success in an undertaking though properly begun; because it is a stronger force of fate which causes acts adversely by overshadowing one's enterprise.[232]

A wise king neither relies on mere fate only nor he depends solely on his exertion, but like an eminent poet who relies on both, words and meaning, he relies as much on luck as on human enterprise.[233] Yājñavalkya has given a detailed account of the strength and *Puruṣākāra*. He says success depends on both fate and human efforts. The actions belonging to past life determine the fate which is inscrutable and beyond our control. Some people wish to achieve their ends by fate only, while some apply their own efforts. But as the chariot cannot move by one wheel, so the fate not associated with human efforts, cannot become effective.[234]

---

230. KA VI. 6 to 12
मानुषं नयापनयौ, दैवमयानयौ ।
देवमानुषं हि कर्म लोकं यापयति । अदृष्टकारितं दैवम्
दृष्टकारितं मानुषम् तच्चिन्त्यम् अचिन्त्यं दैवम् ।

231. Kirā II.34

232. KN XII.19
यत तु सम्यगुपक्रान्तं कार्यमेति विपर्ययम् ।
पुमांस्तन्त्रानुपालम्भे दैवान्तरितपौरुषः ॥

233. Śiśu II.86

234. YS I. 348/350

A person who is contented with his acquired wealth, the destiny does not help him.[235] It helps a valorous and ambitious person. So an ambitious king may not be satisfied with small fortunes, even if fate goes against him.

MATRIMONIAL RELATIONSHIP :

Alongwith the various Saṁskāra-vidhi's the vivāha-saṁskāra is frequently occurred and described in the *Pañcamahākāvyas*. We come across vast poetic descriptions of the *Swayaṁvara* and marriage ceremony of Indumatī and Sītā in Raghuvaṁśa, that of Damayantī in Naiṣadhīyacarita and of Pārvati in Kumārasaṁbhava.

Here we are intended to see the political considerations, if there any, behind the matrimonial relations of the rulers. A prominent motif behind the matrimonial relations of the valorous and 'Vijigiṣu' kings was to increase a circle of alliances, which could supply them a strong backing against their enemies. In this context the marriage of Kuśa with Kumudvatī, the Nāga-princess is worthy to be noted. By this relation, the Nāgas got king Kuśa as their kinsman and Kuśa on his part obtained support of Nāga-power. The Nāga-king left the fear arising from his enemy Garuda and Kuśa also ruled the earth where serpents were made harmless.[236]

An intention behind the marriage of Śiva and Pārvatī, in Kumārasaṁbhava was to create a valorous and eminent commander-in-chief for the gods that he could destroy the demon Tāraka. Thus matrimonial

235. Śiśu II.32

236. Raghu XVI.88
इत्थं नागस्त्रिभुवनपुरोशैरसं मैथिलेयं
लब्ध्वा बन्धुं तमपि च कुशः पञ्चमं तक्षकस्य ।
अेकः शङ्कां पितृवधरिपोरत्यजव्दैनतेयात् ।
च्छान्त व्यालामवनिमपरः पौरकान्तः शशास ॥

relation was a prominent reason of acquiring alliances and military strength and support. Sometimes the matrimonial relation effects into rivalry between two kings. In the sixteenth canto of Śiśupālavadha, while abusing Śrīkṛṣṅa the messanger of śiśupāla charges that Rukmini was decided by the elders to be given in marriage to Śiśupāla. She was betrothed of Śiśupāla so her forceful abuction proves his rebellious nature, not only as a king but also as a relative.[237] So it was one of the prominent causes of the rivalry between Śrīkṛṣṇa and Śiśupāla.

A *swayaṁvara* ceremony was an opportunity to a princess to choose her consort from the assembled princes. After the selection by the princess of her life-partner, probably the unsuccessful candidates. getting insulted used to attack the successful prince. The victorious hero, by his valour and strength defeating the other king, proved himself worthy of acquiring the hand of princess in marriage.[238] That is why the father of the princess, by declaring some difficult condition in the *swayaṁvara* tested the strength and worth of the 'would be guardian' and husband of his daughter. In Sītā's *swayaṁvara*, Janaka had declared the participants, the condition of breaking the divine bow, difficult to be bent. The word 'Vīryaśulka' indicates that Rāma paid the price in the form of an exhibition of his strength, while breaking the bow.[239]

Thus the political considerations are prominently seen in the matrimonial relations alluded in the *Pañcamahākāvyas*.

---

237. śiśu XVI.48/49
238. Raghu VII.67
अितः पराभकहार्यशस्त्रान्वैदर्भि । पश्यानुमता मयासि ।
अेवंविधेनाहवचेष्टितेन त्वं प्रार्थ्यसे हस्तगता ममैभिः ॥
239. ibid. XI.47

CHAPTER III

MINISTERS

A SIGNIFICANT PLACE OF THE MINISTERS :

Among the seven constituents of the State, Ministers have occupied a significant place next to the king. A king, single-handed, cannot bear the burden of the whole administration, as a single wheel is unable to pull the carriage.[1] According to Manu, an easy work becomes difficult if it is done singly; then what to say about the vast kingdom?[2]

The word 'minister' comprises all that is connoted by the words *'amātyas' sacivas* and mantrins. These words are employed in the *Pañcamahākāvyas* as synonyms, though they indicate distinction of grades and functions supposed by ancient writers.[3] It was essential for the ministers that they should be meritorious.[4] They were expected to be well-versed in

1. KA I.7.9
सहायसाध्यं राजत्वं चक्रमेकं न वर्तते ।
कुर्वीत सचिवांस्तस्मान्तेषां च शृणुयान्मतम् ॥

2. MS VII.55

3. Amarkośa II (Kṣatriya Varga)
मन्त्रीधीसचिवोऽमात्योऽन्ये कर्मसचिवास्ततः ॥

4. KA I.8.29
विभज्यामात्यविभवं देशकालो च कर्म च ।
अमात्याः सर्व अेवैते कार्याः स्युर्न तु मन्त्रिणः ॥

statecraft,[5] pure in conduct[6] and loyal to their masters. Loyalty to the master was an important requisite for a minister. Due to this merit the kings in the Pañcamahākāvyas could confide the responsibilities of administration to the ministers. They were matured not only in age but in the knowledge of state-craft. Kāmanḍaka has mentioned these qualities as the special requisites of the ministers.[7]

It was a foremost duty of the ministers to advise the king in administrative functions. In the period of emergency the ministers should assemble and help the king in taking decisions. The king Aja used to take counsel of his ministers day-to-day, who were well-versed in the state-affairs. Atithi consulted every day his ministers.[8] It was essential for a king to acquire the help of competent ministers because even a virtuous king was not able to recollect all the aspects of a problem. Moreover different aptitudes and capacities are seen in different persons.[9] In Śiśupālavadha, Śrīkṛṣṇa reminds of this important tenet while offering chance to Uddhava and Balarāma to forward their opinions.[10]

---

5. KA I.9.1
जानपदोऽभिजातः रुयग्रहः कृतशिल्पश्चक्षुष्मान्प्राज्ञो
धारयिष्णुर्दशो वाग्मी प्रगस्भः प्रतिपत्तिमानुत्साह-
प्रभावयुक्तः क्लेशसहः शुचिमैत्रो दृढभक्तिः शीलबलारोग्य सत्वयुक्तः
स्तम्भचापलहीनः संप्रियो वैराणामकर्तेत्यमात्यसंपत् ।
6. Kirā XIII. 14
7. KN IV.24
कुलीनाः शुचयः शूरा श्रुतवन्तोऽनुरागिणः ।
दण्डनीतेः प्रयोक्तारः सचिवा स्युर्महीपतेः ॥
8. Ragu XVII.50
9. ŚN II.5
पुरुषे पुरुषे भिन्न दृश्यते बुद्धिवैभवम् ।
10. Śiśu II.12
मम तावन्मतमिदं श्रूयतामङ्ग वामपि ।
ज्ञातसारोऽपि खल्वेकः सन्दिग्धे कार्यवस्तुनि ॥

So it is beneficial to consult the wise ministers and they should be given full scope to express their opinions.

Another important responsibility of the ministers is to safeguard their master in a critical moment and to consult him at a suitable time and situation. In Kirātārjunīyam the messenger of Yudhiṣṭhira states that he is the bad counsellor who does not give proper advice to his master and he is a bad master who does not listen to the advice of his well- wishesr.[11] In Raghuvaṁśa it is described that the ministers expert in polity advised the new king Raghu about the proper and improper modes of behaviour from which the king was to choose the first.[12] As the best councellor, Uddhava in Śiśupālavadha shines foremost among all the ministers. Kauṭilya in his Arthaśāstra has mentioned Uddhava by the name of Vātavyādhi. In Śiśupālavadha he gets the similar name as Pavanavyādhi.[13] As a clever minister he gives good counsel to Śrīkṛṣṇa. Between the two courses, either to join the Rājasūya sacrifice of Yudhiṣṭhira or to attack Śiśupāla, Śrīkṛṣṇa and Balarāma express the opinion of attacking the dangerous enemy Śiśupāla; but as an eminent politician, Uddhava forwards all the pros and cons of the situation. His speech is weighty, full of gravity and thoughtfulness, true and accorded by science of polity.[14] Though well-versed in polity he speaks before Śrīkṛṣṇa in a polite manner.[15] He explains importance of a good counsel. According

---

11. Kirā I.5
स किंसरवा साधु न शास्ति योऽधिपं हितान्न यः संशृणुते स किंप्रभुः ।
सदाऽनुकूलेषु हि कुर्वते रतिं नृपेष्वमात्येषु च सर्वसंपदः ॥
12. Raghu IV.10
13. Śiśu II.15
14. ibid. II.69
15. ibid. II.75

to him a king who is assisted by intellectual guidance in deliberation, gets victory.[16] He also explains the proper application of an opportunity, right use of the four expedients, consideration of the time factor and relative strength of the enemy. While suggesting the declaration of war, he says one should account for all these points. Uddhava dares to warn Śrīkṛṣṇa of losing his best friend Yudhiṣṭhira. According to him, if Śrīkṛṣṇa engages all the kings in a battle against Śiśupāla, at the time of the Rājasūya sacrifice, he would lose his best friend and a friend once estranged cannot be won back. This consultation of Uddhava exhibits his deep study of the situation. With regard to the future plans Uddhava suggests that through expert spies Śrīkṛṣṇa should pursuade the circle of friendly powers attending Yudhiṣṭhirās sacrifice. Not bearing the honour offered to Śrīkṛṣṇa, Śiśupāla is likely to wage war and it will be a good ground to get victory. All the coming events happen according to his consultation which is the very proof of his profound knowledge of polity and the foremost councillorship.

Sometimes the ministers had to take important decisions on their own responsibility in the absence of the king. When King Dhṛvasandhi died in accident, his son Sudarśana was a mere child; but due to the pitiable condition of the subjects without a king, the ministers unanimously took decision to coronate the child as a king of Ayodhyā.[17] The ministers could work out the administration in the absence of the king when he was engaged in some religious performance. King Dilīpa in

16. Śiśu II.77
सोपधानां धियं धीराः स्थेयसीं खट्वयन्ति ये ।
तत्रानिशं निषण्णास्ते जानते जातु न श्रमम् ॥

17. Raghu XVIII.36

Raghuvaṁśa confided all the responsibilities of kingdom to the ministers, as he was desirous to perform some religious performance for the sake of progeny.[18] As the responsibility of the kingdom was borne by the ministers, Daśaratha also went for hunting.[19] King Nala in Naiśadhīyacarita obtaining a beautiful wife like Damayantī enjoyed the pleasures, entrusting the kingdom to his ministers.[20] In the nineteenth canto of Raghuvaṁśa we come across a passage mentioning the great responsibility and an extraordinary work performed by the ministers, in the record of Indian polity. In the reign of Agnivarṇa, who swerved from the path of duty was drowned in the passions, the ministers bore the burden of the kingdom on their own responsibility[21] The king, due to his excessive enjoyment of passions died, and he was without any issue, so the ministers placed his pregnant queen on the royal throne with proper rites.[22] The righteous and eminent ministers thought that the drawbacks of their king should not be revealed to the subjects. When the king was seriously ill, because of the excessive enjoyment and there remained no hope of his life, the ministers kept the news of his disease and death confined. They performed the funeral rites, directed by the priest, in the garden of the royal palace quite secretly. The ministers who suspected the danger declared among the subjects, that the king was busy in performing a sacrifice for son.[23] The strategy employed by ministers

---

18. Raghu I.34
संतानार्थाय विधये स्वभुजादवतारिता ।
तेन धूर्जगता गुर्वी सचिवेषु निचिक्षिपे ॥
19. ibid. IX.69
20. Nai XVIII.3
21. Raghu XIX.4
22. ibid. XIX.57
23. ibid. XIX.52

in such a critical condition is in confirmity with the view expressed by Kauṭilya in his Arthaśāstra. He mentions, when a king is on the path of death, the ministers should declare in the subjects that the king would visit the subjects after one or two months, because the king was busy in performing rites for removing calamities of the kingdom or destroying enemies or for the sake of progeny.[24] Thus concealing the news of death of the king for some days, the ministers saved the kingdom from anarchy and from the external attacks of the enemies, who could take an advantage of the kingless state.

Alongwith the administrative responsibilities the loyalty of ministers was needed in other fields also. The ministers were the trustworthy guardians of the harem in the period of emergency. in the *swayaṁvara* of Indumati, The unsuccessful candidates, full of resentment declared war against Aja, the successful one, who directed the trustworthy ministers with a large number of warriors to guard Indumatī[25] In Naiṣadhīyacarita it is described that being in office of the ministers and physician, there were no evils in to disturb his daughter's inner apartment.[26] So the kings could confide such tender responsibilities upon their trustworthy ministers. Searching of a suitable bride for the king was one of the functions of the ministers.[27]

The ministers were not only the trustworthy counsellors of the king, but there was a mutual co-operation between them. The King Raghu was

---

24. KA V.6.1/2
राज्यव्यसनमेवममात्यः प्रतिकुर्वीत ।
प्रागेव मरणबाधयात् राज्ञः प्रियहितोपग्रहेण मासद्विमासान्तरं दर्शनं स्थापयेद् देशपीडापहमायुष्यं पुत्रीयं वा कर्म राजा स्थापयति इत्यपदेशेन ।
25. Raghu VII.36
26. Nai IV.116
27. Raghu XVIII.53

attributed as the friend of the ministers.[28] According to Kāmandaka the ministers are the real friends of the king, who prevent the king from following a dangerous path.[29] Prosperity of every kind delights to live there, where kings and their ministers always act in perfect accord.[30] Though beholder and owner of the royal power, the king obeyed the advice of his ministers. King Agnivarṇa, who was fully drowned in the ocean of passions and who was not desirous to offer even his sight to his subjects, respected the words of his ministers and showed only his feet to his subjects for paying obeisance.[31] Rather it was not possible for the weak king to transgress the words of his ministers. In the case of Agnivarṇa, his passionateness reached the height so much so that it was not perhaps possible for the loyal ministers to protect him from his downfall, Agnipurāna states that ministers should protect the kings against all kinds of vices which bring about his downfall.[32] Kāmanḍaka enjoins the minister to help the king to come out of the ditch of affection, pride and arrogance. He compares a minister with the driver of an elephant who keeps him on the right path.[33] Though the loyal ministers of Agnivarṇa could not protect him from his downfall, they successfully secured the duty of protecting the kingdom in a critical condition of anarchy. A mutual admiration and affection between the king and his ministers are frequently seen in the *Pañcamahākāvyas*. In Naiṣadhīyacarita, we come across a

---

28. ibid. IV.87
29. KN IV.42
    नृपस्य त एव सुहृदस्तअेव गुरवो मताः ।
    य अेनमुत्पथगतं वारयन्त्यनिवारितम् ।
30. Kirā I.5
31. Raghu XIX.7
32. AP 239.42
33. KN IV.47

fine description of King Nala entering the city who met his ministers, like the spring season accompanied by the beauty of flowers meeting the eagerly curious bees that come one by one;[34] king Rāma in Raghuvaṁśa, after killing Rāvaṇa returned Ayodhyā by Puṣpaka-plane, he showed Sītā that ministers, old in age, followed by sage Vaśiṣṭha, had come to receive and to meet their laudable king.[35] The king also fevoured the bowing ministers by his serene looks and by sweet words.[36] In this connection we are tempted to mention a fine description of the affectionate relation between the king and his minister in Rājataranginī. The King (Avantivarmā) and his minister (sūra) were masters of each-other when issuing command, but were servants of each other in receiving commands. Indeed, the combination of a grateful king who is forbearing and a minister who is devoted and modest is rarely found on this earth and that too, only as a result of past good deeds.[37]

This affectionate relation between a king and his minister is not only admirable but it is very essential and helpful for the stability and prosperity of the kingdom. A conflict between the king and his ministers possibly results in the fall of the entire empire. How it results, is fully explained by Yudhiṣṭhira in the second canto of Kirātārjunīyam. Yudhiṣṭhira argues and explains to Bhīma to wait upon some opportunity and not to take any hasty action because king Duryodhana being

34. Nai XVI.124

35. Raghu XIII.66

36. ibid. XIII.71

37. Rājtaraṅgiṇī V. 4/5
शासतां क्षितिपामात्यो तौ द्वावपि परस्परम् ।
आज्ञादाने परिवृढौ भृत्यावाज्ञापरिग्रहे । कृतज्ञः
शान्तिमान्क्ष्मामृन्मन्त्री भक्तः स्मयोज्झितः ।
अभङ्गुरोऽयं संयोगः सुवृतैर्जातु दृश्यते ॥

arrogant by nature would surely insult his own friends and ministers who would decrease his power. Even a small disturbance caused by the disaffection of the internal constituents of the state kills the king.[38] Yudhiṣṭhira further argues that tossed by the wind of disaffection, the ministers and other friends gradually estranged an enemy, though very great, is like a tree, shaken by the wind and with roots shattered, is easy to be uprooted.[39] Thus the insulted ministers are used by the enemies for the strategy of dissension. In Śiśupālavadha also the same strategy is mentioned. Uddhava explains that attending the sacrificial function of Yudhiṣṭhira and thereby the execution of the spies, they could turn the ministers etc. of the enemy to their side by dissension.[40] In a simile it is mentioned that the arrows thrown by Śrīkṛṣṇa destroyed the arrows of the enemy just like the sowing of the seeds of dissension among ministers etc. of the enemy through treachery, by the spies.[41] The insulted ministers are possibly made the target of dissension, so it is very essential for the king to secure the dignity of his own ministers.

Now the point under discussion is the hereditary ministership in the *Pañcamahākāvyas*. From the frequent occurrences of the words as 'old ministers'[42] 'counsellors of the father.[43] it is clear that the ministers were serving the kings hereditarily. From the ancient times heredity was frequently persued in the appointment of the chief government offices including ministers. The psychology working behind the system of hereditary employment

---

38. Kirā II.51
39. ibid. II.50
40. Śiśu II.113
41. ibid. XX.23
42. Raghu XII.57 स्थविरसचिवैः। XVII.8 मन्त्रिवृद्धाः। XIII.71 मन्त्रिवृद्धान् XVIII.50 प्रकृतीश्च पित्र्या।
43. Supra Ref. 27, Kirā XIII.39

was that the length of service for generations deepens an affection and kingly feeling in the heart of the master for their attendants and their sons. Moreover it makes the servants much more responsible towards their service and loyal towards their master. It was believed that hereditary qualities add the efficiency of the servant. The tendency of faithfulness got from inheritance strengthens the tie of attachment and removes the possibility of treachery. For this reason, the hereditary ministership is praised by some ancient thinkers. According to Kauṇapaḍanta the king should make those his ministers who have come as hereditary servants from his father and grandfather since their pure conduct is known. They do not desert him even when he misbehaves.[44] Manu and others prescribe hereditary ministership provided that the son was capable like his father.[45] Thus the loyal hereditary ministers are seen in the *Pañcamahākāvyas* exhibiting their love and devotion towards their masters. It may be the reason that the loyal hereditary ministers of Agnivarṇa in Raghuvaṁśa neglected his vices through affection and could not control his downfall due to his notorious passionatenes, but handled the difficult situation quite successfully.

Thus the ministers had a significant place in the statecraft. Securing all important duties they proved to be the pillars of the state. The state is supported by the dutyful ministers who are loyal, defectless, straightforward and well tested.[46]

---

44. KA I.8
पितृपैतामहानमात्यान् कुर्वीत । दृष्टापदानत्वात् ।
ते ह्येनमपचरन्तमपि न त्यजन्ति ।

45. MS VII.54, AP 220.16

46. Pañcatantra I.127
अंतः सारैरकुटिलैरच्छिद्रैः सुपरीक्षितैः ।
मन्त्रिभिधीयते राज्यं सुस्तम्भैरिव ॥

In short, the meritorious and proficient ministers with their masters regarded as trustees of the interests of subjects, Though the ministers were not constitutionally responsible to the subjects; the dutiful ministers sought to protect and promote the interests of the state and a welfare of the subjects, to the best of their ability.

STATE OFFICIALS : TĪRTHAS

There were only seven departments of administration and later on they became eighteen in number, because the seven departments were insufficient to secure alround development and prosperity of the state.[47] The complicated state administration was possible only by the division of the several departments. The administration of the kingdom was carried on by the king with the high officials termed as *'tīrthas'*. Conventionally their number was fixed as eighteen. A definition of the word *'tīrtha'* is mentioned as follows 'Persons, who are helpers in dharma and state business are called tīrthas.[48] In Raghuvaṁśa and Śiśupālavadha we come across the term *tirtha* which shows that the poets of *pañcamahākāvyas* were familiar with the classification of the functionaries known as *tīrthas*. These functionaries of the state have a very early origin, In the vedic period they were listed as *'Ratnins'* and in the performance of *Rājasūya* sacrifice the offerings were offered which were named as *'Ratnahavīṁṣi'*. After the vedic period the various officers were called as *tīirthas*. The term is used in Mahābhārata also.[49] Kauṭilya enlists

47. Rājataranginī I.119/120
धर्माध्यक्षो धनाध्यक्ष कोक्षाध्यश्च भूपतिः ।
दूतः पुरोधा दैवतः सप्त प्रकृतयो भवन् ।
कर्मस्थानानि धर्म्याणि तेनाष्टदशकुर्वता ।
ततः प्रभृतिभूपेन कृता यौधिष्ठिरी स्थितिः ॥
48. NV (Arthasamuddeśa p.29 II.5
धर्मसमवायिनः कार्यसमवायिनश्च पुरुषास्तीर्थम् ।
49. Sabhāparvan (Critical Edition by BORI) 5.27

the different officers and their departments. They are as follows : *Mantrin, Purohita, Sanāpati, Yuvarājan, Dauvārika* (Chamberlain), *Antardeśika* (Superintendent of harem), *Praśāstṛ, Samāhartṛ, Pradeshṭṛ, Nāyaka* (overseer of city), *Pauravyāvahārika, Kārmāntika, Mantriparisadādhyakṣa, Daṇḍapāla, Durgapāla, Antpala, Ātavika.*

From these officers, the duties and functions of *mantrin, Purohita, Yuvarāja* are stated before, and that of the *Senāpati,* will be discussed later. From the above list the fact is clear that the functionaries help and assist the king in all the spheres of administration as deliberation, field of justice, internal and external security, collection of taxes and their application, commerce and industries etc.

About the functioning of these departments viz. the *tīrthas,* an information is got by the king through his spies. He gathers an information about their inner workings and controls them by using the four expeditients viz. *Sāma, Dāna, Bheda* and *daṇḍa* suitable to circumstances.[50] An administrator has to acquire a strong support, co-operation and belief of these *tīrthas* for the smooth working of the state and direction of the policy. An employment of the four expedients is able to offer him the desired fruit among all the departments of administration. It is very essential for the ruler to be watchful, not creating any scope for treachery among his own officers; and not giving a chance to the enemy to enter through the weak points of the administrative departments viz. the *tīrthas.*

By the same policy of dissension used among the eighteen *tirthas* of the enemy, the king is able to uproot the whole empire of the enemy. In Śiśupālavadha, Uddhava the eminent minister skilled in polity, advises Śrīkṛṣṇa to apply his secret agents in the *tīrthas* of the enemy to get information of their workings and to seek the weak holes where dissension holds a root.[51] Like

50. Raghu XVII.68

51. Śiśu II.111

a skilled swimmer, who only by stepping his foot in water knows the depth of the water, the king employing the network of secret agents should get a conjecture about the relative strength of the enemy. He should seek the insulted and discontented persons who can be turned to his side easily. The enemy, whose functionaries are gradually estranged and tested by the wind of disaffection, is easy to be uprooted.[52] Even a very small revolt caused by discontent of the internal constituents of the kingdom kills the king.[53] So instead of the sudden attack on the enemy, Uddhava suggests the policy of dissension through the spies among the *tīrthas* of the enemy; because a kingdom whose base is shattered is easy to be uprooted. Kauṭilya has stated a necessity of employing the secret agents not only in the surrounding states whether inimical or friendly, to watch their movements but also to keep a watch on the eighteen functionaries of his own state.[54]

Thus a watchful administrator gets a full advantage of the discontent of the functionaries of the enemy; but a full control over the eighteen departments in his own state offers him his desired fruit.

Besides the political meaning to the word *tīrtha,* it occurs in its normal sense as holy water-place in Raghuvaṁśa,[55] and also in the sense of deserving person[56] which is mentioned by Kauṭilya also.[57]

---

52. Kirā II. 50
53. Kirā II.51
54. KA I.12.20
    अेवं शत्रौ च मित्रे च मध्यमे चावपेच्चरान् ।
    उदासीने च तेषां च तीर्थेष्वष्टादशस्वपि ॥
55. Raghu XVI.33
56. Śiśu XIV.9
57. KA I.4.3
    अलब्ध लाभार्था लब्धपरिरक्षणी रक्षितविवर्धनी
    वृद्धस्य तीर्थे प्रतिपादनी च ।

SABHĀ AND SAMITI :

The word *sabhā* is of frequent occurrence and some other words as *samiti, Pariṣad, Vidatha* etc. are used as synonyms to *sabhā*. *Before discussing the significance and functions of sabhā* in the *Pañcamahākāvyas*, it will not be out of place to mention a brief account of *sabhā* and *samiti* in *Vedic* period, when these institutions had got a prominent place in the social and political aspect of ancient India.

Sabhā and *Samiti* were separate assemblies. Sabhā was people's assembly where people met for various functions.[58] According to Spellman, it was a public assembly to which the king, learned men, gamblers and others went. It probably started as a festive hall where people met for religious and social functions. It became a sounding board of public opinion. It is not clear whether *sabhā* had any legislative status in the political administration at this time.[59]

K.P. Jayawal holds that Sabhā was a standing and stationary body of selected men working under the authority of Samiti.[60] According to A.S. Altekar, villages had their own popular assemblies known as *sabhās* and the capital had the central assembly for the whole state which was called *samiti*.[61] *So Sabhā* in vedic period was usually a village-assembly meeting mostly for social as well as political purposes. It was a representative

58. Atharva Veda VII.12.1
59. Spellman, Political Theory of Ancient India Published by Oxford University Press, 1964, p.93
60. K.P. Jayaswal, Hindu Polity Part I Published by Butterworth & Co. (India) Ltd. Calcutta 1924 P.18
61. A.S. Altekar, State and Government in Ancient India Published by Motilal Banarasidass, 1962, p. 139

assembly based on the village.[62] *Samiti* was a powerful political body rather than a mere social gathering of the people, who could keep control over king's power. Though sometimes denoted as a social gathering, usually it referred to a political assembly of the central government. Discussions were held in the *Samiti*. *Samiti* assumed obstructions if the king becomes miserable. So a co-operation of *Samiti* was necessary for the king. The popular element had not ceased to exercise its control in the task of administration. Thus *sabhā* and *samīti* in Vedic period definately had the political rights of discussing and deciding matters of interest and concern for the village and town population. *Samiti* could reinstate an exiled king.[63] Thus these institutions had occupied a prominent position in the political and social life of the ancient community.

In the later period of *Saṁhitās* and *Brāhmaṇas*, the *Samiti* disappeared. After Chāndogya Upanisad[64] there is no literary record of its existence. The reason behind the decreasing powers of these assemblies is stated by A.S. Altekar. According to him, the state was usually expected to enforce the customs and laws mentioned by *dharmaśāstra*, it began to be invested with some powers to make its own regulations from about third century B.C. At the time when these powers were granted, *samiti* or popular assemblies had disappeared from the scene.[65]

---

62. K.P. Jayaswal, Hindu Polity, Part I
Published by Butterworth & Co. (India) p.15 Ltd. Calcutta, 1924
63. Atharva Veda VI.88.3 ध्रुवाय ते समितिः कल्पतामिह ।
64. Chāndogya Upaniṣad V.3.1
65. A.S. Altekar, State and Government in Ancient India, Published by Motilal Banarasidass, 1962; p. 145.

When we turn to our *Pañcamahākāvyas,* the words *sabhā, saṁsad, Pariṣad* frequently occur, but in a new sense. *Sabhā* being transformed from a popular body or public assembly into king's court. The word *sabhā* is used in the sense of assembly of any sort. It may be law-court, royal court, convivial assembly, political assembly or also a royal assembly for social function. In Kirātārjunīyam, the word *saṁsad* is used which means an assemblage of eminent personages.[66] In Naiṣadhīyacarita also, it is mentioned that the assembly was adorned by the scholars of the three worlds.[67]

Sabhā, in the sense of judicial assembly appears in the passage of the third canto of Kirātārjunīyam. The great sage Vyāsa censures the unrighteous party of Duryodhana and praises the virtues of Yudhiṣṭhira, that he has manifested the highest love for virtues in the assembly of the enemies where they swerved from the right path.[68] The sage indicates the incident when Draupadī the queen of Paṇḍavas was dragged into the assembly by Duhśāsana being violently pulled by the hair, when the honourable personalities like Bhīṣma could not prevent the unrighteous act in the assembly, which was the place for justice. Here the word *saṁsad* comes in the sense of judicial assembly. According to Manu the assembly dealt with law, whatever is decided by the assembly gets the force of law.[69] Sabhā in the sense of judicial assembly appears in Mahābhārata also. That is not an assembly where there are no elders, those are not elders, who do not declare the law.[70]

66. Kirā III.51
67. Nai X.71
68. Kirā III.15
69. MS XII.111/112
70. Sabhā Parvan (Critical Edition by BORI) 2.540

Assembly in the sense of royal court is seen in Raghuvaṁśa. The king seated on the royal throne as the supreme head of the state presided over the regular sessions of the council and as such, administers his decisions. In all the important matters the king used to take consent of the royal court and the learned *brāhamaṇas*. The incident of the dream and the narration by the presiding deity of Ayodhyā about the ruined condition of the capital Ayodhyā, Kuśa told the *brāhmaṇas* in his court.[71] They congratulated him for the auspicious dream. The 'sadas'[72] '*saṁsad*'[73] '*samiti*'[74] are used in the general sense of 'royal assembly'.

Assembly, was the 'place of council' where important matters concerning the state were discussed with the ministers. Here the word '*sadas*, is used in the sense of 'ministerial councils.[75] Kauṭilya shows a slight difference between the councillors and members of *mantripariṣad* as he states, the king consulted only the councillors as a matter of course calling the '*mantrins*' only in connection with urgent works.[76] In Śiśupālavadha, Kṛṣṇa had to take a decision between two clashing courses, either to join the *Rājasūya* sacrifice of Yudhiṣṭhira or to make an immediate attack on Śiśupāla. For the urgent decision Kṛṣṇa called an assembly for the consultation with Balarāma and his minister Uddhava, skilled in state-craft.[77] In his short

71. Raghu XVI.24
72. Śiśu XV.59/60; XVII.1
73. Śiśu XV.67
74. ibid. XVI.13
75. ibid. II.2
76. KA I.15.58/59
आत्ययिके कार्ये मन्त्रिणो मन्त्रिपरिषदं चाहूय ब्रूयात् ।
तत्र यदभूयिष्ठा ब्रूयुः कार्यसिद्धिकरं वा तत्कुर्यात् ।
77. Śiśu II.1
यियक्षमाणेनाहूतः पार्थेनाथ द्विषन्मुरम् ।
अभिचैद्यं प्रतिष्ठासुरासीत्कार्यद्वयाकुलः ॥

speech, Kṛṣṇa stressed urgency of attack on Śiśupāla. Balarāma lends support to Kṛṣṇa's view, but Uddhava, a politician of uncommon intellect urged against war stating all the pros and cons of the situation. He also discussed the measures and counter-measures to be adopted against the enemy. Thus a detailed discussion for the decision, took place in the 'place of council', which was an important sense of the word *sabhā*. This assembly was compared to the altar of the sacrifice where the three sacred- fires were present in the form of Kṛṣṇa, Balarāma and Uddhava and assembled for the pacification of the world harassed by Śiśupāla.

In Naiṣadhīyacarita, '*sabhā*' served the sense of 'an assemblage of kings for Damayantīs swayaṁvara.[78] It was brilliant with sunshine and was so beautiful and prosperous with the kings that the great sages like Vālmīki, Bṛhaspati, Śukrācārya could not stay without praising the assembly.[79]

Thus, *Sabhā* which was indicative of the popular assembly in Vedic period and '*Samiti*' which had a considerable influence over the administration, disapperared and the word *sabhā* from epic period exhibited various meanings as shown above, It was a king's court where justice was meted out to the appellant; it was an assembly which discussed important matters concerning state; It was a place of meeting of the king and his ministers for consultation and it was also an assemblage of people for social gathering.

In all the important matters the king took the consent of people's council,[80] in which the citizens[81]

78. Nai XI.1
79. ibid X.56/57/58 to 64
80. Raghu XII.3
81. ibid. XV.42

were represented by the leading and important members in the society.[82]

Thus *sabhā* had an important place in the administration of the of the state, though it loses its importance as a controlling body as in the *Vedic* period.

CHECKS UPON THE KING'S POWER :

It is stated above that in *vedic* age a popular assembly or *samiti* functioned as a constitutional check. The powers of the popular assembly were declined and its place was not taken by another similar body. There was however no popular assembly or form in post vedic period which could effectively control the king if he became oppressive.[83] Though the principle of king's divinity had offered to his office obvious powers it should be stated that it had not given unlimited powers to the king. It should not be supposed that the glorification of the king resulted in the fullfledged theory of divine rights of the kings or that every king, however, bad was looked upon as a divinity or could do whatever, he desired. Only the righteous kings were meant as the essence of gods.[84] The rights and powers of the powerful monarch were restrained by some limitations and checks.

The checks or limitations which we are supposed to mention in this topic, cannot be named as 'constitutional' as the word is used in the modern sense of the term; but the indirect checks were effective enough for the ruler that he could not dare to transgress them.

A ruler was supposed to discharge the heavy responsibilities of the kingdom. From his childhood he

---

82. Raghu XIX.55, 1.55

83. A.S.Altekar, State and Government in Ancient India Published by Motilal Banarasidass 1962; p. 66

84. ŚN 1.70

was given a proper education and training. By the education, the king was expected to show a high respect towards *dharma*, public welfare and enhancement of moral discipline. To secure the heavy duties he had to follow a particular method. His daily duties were situated in the daily time-table prescribed by the ancient law-books. The king could, no doubt, alter it so that it suited himself but the freedom was restricted in limits which he could not transgress. Thus starting from his daily routine, his duties were moulded in rules and regulations prescribed by law- books. He was not to act according to his sweet will, for the life of those in bonds was opposed to the enjoyment of pleasures.[85]

King's office was regarded as a sacred-trust and he was to rule according to the directions of the *Śāstras*. The *śāstras* showed him right path.[86] As a protector of the subjects it was his prime duty to protect his subjects and to endow security to them. His treasury was not for his enjoyment and it was not his private and personal property; but it was a public trust to be utilized for public purposes.[87] The admirable reign of the solar kings or of king Durodhana fulfilled the above expectations as they treated the path of nīti.[88]

Religious and spiritual sanctions had greatest influence on the rulers in ancient India. As a guardian of his subjects the king was specially bound to follow the instructions enjoined by the scriptures and law-books. The established laws and customs were superior to the king. The king was not the maker of the laws but only the follower of them and an observance of

---

85. Raghu XVIII. 18
तमात्मसंपन्नमनिन्दितामकमा कृत्वा युवानं युवराजमेव ।
सुखानि सोऽभुङ्क्त सुखोपरोधि वृतं हि राजाभुपनध्दवृत्तम् ।

86. ibid. XVII.77

87. Raghu IV.86

88. Kirā I.7

dharma was meant to be a great ideal before the rulers. In the *'History of Dharmaśāstra'* it is mentioned that the importance of *dharma* as all-embracing institution was impressed upon the king by the writers so frequently that it must had its psychological effect on every king.[86] Not only for his own interest but as a protector of the subjects the king was advised to perform several rituals to avert national calamities. They were aware of the power of religious rites to avoid the dangers, human and divine. King Dilīpa in Raghuvaṁsa offers a full credit of his prosperous state and of the freedom and security of his subjects from the calamities to the spiritual power of the preceptors.[87] So the religious instructions were particularly followed by the kings. Neglecting the daily-rituals was counted as sin. King Nala in Naiṣadhīyacarita requests Damayantī not to become a cause of her husband's sin of neglecting the established rites.[88] So the influence of *dharma* was an effective check for the kings to keep them on the right path. A vast description[89] of the religious rites and rules particularly obeyed by and performed by the subjects of King Nala shows that not only the rulers but the subjects also were under the profound influence of dharma.

Not only the righteous kings but even the wicked rulers were kept within the bounds of *dharma. Dharma* had enough power to strike down a bad king. Agni Purāṇa states that a king who oppresses the people, is

---

86. MM P.V. Kane, History of *Dharmaśātra*, Vol. III, Published by BORI, Poona, 1964 P.76

87. Raghu I.64
त्वयैवं चिन्त्यमानस्य गुरूणा ब्रह्मयोनिना ।
सानुबन्धाः कथं न स्युः संपदो मे निरापदः ॥

88. Nai XIX.24

89. Nai XVII.163 to 204

destroyed and he has to live in hell for infinite period.[90] Such type of threat was the check of the autocracy of the king. In ancient law-books a sanction to the *śāstras* is seen that it had allowed the subjects to throw away an unrighteous and unjust king or even to kill a misguided tyrant.[91] So by the fear of sin the rulers did not dare to transgress the restrictions and instructions of *dharma*.

It is stated before that the early *Hindu* scriptures provide emancipation from this worldly existence only for those who beget son. An anxiety of the king for a son is hinted many times in Raghuvaṁśa. King Dilīpa exposes his mental agony before the preceptor that he is not happy as he supposes himself to be guilty as unable to offer *swadhā* offering after his death due to the absence of his progeny. He thinks that the ancestors drink the libations of water offered by him made tapid by their sighs.[92] So it can very easily be conjectured that the idea of emancipation from the debt of the manes, laid down by the scriptures, had a strong hold on the rulers.

The rulers in the *Pañcamahākāvyas* had placed before them the law-books as an ideal to perform their kingly duties. An ambition of Duryodhana expressed in Kirātārjunīyam was to reach the line of conduct laid down by Manu.[93] After the abandonment of Sītā, she reminds Rāma of the duty of a king as prescribed by Manu, to protect the different castes and preserve

---

90. AP 223.7
राष्ट्रपीडाकरो राजा नरके वसते चिरम् ।

91. MS VII.27/28 KA I.4.12
दुष्प्रणीतः कामक्रोधाभ्यामवज्ञानाद्वा वानप्रस्थपरिव्राजकानपि कोपयति किमङ्ग पुनर्गृहस्थान् ।

92. Raghu I.67

93. Kirā I.9

life-stages and expects for protection in common with other ascetics.[94]

Though there was an affectionate relation of father and son, between the ruler and the subjects, the subjects could dare to question the king for the injustice or mishap in the society. It was believed that the ruler was responsible for the evils and mishaps in the kingdom. In Raghuvaṁśa, a premature death of a child was attributed by his father to the misrule of king Rāma. The father of the child, censured the king that the earth deprived of the benign rule of Daśaratha had passed into the hands of Rāma and reached to the most miserable condition.[95] Rāma was ashamed of the mishap in his rule and immediately went to root out the reason of the untimely death of the child, and searching out the reason, punished the *śūdra,* who was propitiating penance, prohibited to his caste. This incident shows that a common person in the society could reach to the king to show his mistake. The subjects was a prominent check on the ruler to make him intent and wakeful to fulfill his duties. Another event in Rāma's reign indicates that people expected spotless and pure conduct of their ruler and the rulers has to care for the public opinion. The rulers strongly dreaded public infamy. Though Rāma himself was confident about the spotless conduct of Sītā, he could not overlook the slanderous tale dripped in the subjects and he had to take decision of abandoning his loving wife Sītā. He knew that people could not accept her as chaste after her long stay in Rāvaṇa's prison. So he could not bear a stain on Raghu's unblemished family and tried to avert the slander by

---

94. Raghu XIV.67

95. ibid. XV.43
शोचनीयासि वसुधे या त्वं दशरथाच्च्युता ।
रामहस्तमनुप्राप्य कष्ठात्कष्टतरं गता ॥

leaving his personal happiness in consideration of the public opinion.

The dutiful ministers of the king had an indirect check on the rulers. Though there was an affectionate relation between the administrator and his ministers and they were like his friends, the kings could not dare to overstep their advice and consultation. He could place the responsibilities of the kingdom on them, but he was not free to behave according to his will. We come across frequent allusions indicating that the rulers obeyed the advice of the ministers. King Daśaratha in Raghuvaṁśa went hunting only after the permission of the ministers.[96] Kṛṣṇa in Śiśupālavadha setting aside his own opinion to attack his enemy obeyed the consultation of Uddhava, the eminent minister.[97] Agnivarṇa in Raghuvaṁśa, who had completely lost his sense of duty under the influence of passionateness, had at least somewhat regard for and obedience to his ministers.[98] Instead of the exceptional case of Agnivarṇa all the kings offered a due regard to their dutiful ministers and there occurred no occasions to use the powers of ministers against kings who were aware of their duties. Agnivarṇa's case reveals the fact that sometimes the ministers also were unable to check the kings who were addicted to passions.

The rulers feared the spiritual power of the sages and *brāhmaṇas* to imprecate a curse to the offender. In Raghuvaṁśa a son of the blind and old couple died by Daśaratha's arrow, so the old sage cursed the king that he also would meet death in his old age through the grief for his son. The King lost peace of mind by the

96. Raghu IX.49
97. Śiśu II.118
98. Raghu XIX.7

sinful act which brought on him the curse.[99] In the fifteenth canto, Lakṣamaṇa broke the agreement of not interrupting the conversation between Rāma and *Kāla* (Death), through fear of the curse by the sage Durvāsa, who expected immediate interview with Rāma.[100]

Thus, all these points mentioned above clearly indicate that various types of checks were present to control the ancient rulers. A belief in religious sanctions was so great that the ancient law-books had taken a full advantage of it to control the kings with rules and regulations. Not only for their own interest and happiness but for securing public welfare and prosperity, averting the evils and dangers the rulers themselves had accepted the bindings of the established laws and regulations. The subjects had a great devotion and respect for their kings, but they had a right to show their mistakes which could have caused their sorrow and difficulties. Sometimes, the position of the subjects seems to be above the king. The ministers also had an indirect control upon the ruler. Considering all these aspects we can argue that though there were not the constitutional checks existing in the modern sense of the term, the above remedies were sufficiently effective to keep the king on the right path. In this connection it is notable that maintaining his command over all the administrative departments the king rarely grew into a despot.

RELATIONSHIP BETWEEN A MASTER AND HIS ATTENDANTS :

An ideal relationship between a master and his attendants is occasionally stressed in the

---

99. Raghu IX.82

100. ibid. XV.94
विद्वानपि तयोर्द्वास्थः समयं लक्ष्मणोऽभिनत् ।
भीतो दुर्वाससः शापाद्रामसंदर्शनार्थिनः ॥

Pañcamahakāvyās. It was due to their loyal service to the masters that in many of the missions they could get success. The attendants, who are aware of this fact aptly secure their responsibilities. In Kirātārjunīyam, the messenger of Yudhiṣṭhira, who informs about the ideal reign of Duryodhana, mentions the model relationship between the servant and his master. He says "the masters (the kings) who see through spies, should not be deceived by their servants entrusted with special duties.[101] In turn, the masters also, should possess a forbearance to tolerate disagreeable news alongwith the pleasant works. he is unjust adviser, who does not give proper advice to his master and he is a bad master who does not listen to the advice of his well wishes.[102]

It is the foremost duty of the servant to obey politely the orders of his master.[103] A person, who transgresses the order of his master is like a blemish on the moon.[104] The eminent servants obtain favour of their master by their sweet words.[105] They are always ready to perform their duties. He considers it to be his great honour, when he is employed for a special duty by his master. Madana accepted the gaze of the thousand eyes of his master Indra, as a special favour in the form of the special mission assigned to him.[106]

A prudent servant behaves according to the intention of his master. From a small hint by his master

---

101. Kirā I.4
क्रियासु युवतैर्नृप । चारचक्षुषो न वञ्चनीयाः प्रभवोऽनुजीविभिः ।
अतोऽर्हसि क्षन्तुमसाधु साधु वा हितं मनोहारि च दुर्लभं वचः ॥

102. ibid. I.5

103. Śiśu XIX.91

104. Kirā XI.75
स वंशस्यावदातस्य शशाङ्कस्येव लाञ्छतम् ।
कृच्छ्रेषु व्यर्थया यत्र भूयते भर्तृराज्ञया ॥

105. Ku IX.12

106. ibid III. 1

he gets suggestion of the situation. In the *swayaṁvara* of Damayantī the palanquin- holders lifted the palanquin of Damayantī from one king to the other, getting the knowledge of her heart for the non- approval of the king.[107] In Śiśupālavadha, when Śiśupāla was deprived of the honour of 'Agrapūjā' in Yudhiṣṭhira's sacrifice and the same honour been accorded to his enemy Kṛṣṇa, he abused Kṛṣna in mean words and the followers of Kṛṣṇa though desirous of exhibiting their anger, controlled it realising the stipulation of their master.[108] A servant who understands the importance of time-factor in his special duty, gets success. Madana, who was employed by Indra of the god's mission to prepare Śiva for the marriage with Pārvatī was burnt into ashes by Śiva due to the disturbance in his austerity. But after the marriage-rites, Madana was allowed by Śiva to strike him by his flowery arrows.[109]

It is a duty of the servant to prevent his master from the wrong actions and to direct him on the right path. In the fourteenth canto of Kirātārjunīyam Arjuna asked the messenger of the lord of Kirātās, why he has not showed a right path to his master, who was threatening Arjuna to accept the dominance of his master.[110]

If an attendant is not successful in his mission, he feels guilty and does not dare to step before his master.

---

107. Nai XI.34

108. Śiśu XV.41
न च तं तदेति शपमानमपि यदुनृपाः प्रचक्रुधुः ।
शौरिसमयनिगृहीतधियः प्रभुचित्तमेव हि जनोऽनुवर्तते ॥

109. Ku VII.93
तस्यामुमेने भगवान् विमन्युर्व्यापारमात्मन्यपि सायकानाम् ।
कालप्रयुक्ता खलु कार्याविद्भि विज्ञापना भर्तृषु सिद्धिमेति ॥

110. Kirā XIV.8
विरोधि सिद्धेरिति कर्तुमुद्यतः स वारितः किं भवता न भूपतिः ।
हिते नियोज्यः खलु भूतिमिच्छता सहार्थनाशेन नृपोऽनुजीविना ॥

In the fight between Arjuna and the Lord of the Kirātas. Arjuna's quiver, which was unable to supply arrows to his master did not show his face.[111] When Arjuna's armour fell on the ground, his arrow went towards downside asif unable to show his face by shame, to his master.[112]

After the fruitful completion of the mission by the servant, it is proper for the master to honour the servant, by words of praise and offering of the gifts. When the prosperous capital of Kuśa was built up and decorated by the multitude of artists employed by the king, he honored his followers according to their rank.[113] The riches of Duryodhana were fully bestowed on his servants when their respective duties were accomplished.[114]

By the honour and gifts offered by the master, the attendants are not only pleased but they show more enthusiasm to work for their master.[115] It does not mean that their eyes are fixed on the money and presents given to them by their master; on the other hand the servants yet to be honoured also are eager to fulfill their duties by a great zeal, because the loyal attendants are aware of the fact that master's favour upon his servant seems from the responsibility applied to him through the belief of success.[116] A master, having the sense of appreciation for his servants, is always eager to honour them by gifts. It is mentioned in

111. Kirā XVII.42
112. ibid. XVII.47
113. Raghu XVI.40
114. Kirā I.14; I.26
115. Śiśu XIX.38
116. Ku VI.62
तथाऽपि तावत्कस्मिंश्चिदाज्ञां मे दातुमर्हथः
विनियोगप्रसादा हि किङ्कराः प्रभवविष्णुषु ॥

Śiśupālavadha that between the two soldiers killed on the battlefield, the master felt much grief for the one who was not honored by him.[117] When the servant is not honoured by his master he supposes it as his defeat, which he tries to wipe out by offering his life for his master, in the battlefield.[118]

ROYAL TREASURY :

Surplus treasury is the mainstay of the stable government. Treasury is counted among the seven constituents of the state. To carry out the schemes of public welfare it is necessary to replenish the treasury. Without the help of treasury it is very difficult to run the administration. A king obtains his supreme position among the other kings, depending on his treasury. The kings in the *Pañcamhākāvyas,* possessed the prosperous treasury because they had recognized the unique position of wealth in the administration of their kingdom.[119]

Here it is proposed to state the sources of income from which the treasury of the king was replenished. Generally the king gets finance from the following sources:

1. From the tax collection
2. From the Natural sources
3. From the gifts from feudatories
4. From the friendly gifts acquired in religious performances.
5. Gifts from the divinities.

---

117. Śiśu. XVIII.52
118. ibid. XIX.58
119. Raghu XVII.60
कोशेनाश्रयणीयत्वमिति तस्यार्थसंग्रहः।
अम्बुगर्भो हि जीमूतश्चातकैरभिनन्दते ॥

Taxes : A king was entitled to taxation by virtue of his protecting the people. It seems that the theory of public finance in ancient India was intimately bound up with the theory of protection. From the theories mentioning the origin of kingship the fact is revealed that, people admitted to give taxes in return of their protection by the King. It is mentioned before that Manu accepted rulership only after he has been promised material and spiritual benefits. A fullest illustration of the compact theory of taxation is found in *Dīgha Nikāya* of the Buddhist literature. After the gradual decay of society and righteousness, the people decided to pay someone (who ruled) portion of rice so that he might punish the wicked.[120]

The king collected taxes only for the welfare of his subject.[121] Here the word 'bali' is applied in the sense of taxes. In Vedic period, the term 'Bali' connoted 'voluntary offerings by the subjects'.[122] According to A.S. Altekar the term 'bali' originally used to denote voluntary offering made to gods for securing their favour. Later it came to be applied to presents and taxes offered to king more or less voluntarily.[123] Afterwards the word *'Bali'* denoted 'regular taxes' from the subjects for their protection and welfare.

---

120. Dīgha Nikāya III.93.

121. Raghu I.18
प्रजानामेव भूत्यर्थं स ताभ्यो बलिमग्रहीत् ।
सहस्रगुणमुत्स्रष्टुमादत्ते हि रसं रविः ॥

122. Prof. Zimmer, Quoted by B.N. Salatore, Ancient Indian Political Thought and Institutions, Published by Bombay p.441.

123. A.S. Altekar, State & Government in Ancient India Published by Motilal Banarasidas. Delhi, 1962. P. 262 MS III.74/108/265.

From the *Pañcamahākāvyas* it does not appear that there was marked development on the financial precept and practice as described in the law-books. The taxation was suited to the simple conditions in which the state was placed. Except the frequent denotation of one sixth share of produce,[124] the tax in kind, we get no special injunctions that could help us to suppose the existence of developed theory of finance.

A noteworthy feature of the taxation mentioned in the *Pañcamahākāvyas* is the moderate collection of the taxes from the subjects. The kings collected reasonable taxes and the subjects had not been oppressed by the burden of the heavy taxes. In the second canto of Raghuvaṁśa the celestial cow, pleased by the devotion of king Dilīpa asks him to take her milk. The King humbly replies to her that he will take the milk remaining after drinking by her calf, as he (the king) receives the one sixth of the produce from the subjects. The King collected taxes only for the welfare of his subjects as the sun takes water only to shower it again in much increased from.[125] Thus the great return was used and reserved for the welfare of the subjects. Ancient thinkers had stated the same principle about taxation. Manu says - As the leech, the calf and the bee take their food little by little, even so must the king draw from his similar realm moderate annual taxes.[126] Pañcaṭantra states the similar principle. As the gardener plucks fruits and flowers, but does not harm the trees, the king should collect his taxes, but should not cause

124. Raghu II.66; V.8; XVII.65

125. Supra Ref.124

126. MS VII.129
यथाल्पाल्पमदन्यार्थं वार्योकोवत्सषट्पदाः ।
तथाल्पाल्पो ग्रहीतव्यो राष्ट्राद्राज्ञाब्दिकः करः ॥

any suffering to the subjects.[127] People hate the kig who takes oppressive taxes.[128]

Taxes were collected from all classes of the society.[129] According to some *smṛtis brāhmaṇa-* class was exempted from the taxes.[130] Manu says that in the case of emergency also a king should not take taxes from the learned *brāhmaṇa*.[131] But exemption is not seen in Pañcamahākāvyas. As Raghu asks the ascetic named Kauṭsa about the holy-places, the sixth part of which, was marked for the king.[132] As a general rule all the classes including *brāhmaṇas* had to pay the taxes. As states Mahābhārata, the students studying in *gurukula* and hermits practicing penance were not the earning members of society and so were exempted from the taxes.[133]

The ancient law-givers had permitted the king to draw taxes in times of financial stringency. Manu enjoins that if a *kṣatriya* (king) in times of distress takes even the fourth part of the crops, he is free from guilts, if he protects his subjects to the best of his ability.[134]

---

127. Pañcatantra I.243
फलार्थी नृपतिर्लोकान्पालयेद्यत्नमास्थितः ।
दानमानादितोयेन मालाकारोङ्कुरानिव ॥

128. ŚP (Critical Edition by BORI) 88.17
प्रद्विषन्ति परिख्यातं राजानमतिखादनम् ।
प्रद्विष्टस्य कुतः श्रेयः संप्रियो लभते प्रियम् ॥

129. Raghu XVII.65

130. VS III.25
ब्राह्मणेभ्यः करादानं न कुर्यात् ते हि राज्ञो धर्मकराः ।

131. MS VII. 133
म्रियमाणोऽप्याददीत न राजा श्रोत्रियात्करण् ।
न च क्षुधास्य संसीदेच्छ्रोत्रियो विषये वसन् ॥

132. Raghu V.8

133. ŚP (Critical Edition by BORI) 76.4/8

134. MS X.118

Mahābhārata also excuses the king, who harasses the people in emergency period by heavy taxes.[135] But this view is not approved by the kings in the *Pañcamahākāvyas*. For, paternal kingship was their ideal. They did not think of the idea of collecting heavy taxes by harassing the people even in financially distressed condition of the state. Raghu was unable to offer the desired gift to Kauṭsa, because of the empty treasury due to a performance of sacrifice; but he never thought of replenishing his treasury by heavy taxes.

The king received fines levied against all grades of criminal and civil offenses. It was one of the sources of income in ancient India. But it could have produced only a small amount for the states in the *Pañcamahākāvyas,* due to the ideal arrangement of security and protection by the kings. The word 'Robbery' was only in hearing and there were no prisoners to be set free at the happy occasion of the birth of prince Raghu. Though gambling was included in the vices, the game of gambling had a royal support as it was played between the two kings Yudhiṣṭhira and Duryodhana. Of course, we get no reference of the tax received on this game; but it might have been a source of royal income.

Natural Sources : The fruitful land, in the state was the main source of income. So the huge property and riches of the state are frequently reflected in the *Pañcamahākāvyas*. The land even in the forests was cultivated for agriculture.[136] The land was prosperous by the plentyful crops.[137] In the reign of Duryodhana,

---

135. ŚP (Critical Edition by BORI) 128.36
नान्यनपीडयित्वेह कोषः शक्यः कुतो बलम् ।
तदर्थं पीडयित्वा च दोषं न प्राप्तुमर्हति ॥

136. Raghu V.9

137. ibid. IX.4

people did not depend upon rain for the fertilization of the land and the farmers obtained the crops at ease.[138] As mentioned before, the minute details in the taxation are not seen in the *Pañcamahākāvyas*. We know them only from the law books.

Fields, mines, forests, Cattle-breeding were the permanent sources of income to the treasury. In Duryodhana's reign the earth showered the treasures inside her, like a cow overflowing with milk offers milk in plenty.[139] The treasury of the kings was being replenished by the gems from the mines, crops from the fields and elephants from the forests.[140] The earth is named as the begetter of numerous gems.[141] Kuśa's treasury was surplus due to the sources from all sides, by the bridges and dams, by agriculture, cattle breeding, trade and by elephants.[142] It reminds us of the mention by Kāmanḍaka of the eight-fold sources of replenishing the treasury.[143] Camels and mares also formed the part of king's treasury.[144] Fine horses, heaps of gold formed the main bulk of king's treasury.[145]

Gifts from the Feudatories : bowing to the might of the emperor, the feudatories accepted his rulership and they had to pay him regular taxes.[146] The

---

138. Kirā I.17
139. Kirā I.18
140. Raghu XVII.66
खनिभिः सुषुवे रत्नं क्षेत्रैः सस्यं वनैर्गजान् ।
दिदेश वेतनं तस्मै रक्षासदृशमेव भूः ॥
141. ibid VII.28
142. ibid XVI.1
143. KN V. 77/78
144. Raghu V.32
145. Raghu IV.70
146. Śiśu II.9
करदीकृतभूपालो भ्रातृभिर्जित्वरैर्दिशाम् ।
विनाप्यस्मदलम्भूष्णुरिज्यायै तपसः सुतः ॥

feudatories also offered valuable gifts to the monarch. We come across frequent references in the *Pañcamahākāvyas*, of the feudatories offering the precious gifts. In the fourth canto of Raghuvaṃśa, there is a vast description of the conquest of Raghu and the gifts offered by the feudatories. So the treasury of the kings was in a greater part, supplemented by the tribute from the feudatories.

The loot and booty in the war also formed a notable part of king's treasury. In the expedition of conquest Raghu took the wealth of Kaling king.[147] It is described in Naiṣadhīyacarita that king Nala in his youth achieved the conquest of world and by that got the acquisition of inexhaustible treasure.[148] The valorous kings due to their prowess acquired great riches from all directions.[149]

Gifts from the friends: The kings received gifts and presents on the occasion of sacrificial ceremonies and functions. When Rāma set free the sacrificial horse, his friends Sugrīva, Vibhīṣaṇa showered him by precious gifts like the clouds showering the crops.[150] In the Rājasūya sacrifice performed by Yudhiṣṭhira, the kings awaited for offering the presents of precious gems to him. One of the kings offered a countless wealth to Yudhṣṭhira, that it was enough to complete the sacrifice[151] Daily presents also were offered by the citizens to their king, as a token of love and respect.[152]

---

147. Raghu IV.43
148. Nai I.19
149. Raghu III.10; VII.99; VI.46; IX.20
150. ibid XV.58
     तमध्वराय मुक्ताश्वं रक्षः कपिनरेश्वराः ।
     मेघाः सस्यमिवाम्भोभिरभ्यवर्षन्नुपायनैः ॥
151. Śiśu XIV.39
152. Raghu I.45

Gifts from the divinities : Sometimes, the treasury of the king was replenished by the help of divine sources. In Raghuvaṁśa, the shining instance supports this point under discussion. After performing the Viśvajit sacrifice the treasury of King Raghu was completely exhausted due to the constant donations and it was not possible for him to fulfill the desire of Kauṭsa who demanded fourteen crore coins from his treasury. Relying on his strength he prepared to attack Kubera, the god of wealth; and Kubera recognizing the strength of Raghu showered heaps of gold in the treasury of Raghu.[153]

Thus the kings kept their financial position sound by receiving the income from all the sources mentioned above. The treasury was inherited to the kings and was increased by them. Treasury mainly comprises gold, jewels and also of elephants, horses etc. While explaining the 'Kośa sampad' in Arthaśāstra, Kauṭilya has stated that Gold reserve is the best treasury. That which is obtained either by inheritance or by self-acquisition, rich in gold and silver, filled with an abundance of big gems of various colours and of gold coins and capable of withstanding calamities of long duration, is the best treasury.[154]

After a due consideration of the sources of income we shall turn to some items of expenditure from the royal treasury. As the theory of public finance was closely related to the protection and security of the people, it is natural that a king should use a great deal of the finance on the plans of public security. Inspite of special mention about the plans of expenditure for the civil defence, in the *Pañcamahākāvyas* spending of the good deal of amount can be inferred from the

153. Raghu V.29

154. KA VI.1.10
धर्माधिगतः पूर्वः स्वयं वा हेमरुप्यप्रायश्चित्रस्थूलारत्नहिरण्यो
दीर्घामप्यापदमनायतिं सहेतेति कोशसंपत् ।

prosperous and well protected kingdoms.[155] The right of the kings of collecting the taxes without fulfilling the duty of protection of the people is refused by the law-books also, Manu enjoins that a king who does not afford protection and yet takes his share in the form of taxes, tolls, daily presents and fines, will soon sink into hell.[156] If the king failed in the affairs of administration and did not render security and protection to the people, the people were authorized to claim for the refund of wages in proportion to their loss.[157]

A king had to protect the people from the external attacks of the enemies. Before they started the expedition of conquest, they properly guarded their kingdoms from the enemies.[158] As, an obtainment of the title of 'Cakravartin' was the aim of their life, they frequently arranged the expeditions of conquests and they had to spend a great share of expenditure on the maintenance of the standing army. An application of finance for the vast army was the prominent item which was taken into account by the ancient thinkers.[159] So the execution of war-efforts was dependent on the treasury.

War was the last policy to conquer the enemy. But a 'Vijigīṣu' always tried to conquer the enemy by applying the first three expedients of the four-fold policy in the field of polity. The successful application of the first three expeditions viz. *Sāma, dāna* and *Bheda* or dissension is not possible without the help of finance.

---

155. Raghu IX.4
156. MS VIII.307
     योऽरक्षन्बलिमादत्ते करं शुल्कं च पार्थिवः ।
     प्रतिभागं च दण्डं च स सद्यो नरकं व्रजेत् ॥
157. YS XI.36 (Mitākṣarā)
     प्रत्याहर्तुमशक्तस्तु धनं चौरैर्हृतं यदि ।
     सकोशाद्धि देयं स्यादशक्तेन महीक्षिता ॥
158. Raghu IV.26
159. ŚN IV.880 to 890

A large amount is to be spent on present to the inimical as well as friendly kings, on bribes to create dissension in the rank of file of the enemy and on preparation of the war efforts. This policy of uprooting the enemy is explained in details by Uddhava in Śiśupālavadha. Inspite of the hasty action of declaring a war against Śiśupāla, Uddhava consults the policy of dissension by the spies taking pay from both sides.[160] Thus the first three aspects of the fourfold policy are mainly dependent on the organizations of spies who relied on good wages, good gifts and presents.[161] So the execution of war-efforts and actual military expenditure was the notable disbursement or royal treasury. Kauṭilya has stated that the finance in the welfare state contains the finance designed for peace time and also for war time.[162]

When we look at the financial policy and the approach towards 'Artha', of the kings in the *Pañcamahākāvyas*, we realize one thing that obtaining *Artha* was not their aim of life but it was an instrument to fulfill the needs of the people. They collected wealth not out of greed but for the welfare of the state.[163] Their financial directive was situated in the four aspects. Earning money through just ways, protecting the treasury and using it in right ways.[164] Their gaining was only for giving. After the successful universal conquests the kings, in the religious performances as *Viśvajit, Rājasūya, Aśvamedha* sacrifices distributed all of the conquered wealth. In the *Viśvajit* sacrifice performed by Raghu he emptied all his treasury and in the *Rājasūya* of Yudhiṣṭhira, he gifted not only gems and jewels but

---

160. Śiśu II. 113
161. ibid II.112
162. KA II. 8. 1/2
कोशपूर्वाः सर्वारम्भाः । तस्मात्पूर्वं कोशमवेक्षेत ।
163. Raghu I.21
164. Śiśu XIV.9

even the lands of his own seal to the pititioners.[165] This great virtue of charity of the kings was supported by the law books. As Kāmanḍaka states - "A righteous king should preserve his treasury for religious deeds for protection of servants and subjects and for the period of emergency.[166]

Thus though we do not get the details of the system of taxation and items of expenditure, we can mention the sources of income and items of expenditure from which a good picture of the welfare-state in the *Pañcamahākāvyas* stands before us.

---

165. ibid. XIV.36

166. KN IV.62
धर्महेतोस्तथार्थाय भृत्यानां शरणाय च
आपदर्थं च संरक्ष्यः कोशो धर्मवता सदा ॥

CHAPTER IV

DIPLOMATIC POLICY

THE MEANS OF DIPLOMACY :

The principle methods by which a king was to extend his dominions and to govern his own kingdom were called *Upāyas* or expedients. *Nīti*, *Naya* are the synonyms used for expedients, which are four in number. These are *Sāma* (conciliation), *Dāna* (bribery), *Bheda* (dissension) and *Daṇḍa*. Besides these traditionally accepted means or expedients, three additional expedients viz. *Māyā*, *Upekṣā* and *Indrajāla* are mentioned by some politicians like Kāmanḍaka.[1] A king, who knows the code of diplomacy,[2] which contains four expedients, is sure to be the victor over the earth. These four *upāyas* are the definite means to get success.[3] The newly wedded four sons of Daśaratha are described as the winners of success, as are the four means.[4] Rāma was symbolized for a union of the four means, expedients, because he was fanned by Lakṣmaṇa and Śatrughna and also by Bharata who held the royal umbrella.[5]

These four expedients offer success to the king if they are applied in a suitable manner. The treasury of

---

1. KN XVII.3
2. KA VI.1.18
   आत्मवांस्त्वल्पदेशोऽपि युक्तः प्रकृतिसंपदा ।
   नयज्ञः पृथिवीं कृत्स्नां जयत्येव न हीयते ॥
3. Raghu X.86
4. ibid. XI.55
5. ibid. XIV.11

the state becomes prosperous by the proper employment of the four *upāyas*. In Kirātārjunīyam, while describing the ideal reign of Duryodhana the poet says "The four expedients of success used by him in their suitable places of action and thus honoured by being rightly employed as if emulating to eachother, ever produce happy results and prosperous future.[6] In Raghuvaṁśa, it is described that the intelligent king Ahīnagu, taking birth through Viṣṇu became a lord of four directions due to the unobstructed use of four expedients.[7] In the description of the marching of the army of Kṛṣṇa, it is imagined that the army follows Kṛṣṇa, as the fruits of actions performed by the excellent diplomats follow them on their heels.[8]

Like the internal gains for the state, these expedients are very helpful in maintaining the inter-state relationship. An ambitious king can conquer the world by the means of diplomacy. A successful ruler was considered to be one, who conserved all his energies and forces for using them in extreme cases and generally depended on the art of diplomacy to secure the ends of the state. A success or failure depends on the policy that the state adopts. In the absence of the policies the war would be a frequent matter. So the battle of wits is preferred to the battle of arms. Diplomacy is a nature of a method of negotiation, persuasion and conciliation for promoting the common interests of different matters.

These four expedients were the cardinal points of the diplomatic system and were effective instruments in acquiring prosperity and averting many a war which would otherwise have resulted in much bloodshed and

---

6. Kirā I.15
अनारतं तेन पदेषु लम्भिता विभज्य सम्यग्विनियोगसत्क्रियाः ।
फलन्त्युपायाः परिबृंहितायतीरुपेत्य संघर्षमिवार्थसम्पदः ॥
7. Raghu XVIII.15
8. Śiśu III.26

economic distress. Through the application of these expedients the enemy was easy to be controlled like a serpant which is controlled by the charmer.[9]

Sāma (Conciliation)- Through the policy of conciliation, a clever diplomat turns even an enemy to his side.[10] When two kings enter into a friendship and promise to do no harm mutually and to help in the time of distress, the policy is known as *Sāma.*[11] A real diplomat entering into the insight of the things becomes successful. With the strong enemy the policy of *sāma* should be applied. The application of conciliation necessitates the virtue of forbearance. A king's power of tolerance and spirit of forgiveness helps him in his policy of conciliation. Yudhiṣṭhira observes that anger destroys the utility of opportune time, takes away the success and inflames the body and senses;[12] so in the expedient of *sāma* forbearance helps the person, which is itself indestructive but can destroy the vile enemy.[13] Dāna (Bribery) : Dāna is the second expedient in order, An employment of *sāma* when accompanied with *dāna* becomes more effective. The seditious parties from the enemy-side are easy to be diverted through the use of *dāna* accompained with *sāma.*[14] Money or gift-giving is necessary to conciliate those who are in distress or in

---

9. Śiśu II.88
10. MS VII.107
11. ŚN IV.28
    परस्परमनिष्टं न चिन्तनीयं त्वया मया ।
    सुसहाय्यं हि कर्तव्यं शत्रौ साम प्रकीर्तितम् ।
12. Kirā II.42
    अतिपातितकालसाधना स्वशरीरेन्द्रियवर्गतापनी ।
    जनवन्नभवन्तमक्षमा नयसिद्धेरपनेतुमर्हति ॥
13. ibid. II.43
14. KA I.14.12
    लभेत सामदानाभ्यां कृत्यांश्च परभूमिषु ।
    अकृत्यान्भेददण्डाभ्यां परदोषांश्च दर्शयन् ॥

need of money. The king Duryodhana was well versed in diplomacy and he knew the proper use of dāna. His policy of sāma was always successful as it was accompanied with dāna. He offered gifts to the worthy persons.[15] His attendants, servants and followers were sure that after the completion of their work they would get favourable gift from their master.[16] His mighty warriors were properly paid and honoured with money gifts, so there was no chance for treachery by them towards him.[17] Supreme importance is given for keeping the army contended and gratified; for discontent army-troops is a source of grave danger to the state. On the eve of expedition special allowances and rewoards were given (Śiśu XIX.57). Thus his policy of dāna was completely successful in keeping his servants and subjects to his side. A benefit of the good policy, internal as well as in foreign affairs, is obtained when the policy of *dāna* is comprised of prosperous pay and proper prizes to the attendants, executives and spies, after a successful accomplishment of the mission (Śiśu II.112) Importance of *dāna* is also mentioned by Kāmanḍaka. He says "Conciliation applied without gifts is useless as a straw. Even women refuse such *sāma* unaccompanied by gifts."[18]

The policy of *dāna* is necessary for an ambitious king who wants to divert other kings to his side. While stating an importance of *dāna* in keeping friendship, Uddhava in *Śiśupālavadha* explains that Śiśupāla has a strong support of his friends, as he has offered many horses and elephants in gift to Bāṇāsura and thus

---

15. Kirā I.12
निरत्ययं साम न दानवार्जितं न भूरि दानं विरहय्य सत्क्रियाम् ।
प्रवर्तते तस्य विशेषशालिनी गुणानुरोधेन विना न सत्क्रिया ॥
16. ibid. I.14
17. ibid. I.19
18. KN XVIII.64

obliging him, he has turned *Bāṇāsura* to his side; so Bāṇāsura will unite with Śiśupāla just like a sharp arrow uniting with the bow.[19]

The success of the third policy viz. dissension is mainly dependent upon the application of *dāna*. Among the four classes of seditious people[20] the greedy are easily diverted to another side through the use of bribery.

Bheda (Dissension) : Bheda or dissension is the third strong policy in the field of polity. It is the policy of divide and rule. The policy of dissension when applied to the internal constituents of the enemy is able to uproot him. "Tossed by the wind of disaffection of the ministers and their friends gradually estranged, an enemy even though powerful is like a tree shaken by the wind and with its roots gradually shattered is easy to be uprooted.[21] So a dissension among the ministers etc. causes a downfall of a vast kingdom of the enemy. In Śiśupālavadha a similar instance is given to show the result of dissension. While describing the effective diplomacy of Śiśupāla his messenger says "seeking holes in the circle of ministers and making dissension, he cuts even the roots viz. the chief minister crown prince etc. of the tree of the kingdom of enemy".[22]

---

19. Śiśu II.97
सम्पादितफलस्तेन सपक्षः परभेदनः ।
कार्मुकेणेव गुणिना बाणः संधानमेष्यति ॥

20. KA I.13.22 I.14.12
क्रुद्धलुब्धभीतमानिनस्तु परेषां कृत्याः ।
लभेत सामदानाभ्यां कृत्यांश्च परभूमिषु ।

21. Kirā II.50
अपरागसमीरणेरितः क्रमशीर्षाकुलमूलसंततिः ।
सुकरस्तरुवत्सहिष्णुना रिपुरुन्मूलयितुं महानपि ।

22. Śiśu XVI.73
अधिगम्य च रन्ध्रमन्तरा जनयन्मण्डलभेदमन्यतः ।
खनति क्षतसंहति क्षणादपि मूलानि महान्ति कस्यचित् ॥

Even a very small disturbance caused by disaffection of the internal constituents kills the king, as the fire produced by the friction of the branches of a tree burns the whole mountain.[23] Balarāma in Śiśupālavadha suggests that the ministers who are unable to employ a right policy are really enemies in the guise of ministers.[24]

The wicked nature of a king itself creates scope for dissension. His arrogant behaviour becomes unbearable to others. In such a condition a seed of dissension sown by the enemy becomes fruitful. In Kirātārjunīyam, Yudhiṣṭhira is not willing to take any hasty action against Duryodhana as Yudhiṣṭhira hopes that he will surely get an advantage of the arrogant nature of Duryodhana. According to Yudhiṣṭhira's argument, overpowered by arrogance Duryodhana, insulting other kings will make them ready for dissension. Even an ordinary perṣon does not suffer insults how then, can the group of kings bear it?[25] Due to the king's haughty nature the ministers, subjects, friendly kings are enraged and get seduced and the enemy takes an advantage of the situation. It is just like a river which overruns and sweeps away the loose bank broken inside and outside.[26] Thus king's conduct gives scope for dissension.

The policy of dissension becomes effective when regulated through the secret agents or spies, taking pay from both sides. These spies work for one king, entering into the enemy-country, the spies work there by showing secret letters written by the king to his ministers and make dissension among the king and his ministers. Uddhava in Śiśupālavadha states the necessity

23. Kirā II.51

24. Śiśu II.56

25. Kirā II.47
उपजापसहान्विलङ्घयन्स विधाता नृपतीन्मदोद्धतः।
सहते न जनोऽप्यधःक्रियां किमु लोकाधिकधाम राजकम् ॥

26. ibid. II.53

of employment of such spies.[27] Enemy is easily captured, if the loopholes in the eighteen departments of his state are detected by the spiės.[28] Uddhava advises Kṛṣṇa to sow dissension in the enemyside and his ministers through spies. Kauṭilya has urgefully stated the necessity of double-paid spies to employ the policy of dissension.[29]

The four steps in the process of policy of dissension, which are recommended for a king for the complete annihilation of the enemy are suggested in Śiśupālavadha. They are securing an opportunity in the middle of the circle of ministers; creating a rift among them; destroying their main supporters and destroying the union of the enemy-kings.[30]

The work for seducing from the allegiance is not easy. Only those who are bold-speakers, false narrators and receivers of payment from both sides can very well do this job. The persons to be seduced from allegieance thus are described as *'Kṛtya'* or *'Bhedya'*[31] *-Upajāpa'*[32] or Intrigue is the name given to the work of sowing seeds or dissension which is mentioned with emphasis in Arthaśāstra.[33] Thus dissension is very useful against a

---

27. Śiśu II.113
28. ibid. II.111
29. KA I.12.18
    कण्टकशोधनोक्ताश्चापसर्पाः परेषु कृतवेतना
    वसेयुरसंपातिनष्चारार्थम् । त उभयवेतनाः ।
    I.12.19
    गृहीतपुत्रदाराश्च कुर्यादुभयवेतनान् ।
    तांश्चारिप्रहितान्विद्यात्तेषां शौचं त तद्विधैः ।
    I.12.23
    य परप्रवृत्तिज्ञानार्था शीघ्राश्चारपरम्पराः ।
30. Supra Ref. No.20
31. Śiśu XX.23
32. ibid. II.99
33. KA IX.6

strong king. It keeps him occupied with domestic troubles as to make it impossible for him to launch upon a foreign expedition. Dissension, if well directed is able to divide even a firm king as a mighty stream of water divides mountains of solid rock.

It is very essential for an ideal diplomat to cover his weak points and not to create a chance for the enemy to enter in his internal constituents. He should be cautious about detecting the weak-points of the enemy. By the proper application of the policy he should wipe out the dissension applied by the enemy.[34] On the other hand an ambitious king by his policy unknown to the enemy, should sow dissension in his constituents of the state.[35]

The policy of dissension is more effective than the policy of conciliation. Uddhava argues that though Pāṇḍavas have done compromise with Bāṇāsura, he will not unite with them; on the other hand Śiśupāla by the application of dissension may enrage him against Pāṇḍavas,[36] In addition to this, Śiśupala has diverted Bāṇāsura to his side by offering him valuable gifts.[37] Thus dissension through bribery proves to be a very effective policy in the political field.

Daṇḍa : Daṇḍa is an effective expedient applied by a king, through which he protects his subjects and controls the internal and external enemies. The kings used this expedient to punish the criminals for the preservation of law.[38] The kings employed *daṇḍa* in a

---

34. Kirā XVI.42
    तमाशु चतुःश्रवसां समूहं मन्त्रेण ताक्ष्योंदयकारणेन ।
    नेता नयेनेव परोपजापं निवारयामास पतिः पशूनाम् ॥
35. ibid. XVII.27
36. Supra Ref.No. 32
37. Śiśu II.97
38. Raghu I.25

proper manner, pleasant like a southern wind, attracted the minds of the subjects.[39] People get agitated if the harsh *daṇḍa* is applied, on the other hand the ruler is defeated by the mild use of *daṇḍa;* So a proper application of *daṇḍa* is much honored by all the ancient thinkers.[40] A prime duty of the beholder of *daṇḍa* was to protect the weak.[41] This *daṇḍa* power is described as non-separable from the kings's body.[42] *Daṇḍanīti* is like the reins of a horse or the goad of an elephant, to the men of four varṇas to keep them in the ordained path of *'dharma'*[43] An impartial king uses it equally to his son as well as towards a foe.[44] The proper observance of *'trivarga'* comes as a result of the application of *daṇḍa*[45] Thus on *daṇḍa* alone, depends the successful prosecution of the ends of life of the subjects and peace in the internal administration of the king.

While stating the necessity of the fourth expedient *daṇḍa* to check the attacks of the external enemy, it must be noted that *daṇḍa* is not actual punishment or opening of hostility. It is a diplomatic war, nor an armed contest. "It is a threat of war, generally applied as a last resort before the actual commencement of

---

39. Raghu IV.8
स हि सर्वस्य लोकस्य युक्तदण्डतया मनः ।
आददे नातिशीतोष्णो न भस्वानिव दक्षिणः ॥
40. KA I.4.10
तीक्ष्णदण्डो हि भूतानां उद्वेजनीयो भवति ।
मृदुदण्डः परिभूयते । यथार्हदण्डः पूज्यते ।
Kn II.37 MS VII.19 ŚP (Critical Edition by BORI) 56.21/40
41. Nai I.133
42. Raghu XVII.62
43. V.R.R. Dikshitar, Hindu Administrative Institutions, published by University of Madras, 1929, p.28.
44. Kirā I.13
45. KN II.38

fighting.[46] A threatening by the envoys in Kirātārjunīyam and Śiśupālavadha to Arjuna and Kṛṣṇa respectively, exhibiting the tremendous strength of their masters can be described as the application of *daṇḍa*.[47] Thus only an exhibition of one's strength is able to discourage and conquer the enemy.

With these four important traditional expedients other three also are mentioned by ancient thinkers. These are *māyā*, *Upekṣā* and *Indrajāla*.[48] *Upekṣā* is the policy of showing a lack of interest towards the enemy. According to Agnipurāṇa it is a policy of neutrality.[49] It is just only a time-saving device to get prepared to attack one's enemy. But according to bhīma and Balarāma in Kirātārjunīyam and Śiśupālavadha respectively, one should not neglect the rising power of the enemy.[50] If the destruction of his enemy is near at hand and of serious consequence and that with regard to himself it is the reverse, then he should overlook it but otherwise he should take action to check it.[51] A person whose enmity has risen to extremity, should not be neglected, otherwise it should be like an act of sleeping against the wind which spreads through dry grass.[52] Thus one should apply the policy of *Upekṣā* duly calculating the situation. *Māyā* and Indrajāla comprise base diplomacy. Māyā means allusion. So the invader uses all the illusory powers to deceive the enemy and strikes him at his weak point. In the fight between

---

46. V.R.R. Dikshitar, War in Ancient India. published by University of Madras 1944 p.329.
47. Kirā XIV.70
48. KN XVVII.3
49. AP 241.66
50. Kirā II.8
51. ibd. II.9
52. Śiśu II.42

Rāma and Rāvaṇa, the latter deceived Sītā showing the cut-off head of Rāma, by the sight of which Sītā became unconscious.[53] In the policy of *Indrajāla* actual war is not implied but the success over the adversary is achieved by a net-work of intrigues and counter intrigues.

The four expedients applied at opportune time and place offer desired fruit. Vibhīṣaṇa, the youngest brother of Rāvaṇa allied the Rāma, who promised him the sovereignty over the rākṣasas.[54] It was a great loss for Rāvaṇa but a great gain to Rāma who acquired a powerful friend and Vibhīṣana got his desired fruit.[55] Thus, the proper application of the four *upāyas* is sure to bear fruit, but the employer must have a discriminative power to use them. According to Bhīma and Balarāma in Kirātārjunīyam and Śiśupālavadha respectively, the polity though difficult can be grasped by its close study, but a guide to show the way is rare.[56] A mediocre man also gets the knowledge through the books, but the proper application of the theories can be employed by a clever diplomat only.[57] Sometimes all these expedients prove futile against a strong enemy.[58]

---

53. Raghu XII.74

54. ibid. XII.69
तस्मै निशाचरैश्वर्यं प्रतिशुश्राव राघवः।
काले खलु सभारब्धाः फलं बध्नन्ति नीतयः ॥

55. ibid. XII.68

56. Kirā II.3

57. Śiśu II.26
षड्गुणाः शक्तयस्तिस्त्रः सिद्धयश्चोदयास्त्रयः।
ग्रन्थानधीत्य व्याकर्तुमिति दुर्भेधसोऽप्यलम् ॥

58. Ku II.48
तस्मिनुपायाः सर्वे नः क्रूरे प्रतिहतक्रियाः।
वीर्यवन्त्यौषधानीव विकारे सान्निपातिके ॥

A prudent diplomat employs these four expedients in accordance with their due order. The first three expedients should be tried in the beginning and if they do not achieve any fruit, then war should be undertaken as the last resort. As an outcome of war is always full of risks, it should be a last measure only. The first expedient of conciliation was held to be the best, because it did not entail any loss of money and strength while the last one viz. *daṇḍa* means destruction of human life and property. The prudent rulers in the *Pañcamahākāyas* employing the expedients by their due order gained good results without any obstruction.[59] Duryodhana, by employing conciliation and bribery has got the support of his attendants and army, not giving a way to dissersion. By employing *daṇḍa* impartially he controlled his subjects. Thus by the proper use of means, happy results were seen in the reign of Duryodhana. If conciliation with bribery gets no fruitful results then one should apply dissension against a powerful enemy to uproot his power. When all the three remedies become exhausted then alone the last remedy of force was resorted to. Ancient thinkers also suggested the fourth expedient as the last resort when the first three prove to be futile.[60] This attitude towards *daṇḍa* was not only the maxim of perfection only but it was put in practice by the prudent rulers. The wars in Kirātārjunīyam and Śiśupālavadha are only the outcome of the futility of the first three expedients. Thus it is suggested that wars should be avoided by all the possible means.

But in Śiśupālavadha, Balarāma is not ready to accept this principle of avoiding war. He favours the view that when an enemy can be subdued by means of fourth remedy viz. *daṇḍa*, the use of *sāma* would be

---

59. Raghu XVII.68
60. MS VII.198/200

a wrong policy. the strength and valour of the army of Kṛṣṇa are on the climax of prosperity. Sc he suggests only the war- policy. According to him the whole science of polity rests on only two sides; The rise of the self and fall of the enemy.[61] So when the fourth means is applicable why should we apply conciliation which is useless in the case of a wicked enemy like Śiśupāla ? A wise person does not sprinkle water on a fever which is wiped out by the sweat.[62] On the contrary, the conciliatary words increase an anger of the enemy, like the drops of water sprinkled in the clarified butter inflame it[63] Almost all the books on polity state that daṇḍa should be a last resort which should be applied after a due consideration; but according to Balarāma, a ruler having a tremendous strength should neglect the saying of *Śāstras.*[64]

To launch a policy of either aggression or defence, internal peace in the reign of the king is essential. The rulers in the *Pañcamahākāvyas* were watchful in not creating even a chance for the discontentment in their subjects.[65] The ideal rulers like Duryodhana satisfied their subjects through *sāma* and *dāna*. Sometimes the discontented local-chiefs or leaders join hands with foreigners and rise against the king, which causes the destruction of the king. In such cases the policy of *sāma* and *dāna* should be applied so that the discontented subjects may give their unholy alliance to the enemy. The internal danger must be suppressed first before dealing with the external danger. After ensuring peace

---

61. Śiśu II.30
62. Śiśu II.54
    चतुर्थोपायसाध्ये तु रिपौ सान्त्वमपक्रिया ।
    स्वैद्यमामज्वरं प्राज्ञः कोऽम्भसा परिषिञ्चति ॥
63. ibid. II.55
64. ibid. II.62
65. Raghu XVII.55

at home the conqueror is asked to apply the policy of dissension towards the enemy, as is advised by Uddhava in Śiśupālavadha.

While applying these expedients one should take into account the circumstances and the nature of the person of the hostile party. One should face the enemy in the same mode and manner in which he is coming to face. In Śiśupālavadha, Sātyaki replies to the messenger of Śiśupāla "We are ready to reply to Śiśupāla in the same manner in whatever capacity, either of a friend or of a foe, he will come.[66] If the enemy is wicked and deceitful then there is no use of conciliation as states Draupadī. The man of dull intellect, who does not apply fraud against fraud, gets defeat.[67] In Naiṣadhīyacarita, Nala expresses the similar opinion when he comes to know that gods deceitfully requested him to be their messenger. According to him sincerity is not the right policy towards those who are insincere.[68]

Thus considering the effect of the expedients a diplomat should apply them in suitable circumstances. A Campaign should be conservant with *'tantra'* viz. home-affairs and 'Āvāpa' viz. foreign matters.[69] through the expedients. A diplomat, who uses these different modes of policy with due regard to place, time and resources against enemy, obtains success. With the help of policy even snakes, elephants, tigers are brought under control and men can attain heaven. Even a stone can be pierced easily.[70]

---

66. Śiśu XVI.33

67. Kirā I.30

68. Nai V.103
तेन तेन वचसैव मघोन: स स्म वेद कपटं पटुरुच्चै: ।
आचरत्तदुचितामथ वाणीमार्जवं हि कुटिलेषु न नीति: ॥

69. Śisu II.88

70 ŚN IV.22
उपायेन यथा व्यालो गज: सिंहोऽपि साध्यते ।
भूमिष्ठा: स्वर्गमायान्ति वज्रं मिन्द्रस्युपायत: ॥

DIPLOMATIC AGENTS :

Now we turn to the topic of the diplomatic agents, appointed by a king. These diplomatic agents viz. *'Cāra'* and *'Dūta;* or spies and envoys were indispensable instruments of security for a king which he achieved by keeping a vigilant watch through them. Spying was a very ancient institution, as the references to it are found as far back as *Rgveda*. The spies of Varuṇa are pictured to be seated around him.[71]

An institution of *Cāra* and *Dūta* was very important for the maintenance and progress of the state. It was essential for an administrator to keep contact with his subjects and officials and to keep watch over the neighbouring countries to know their exact strategy. A stability of the kingdom was relied on the information brought by the informants about the loyalty and disaffection of the people and the relative strength and loopholes of the enemies. In the *Paṇcamahākāvyas* the kings are rightly said to be *Cāracakṣuṣah* as they saw through the spies.[72] The spies were spread all over the kingdom like the rays of the sun, that the kings were not ignorant of anything in their states and outside the country.[73] Though the kings slept every night, they were wakeful on account of the informants sent in their own countries and also in the country of enemy.[74]

Before stating the significant role performed by the spies and *Dūtas* in the *Pañcamahākāvyas,* it should be noted that there was not a functional difference between these two offices. *Dūta* or ambassador was an open

71. Rgveda I.25.13 परि स्पशो निषेदिरे ।
72. Kirā I.14 Nai I.13 Śiś II.82
73. Raghu XVII.48
74. ibid. XVII.51
परेषु स्वेषु च क्षिप्तैरविज्ञातपरस्परैः ।
सोऽपसर्पैर्जजागार यथाकालं स्वपन्नपि ॥

representative of his master while *'cāra'* or spy was a secret agent. Execpting the difference in rank, the political theorists did not appear to think that there was a very great difference between the spy and the ambassador. Indeed, one of the functions of the ambassador was to spy. An ambassador was but an open spy and a spy was but an envoy, roaming about in the enemy's country in various disguises. Secrecy was the characteristic feature of the spies which distinguished them from envoys. An ambassador was an open spy officially sent by the king. Only by a previous permission an envoy could enter into the country of the enemy while the identity of a spy was unknown and secret in his own country as well as in the foreign country.

The kings used to get the latest information of the events in their kingdoms. The spies were appointed by the king to find out the rumours among the subjects. The king used to hear the secret reports from the spies in complete privacy. King Rāma got the news of the scandal about Sīta from his spy. According to his report people suspected Sītā's character because of her stay at Rāvaṇa's place.[75] Rāma could not bear the stain on the unblemished family sprung from the Sun; so though fully confident in Sīitā's purity, he had to take the decision of the abandonment of Sītā.[76] This event reveals the fact that important decisions of the kings were influenced by the reports of the spies.

The king was ever in contact with the happenings in his country and he knew even about his own high or low officers. In connection with the activities of the spies it was important that they should be unknown

---

75. Raghu XIV.32
76. ibid. XIV.40
    अवैमि चैनामनघेति किंतु लोकापवादोबलवान्मतो मे ।
    छाया हि भूमेः शशिनो मलत्वेनारोपिता शुद्धिमतः प्रजाभिः ॥

to eachother and should be ignorant of the fact that their master is common.[77] Kāmandaka suggests the same principle that a king should appoint spies in the territory of the enemy as well as among his own people. The spies should be mutually unknown and nobody should recognize them.[78] Like the functions of the spies inside the kingdom, their significant role in the foreign policy is prominently discussed in Śiśupālavadha. In Śiśupālavadha, the prudent minister Uddhava advises Kṛṣṇa to attend Yudhiṣṭhira's sacrificial function and not to make an hasty attack on Śiśupāla. In the meanwhile they should collect information about enemy's strength through the spies. According to Uddhava, an expert boat-man knows the depth of water by stepping a leg in water, so also an expert is policy should appoint spies among the eighteen *tīrthas* and should get an information about the seditious and non-seditious persons in the enemy's party.[79] The spies spread among the kings, gathered for the ceremony, would search out the friends of Kṛṣṇa and would deliver his massage to be favourable to his side.[80] Uddhava states the necessity of employing double-paid spies for the policy of dissension. This type of spies appointed by one king receives pay from the opposite party also. They spy for their master, entering into the secrets of the enemy without any suspicion. Kauṭilya has mentioned the necessity of employing the double paid spies.[81]

A king should penetrate everywhere is his country as well as in the foreign country, the ministers, officials of the government from their heir-apparent down to

---

77. Raghu XVII.51
78. KN XIII 37/38
79. Śiśu II.111
80. Śiśu II.114
81. KA I.12.18

the lowest officials, as a wind, which moves everywhere and penetrates all created beings.[82] Concealing of his own identity and searching 'holes' in the secret counsels of the enemy is the foremost duty of a spy. So the king should be quick in action after the completion of the counsel; otherwise the secrets would be disclosed by the spies of the enemy.[83] A comparison of a spy to a serpent is very sifnificant.[84] Like a serpent, a spy works stealthily and windingly, so that none easily suspects him and detects his intention. The keen intellectual insight of *apasarpa* is compared with the high sensibility of the serpent. His eyes sought the vices, crimes, acts of treason and the holder of those in the foreign court.[85] To keep secrecy about their identity and their mission, the spies wandered in various disguises. In the very commencing part of Kirātājunīyam we come across an account by the spy who was in the guise of a religious student.[86] The ascetics, monks, nuns were honoured in the society, so the secret agents in the disguise of ascetics could easily get entrance in the society and even in the royal palace. Kauṭilya mentions various disguises of the spies.[87] It is essential for these persons in secret service to be expert in different kinds of manners and behaviors, as they have to assume different forms according to the demand of the occasion. The king learns the plans of other kings through his

---

82. MS IX.306
83. Śiśu II.29
84. Raghu XIV. 31
85. Rudrakānta Mishra, An Article in the Journal of the Ganganath Jha Research Institute, Allahabad, January 1967, Vol. XXIII
86. Kirā I.1
87. KA I.11.1
उपधाभिः शुद्धामात्यवर्गो गूढपुरुषानुत्पादयेत् ।
कापटिकोदास्थितगृहपतिकवेदेहकतापसव्यञ्जनान् सत्त्रितीक्ष्णरसदभिक्षुकीश्च ।

faithful emissaries.[88] A king, well versed in diplomacy employs secret agents, skilled in discord to watch the doings of his own party as well as that of the enemy and deals with them with an unsuspecting air.[89] His own plans are not disclosed but are guessed through the results. Thus a king becomes able to take action relying on the reports by the spies.

Dūta viz. envoy was another prominent factor of cultivating diplomatic relations between different states. The relation between the two states depended upon the mission of an envoy. The way in which an envoy delivers the message of his master may make or mar his master's relations with others. *Dūta* transacts that business by which kings are separated or united.[90]

Though in ancient India a theory of international law and ethics was developed, the ambassadors were not permanent agents in foreign countries. They were sent on a special mission and were expected to return after having carried out their missions. A practice of sending ambassadors to declare war is prominently seen in the *Pañcamahākāvyas*. It is stated before that an envoy was open spy, his functions were to plead for his master, to exhibit his master's greatness, to hide his master's drawbacks and to search out the 'holes' of others. The envoys in the *Pañcamahākāvyas* reveal all these characteristics. In Śiśupālavadha, Śiśupāla sent an envoy to declare war against Kṛṣṇa[91] Śiśupāla had been insulted, as the honour was offered to his enemy Kṛṣṇa at the sacrificial ceremony of Yudhiṣṭhira. The envoy sent by Śiśupāla was clever enough to employ the words

---

88. Kirā I.20
महीभृतां सच्चरितैश्चरैः क्रिया स वेद निश्शेषमशेषितक्रियः।
महोदयैस्तस्य हितानुबन्धिभिः प्रतीयते धातुरिवेहितं फलैः॥

89. Kirā I.14

90. MS VII.65/66

91. Śiśu XVIth canto

of double meaning in his speech. Openly he exhibited the policy of peace but tried to threaten the enemy by declaration of war. He exhibited his master's strength and valour. The assembled followers of Kṛṣṇa did not bear the provocative language by the envoy though he was a mere mouthpiece of his master. Sātyki told him to stop his talk but then also the bold envoy fearlessly pleaded for his master. The messenger in Kirātārjunīyam, sent by Kirātarāja reveals the similar characteristics, whose mission was to declare war against Arjuna. He proceeded with the four political expedients step by step. In the beginning of his speech, the envoy praised the high birth and luster of Arjuna and after that he made a charge on Arjuna that he had stolen an arrow of his master.[92] He suggested Arjuna to make friendship with his master, who in return was ready to give Arjuna whatever he desired. He assured Arjuna that his master was ready to give even his life, if begged.[93] The clever envoy pleaded for his master and praised his valour.[94] He even threatened Arjuna as the last resort. Outwardly showing compromise the envoy reached the stage of the declaration of war. Arjuna though angry by the speech of envoy, praised it saying "The envoy, who is appointed by his master to employ the policies as compromise etc. speak fearlessly and he has placed himself on the top of the people who had a command on language.[95] Thus these envoys, fearlessly delivering the message of their masters fulfilled their duty as ideal diplomatic envoy. In Raghuvaṁśa, Hanūmāna's message to Rāvana is of

---

92. Kirā XIII.41

93. Kirā XIII.56

94. ibid XIII.59
मार्गणैरथ तव प्रयोजनं नाथसे किमु पतिं न भूभृतः।
त्वद्विधं सुहृदमेत्य सोऽर्थिनं किं न यच्छति विजित्य मेदिनीम् ॥

95. ibid. XIV.6

a historical value. Hanūmāna was not an ordinary person and was the chief counsellor of Sugrīva. He was versed in all arts and sciences. He boldly delivered the message even at the risk of his life. Rāvaṇa ordered Hanūmāna's tail to be burnt, but Hanūmāna with undaunted courage set the whole city on fire with his burning tail.[96]

It would not be out of place to mention two more envoys who are not sent on a political mission but are sent for some delicate mission. These envoys are Hanūmāna in Raghuvaṁśa and the 'Golden Swan', a non human being in Naiṣadhīyacarita. In Raghuvaṁśa, Hanūmāna, introduced himself to Sītā as a messenger from Rāma, assured her of his safety and enquired after her.[97] When he convinced her of his identity, he delivered the message, received her message to Rāma and took leave of her. In this case it was not a message to enemy, but a loving partner. In Naiṣadhīyacarita also, the golden swan, a non-human being, invested with plenary powers, on behalf of King Nala, delivered the love-message to Damayantī and praised Nala. Realising the intention of love for each-other the swan increased the sentiment in them by his sweet words. Thus the delicate task of creating an opportunity of union of lovers was done by the golden swan.

The *Pañcamahākāvyas* are fully aware of the threefold traditional classification of the envoys.[98] This threefold classification of the envoys is due to the authority given by the master to the ambassador for his mission. The types are Nisṛṣṭārtha, Parimitārtha and Śāsanahara.[99]

96. Raghu XII.63
97. Raghu XII.62
98. Raghu III.68
99. KA I. 16.2 to 4
अमात्यसंपदोपेतो निसृष्टार्थः । पादगुणहीनः परिमितार्थः । अर्धगुणहीनः शासनहरः ।

The Nisṛṣṭārtha are those who are vested with full powers and possess abilities to plead the case of the king with due consideration of time and place. He resembled in his powers to modern ambassador. His qualifications were the same as those necessary for a minister and he had full powers of negotiation. Having fulfilled his principal purpose, he accomplished many more, without marring the prime one. For instance, though the specific mission of Hanūmāna was to find the whereabouts of Sīta, he behaved in Lanka as if he was entrusted with absolute authority. The golden swan in Naiṣdhīyacarita falls in the same category. The Parimitārtha type of Dūta was supplied with definite instructions for a particular mission and could not deviate from them. They enjoy limited powers and scope. They are to speak only about the assignment entrusted to them. The third category of ambassadors viz.Śāsanahara is required only to carry the king's letters and messages to other king. He had no powers of negotiation. In the first canto of Kirātārjunīyam, after delivering the massage to Yudhiṣṭhira the messenger suggests Yudhiṣṭhira to decide the policy. According to him, his duty is to gather information and communicate the same to his master. There ends his duty. It is for the master to see what line of policy is to be followed or what measures are to be adopted to thwart the plans of the enemy.[100]

The envoys who were invested with plenary powers on behalf of a state, had to discharge their duties very cautiously. In communication of the messages they had not to come under anyone's influence. Dūta was a mere mouthpiece of his master. Even if arms were raised against him, he was not to tell lies, but to deliver the message faithfully. He was to deliver his master's message and was to speak truth, howsoever unpalatable

100. Kirā I.25

it was. The messenger of Śiśupāla spoke fearlessly before Kṛṣṇa, though Sātyaki threatened him that he should be punished.[101] An envoy or a spy should narrate the exact position of the enemy, though it may be unfavourable to his master. He should never mislead his master delivering a false report. In Kirātārjunīyam the messenger sent by Yudhiṣṭhira narrates that he experienced no pain, as he delivers the message of the prosperous condition of his enemy; for true well-wisheres do not wish to utter an agreeable falsehood.[102] According to *Nītivākyāmṛta,* truthfulness is one of the four attributes of the persons employed in secret service.[103]

An essential qualification of the spy and envoy is that they should be pure in conduct,[104] and skilled in language.[105] Their loyalty was detected by secret tests. A skill in the speech of the envoys is highly praised in the *Pañcamahākāvyas*. The speech of the messenger sent by Yudhiṣṭhira was brilliant with perculiarly graceful and highly significant expressions and the import where of was well-decided, clear and definite.[106] In the fourteenth canto, Arjuna, though angry due to the arrogant speech of the messenger, praised his speech.

A mind and wisdom of a messenger should be steady and firm. He should not exhibit any hesitation of mind on his face. In Naiṣadhīyacarita, King Nala was sent by the gods as their envoy to Damayantī who

---

101. Śiśu XVI.38

102. Kirā I.2

103. NV XIV.2

104. Kirā I.20

105. ŚP (Critical Edition by BORI) 86.27
कुलीनः शीलसंपन्नो वाग्मी दक्षः प्रियंवदः।
यथोक्तवादी स्मृतिमान्दूतः स्यात्सप्तभिर्गुणैः॥

106. Kirā I.3

was his beloved. He, the firm-minded king, did not consider the loss of Damayantī as hindrance in the path of carrying his mission.[107] The envoy should concentrate his mind on the mission and he should be prompt in his work. It is described that the messenger's eye was faltering and losing its footing, seeing the beauty of Damayantī.[108] King Nala blames himself as he says "fie on me, slow in matter requiring haste, in whom is absent even the quality of a servant of others.[109] Nala, firmly tried to secure his mission as he did not wish to deviate from his duty as a messenger.[110] From the point of view of ethics of the messengership it should be noted that an envoy who is mediocre in beauty should be sent to a woman.[111] King Nala met Damayantī as an envoy of the gods. Seeing the cupid-like form and personality of the messenger, Damyantī asserted that the gods had no political wisdom as they sent the cupid of earth, to a woman, as an envoy.[112]

From the point of view of diplomacy, the institution of spies had a greater utility as the king could take action on the report of the spies. It was their important duty to understand the degree of loyalty of the subject and detecting the seditious parties in the state as well as in the enemy country. During the stay of an envoy in a foreign court, he was to cultivate friendly relations

---

107. Nai VI.2
108. Nai VII.7
109. ibid. IX.21
इयच्चिरस्यावदघन्ति मत्पथे किमिन्द्रनेत्राण्यशनिर्न निर्ममौ ।
धिगस्तु मां सत्वरकार्यमन्थरं स्थितः परप्रेष्यगुणोऽपि यत्र न ॥
110. ibid. IX.73
111. Commentary on Nai by Nārāyaṇa
स्त्रीष्वभव्यः सामान्यो दूतः प्रेषणीय इति नीतिः ।
नोज्ज्वलं रुपवन्तं च नार्तवन्तं न चातुरम् ।
दूतं वापि हि दूतीं वा नरः कुर्यात्कदाचन ॥
112. Nai IX.22

with the officials with a view to get a clue to the real policy of the government. he was to impress upon the king, how his own king was strong and had rich resources.

Thus the institution of a spy and envoy was a permanent and prominent feature of state. Kauṭilya has stated the necessity of appointing the secret agents everywhere in his state as well as in foreign country.[113]

Śiśupālavadha expresses the significance that the science of polity is not embellished and suitably employed without the appointment of spies.[114]

SIGNIFICANCE OF ALLES AND ENEMIES :

A necessity of a friend-power is accepted by the ancient thinkers as they added allies among the seven constituents of the state.

A king though valourous cannot win the enemy without the help of his allies. An illustration mentioned in Kirātārjunīyam is significant, Cupid though himself powerful demands the help of his friend Moon.[115] It becomes difficult to conquer a king who is backed by his allies. In Śiśupālavadha, while taking the decision of declaring war against Śiśupāla, Uddhava warns Balarāma to take into account the friend-power of Śiśupāla, According to him as the pulmonary disease is a group of diseases, Śiśupāla also having a group of

113. KA I.12.20
एवं शत्रौ च मित्रे च मध्यमे चावपेच्चरान् ।
उदासीने च तेषां च तीर्थेष्वष्टादशस्वपि ॥

114. Śiśu II.112
अनुत्सूत्रपदन्यासा सद्वृत्तिः सन्निबन्धना ।
शब्दविद्येव नो भाति राजनीतिरपस्पशा ॥

115. Kirā IX.33
ओजसापि खलु नूनमनूनं नासहायमुपयाति जयश्रीः ।
यद्विभुः शशिमयूरवसखः सन्नाददे विजयि चापमनङ्गः ।

his friends is difficult to be conquered.[117] A king, who has lost the attachment and love of his ministers and friends and thus, is helpless is easy to be uprooted. It is essential for a conquering king to increase his friend-circle by maintaining good relations with them. Unity gives success to the powerful king. In Kirātārjunīyam, it is stated that when the warriors of Śiva came near Arjuna, everyone of them thought that he would conquer Arjuna, but none could get success, so they unitedly attacked Arjuna, because success needs helping hands.[118]

It will be interesting at this juncture to consider what are the characteristics of a good friend. From the frequent references in the *Pañcamahākāvyas,* we can mention the requirements and merits of a person liable to be called a real friend. A person, who helps the other in need and in the adversity should be called a friend. In Kirātārjunīyam the messenger sent by the chief of the Kirātas said to Arjuna that the king of Kirātas has saved him from the attacking boar and thus has became a desired friend of him so he should not behave like his enemy. On the other hand he should be grateful to him.[119] Arjuna was not willing to keep down even the vacant quiver, because it had helped him in the tough fight against the Kirātarāja.[120] In Raghuvaṁśa Rāma mentions Sugrīva as a friend in calamity.[121]

A real friend helps in acquiring success. Arjuna had taken an arrow from his quiver, the arrow which

---

117. Śiśu II.96
मा वेदि मदसावेको जेतव्यश्चेदिराडिति ।
राजयक्ष्मेव रोगाणां समूहः स महीभृताम् ॥

118. Kirā XIV.44

119. Kirā XII.51

120. ibid. XVII.41

121. ibid. XIII.72

was desirous of securing success like an agreeable friend.[122] A real friend helps his friend in retaliation against an enemy. the missiles of Arjuna are compared to the friends who are able to retaliate against the foe.[123] A friend is always agreeable. It is described that the bow of Arjuna was easily bent because it was like an humble friend, who was always agreeable and firm in maintaining friendship.[124] In Śiśupālavadha a similar simile is used through which an excellence of a friend is depicted. The bow of Śrīkṛṣṇa was very firm like a friend, who is not bent by anyone else.[125]

A real friend should offer a valuable advice to his friend at the opportune time. He is a bad friend who does not give proper advice to his friend or master and he is the bad master who does not listen to the advice of his well-wisher.[126] Thus a real friend is always helpful, agreeable, firm in maintaining friendship. For the sake of friendship he can surrender his life also. Jatāyu, the friend of king Daśaratha faught at his best with Ravaṇa and tried to obstruct Rāvaṇa on his way. In all possible ways he helped Rāma.[127] Rāma also personally performed the funeral ceremonies of Jatāyu, as respectfully as he did those of his own father.

To recognize a friend or foe, a simple test is mentioned in Kirātārjunīyam. Seeing a person in front, a favourable or adverse state of mind gives the indication

---

122. Kirā XIV.36

123. ibid. XVII.1
अथापदामुद्धरणक्षमेषु मित्रेष्विवास्त्रेषु तिरोहितेषु ।
धृतिं पुरुश्रीर्गुरुणामिपुष्यन् स्वपौरुषेणेव शरासनेन ॥

124. ibid. XII.15

125. Śiśu III.20
न नीतमन्येन नतिं कदाचित्कर्णान्तिकप्राप्तगुणं क्रियासु ।
विधेयमस्याभवदन्तिकस्य शार्ङ्गं धनुर्मित्रमिव द्रढीयः ॥

126. Kirā I.5

127. Raghu XII.54

of a friend or an enemy.[127] A person, towards whom the mind becomes agreeable and jubilanṭ, should be called a friend and seeing whom, the mind becomes agitated should be called an enemy.

But the friendship is not formed with all the people. There are some ties which unite the two persons in a friendship. For the formation of friendship equal valour, equal merits and equal status of the two persons is necessary. Arjuna was not ready to become a friend of Kirātarāja as Arjuna himself was the protector of *Varṇāśramadharmas* and the latter was the hunter of the animals; so according to Arjuna, the high personalities are not interested in keeping friendship with persons of a low status as an elephant does not make a friendship with a fox.[128] If a man of a high birth makes a friendship with a person of low rank the merits of the former become tarnished. If a great person fights against the low one then also he is defamed. So a friendship or enmity both are not suitable with a person of a low rank.[129] Arjuna gives a reason why Pāṇḍavas could not keep friendship with Kauravas.[130] As one is unable to predict the fate in future one cannot assure about the wicked people as they can do treachery to a friend also.[131]

A friendship is possible between the persons suffering from an equal calamity. As Rāma and Surgīva

---

127. Kirā XIII.6
न मृगः खलु कोऽप्यथं जिघांसुः स्खलति ह्यत्र तथा भृशं मनो मे ।
विमलं कलुषीभवच्च चेतः कथयत्येव हितैषिणं रिपुं वा ॥

128. Kirā XIII.6 XIV.22
वयं क्व वर्णाश्रमरक्षणोचिताः क्व जातिहीना मृगजीवितच्छिदः ॥
सहापकृष्टैर्महतां न संगतं भवन्ति गोमायुसखा न दन्तिनः ॥

129. ibid. XIV.24

130. ibid. XI.55
धार्तराष्ट्रै सह प्रीतिर्वैरभमस्मास्वसूयत ।
असन्मैत्री हि दोषाय कूलच्छायेव सेविता ॥

131. ibid. XI.56

were passing through a similar adversity, they came nearer by the tie of friendship.[132] Sugrīva was devoid of kingdom and Rāma was deprived from the right of the royal throne; moreover his wife was abducted by Rāvana. Rama and Sugriva helped eachother[133] Rāma killed Vālin and placed Sugriva on royal throne. In return Sugrīva helped Rāma in the mission of searching Sītā and also allied in the war against Rāvaṇa. Friendship is found in persons having equal vices. The kings Kālayavana, Śālva, Rukmi etc. who were of a vicious nature followed Śiśupāla having the same nature, like the darkness following the evening.[134]

One should have a friendship with a person having middle position i.e. neither superior nor inferior to him, because the person of a low capacity cannot help and offer any favourable return. In the case of the powerful person, there is a risk of being suppressed by him. So one should have a friend of his equal power, who can keep good and just relationship as a friend. The ideal king Atithī has followed this policy.[135]

While discussing the topic of allies and enemies in the *Pañcamahākāvyas,* one finds a deep influence of the classification of allies and enemies formed by the ancient thinkers. We should note here the three categories of friends and enemies classified by Kauṭilya in his *Arthaśāstra*.

---

132. Raghu XII.57
वधनिर्धूतशापस्य कबन्धस्योपदेशतः।
मुमूर्च्छ सख्यं रामस्य समानव्यसने हरौ॥

133. ibid. XII.58

134. Śiśu II.98
ये चान्ये कालयवनशाल्वपरुक्मिद्रुमादयः।
तमः स्वभावास्तेऽप्येनं प्रदोषमनुयायिनः॥

135. Raghu XVII.58
हीनान्यनुपकर्तॄणि प्रवृद्धानि विकुर्वते।
तेन मध्यमशक्तीनि मित्राणि स्थापितान्यतः॥

Inborn friends and foes: Parent's sisters and their sons are inborn friends. Father's brothers and their sons are inborn enemies.[136]

Natural allies and enemies : Possessing a land, after that of the foe is the natural friend and the king having a neighbouring king with a common boundary is a natural enemy.[137]

Artificial allies and enemies : Artificial friendship is formed by deed helping the persons by giving money, protecting their life etc. An artificial enmity is formed by contrary action towards another person.[138]

The above classification and the technical terms used by Kauṭilya are found in the *Pañcamahākāvyas*. In the second canto of Kirātārjunīyam, Yudhiṣṭhira prevents Bhīma from taking any hasty step against Kauravas. He explains that the Vṛṣṇis are apparently in the side of Duryodhana, but they will help the Pāṇḍavas if the war is declared, because having a maternal relation with Kṛṣṇa they are inborn friends of Pāṇḍavas. Though Yādvas seem to be helping Duryodhana, it is only for their own interest. Actually their minds are tied with those of the Pāṇḍavas due to natural affection.[139] On the other hand, the affectionate be-

136. KA VI.2.19/20
मातृपितृसंबद्धं सहजम् मित्रम् ।
तुल्याभिजनः सहजः शत्रुः ।

137. ibid.
भूम्येकान्तरं प्रकृतिमित्रम् ।
भूम्यनन्तरः प्रकृत्यमित्रः ।

138. ibid.
धनजीवितहेतोराश्रितं कृत्रिमं मित्रम् ।
विरुद्धोविरोधयिता वा कृत्रिमः शत्रुः

139. Kirā II.44/45
प्रणतिप्रवणान्विहाय नः सहजस्नेहनिबद्धचेतसः ।
प्रणमन्ति सदा सुयोधनं प्रथमे मानमृतां न वृष्णयः ।

haviour of Pāṇḍavas with the sons of Dhṛtarāṣṭra gives birth to enmity.[140] Kauravas are the inborn enemies of Pāṇḍavas, so a friendly behaviour with them also turns into enmity. Thus the prominent cause of enmity is explained here. While rejecting the offer of friendship by Kirātarāja, Arjuna argues that there should be no friendship between them. The wicked are the inborn enemies of the good people because the wicked are always jealous of the merits of the good people.[141] According to Arjuna a person who charges a lot of blemishes on the ascetic, cannot be his real friend.

A king or a ruler of the neighbouring land, having common boundary is supposed to be a natural enemy. The immediate neighbouring king takes an opportunity and advantage of the dissension in the internal constituents of the state and attacks the neighbouring country. Thus, due to the common natural boundary, there is always the possibility of attack by the neighbouring king.

The third category is of on artificial friendship which is dependent on giving wealth etc. to a needy or protecting his life etc. A conqueror, after usurping the territory of another king, places him again on his royal throne and forms friendship with him. King Rāma killed Vālin and placed Sugrīva on the royal throne. After the Lankā-war Rāma offered Vibhīṣaṇa the kingdom of Lankā[142] because Vibhīṣaṇa wanted an affectionate friendship with Rāma.

सुहृदः सहजास्तथैतरे मतमेषां न विलङ्घ्यन्ति ये ।
विनयादिव यापयन्ति ते धृतराष्ट्रात्मजमात्मसिद्धये ॥

140. ibid. XI.55

141. Kirā XIV.21
सखा स युक्तः कथितः कथं त्वया यदृच्छयाऽसूयति यस्तपस्यते ।
गुणार्जनोच्छ्रायविरुद्धबुद्धयः प्रकृत्यमित्रा हि सतामसाधवः ॥

142. Raghu XII.104

Sometimes an enmity is created by persons by their hostile deeds. It is an artificial type of enmity. Śiśupāla was a son of the father's sister of Kṛṣṇa. So he should been inborn friend of kṛṣṇa. But by his hostile deeds he proved himself to be an artificial enemy of Kṛṣṇa. Kṛṣṇa also became an enemy of Śiśupāla by abducting Rukminī who was betrothed to Śiśupāla.[143] In this context, are declared to constitute the deep roots of the tree of enmity. In reaction to Kṛṣṇa's act Śiśupāla surrounded the city of Dwārakā, and abducted the wife of Babhru.[144] Thus, by perpetrating hostile actions against eachother Śiśupāla and Kṛṣṇa proved to be the enemies by deeds.[145] A friendship or an enmity should be determined by the deeds of person. A friendship of an artificial friend is based upon self-interest and the enmity of an artificial enemy is based upon his attitude and dealing originated in a clash of interest. Therefore as long as these circumstances exist, so long these friends and enemies remain unchanged. Balarāma emphasizes the importance of this type of allies and enemies.[146] According to him friendship and conciliation should be a policy even with an enemy also, who proves to be beneficial to us; on the contrary, there should not be friendship with a harmful person though he is a relative and thus is classified as an inborn friend.[147] In this way help or evil intention are the tests of recognizing alliance or enmity. It should also be noted that improper deeds in dealing with a real friend convert him into an enemy. In Śiśupālavadha Uddhava pleads

143. Śiśu II.38

144. ibid. II.40

145. ibid. II.39

146. ibid. II.36
सखा गरीयान् शत्रुश्च कृत्रिमस्तौ हि कार्यतः ।
स्यातामभित्रौ मित्रे च सहजप्रकृतावपि ॥

147. ibid. II.37

that the declaration of war against Śiśupāla will result in the enmity of Kṛṣṇa with his real friend Yudhiṣṭhira. He explains his arguments as follows. If Kṛṣṇa declares war against Śiśupāla then the enemeis of kṛṣṇa and friends of Śiśupāla will join Śiśupāla while the enemies of Śisupāla and friends of Kṛṣṇa will help Kṛṣṇa and there will remain no king who could attend the sacrificial ceremony of Yudhiṣṭhira. Declaration of war at this time would spoil the whole function of *Rājasūya* and by this deed there would be a split in their friendship. A friend once insulted cannot be won back.[149] So one should not spoil a real friendship by hasty action.

One more cause of enmity should be thoroughly discussed here. At the time of the transition of the kingdom from one king to his successor, the new king becomes a target of other kings, as the new king is yet to be established among his constituents of the state and is easy to be conquered.[150]

A POLICY TOWARDS AN ENEMY :

A policy towards an enemy depends upon the proper judgemtnt of time and place. Fixed rules cannot be useful in dealing with an enemy. Generally a policy of conciliation is employed towards the other kings. The conquering monarchs of the Raghu race used conciliation to conquer other kings. But in the case of the enemies whose enmity was deep-rooted the policy was of aggression.

In Kirātārjunīyam we find an aggressive and firm attitude towards the enemy. In the first canto, Draupadī could not bear the onslaught of their adverse condition brought out by the peace-policy of Yudhiṣṭhira. She

149. Śiśu II.105
चिरादपि बलात्कारो बलिनः सिद्धयेऽरिषु ।
छन्दानुवृत्तिदुःसाध्याः सुहृदो विमनीकृताः ॥

150. Raghu IV.2

argues that forbearance towards an enemy suits to sage and not to an ambitious king. She advises Yudhiṣṭhira to break down the conditions of the agreement of passing thirteen years in exile.[150] Kauṭilya has stated this principle in his Arthaśāstra.[151] Draupadī further states that one should be deceitful towards the deceitful enemy, otherwise he has to face defeat, because the deceitful persons get the secrets from the straight-forward people, like the sharp arrows entering into the body without armour.[152]

While deciding a policy against an enemy, the foremost principle should be recognized that an enemy though insignificant should never be neglected, A minor enemy can increase his power in the nearest future. An enemy though minor in power should be uprooted at the proper time. Seeing the valour of Kirātarāja Arjuna thinks "The extra-ordinary power of Kirātarāja should be destroyed by the Brāhmamissible, because a minor enemy like a minor disease decteriorating by stages is very dangerous.[153]

The enemy should not remain uncaptured when one gets a chance to capture him. It is the greatest gain to destroy an enemy in hand.[154]

He who offends to a small degree and that too not repeatedly is to be forgiven but in the case of a hostile enemy who has done repeated insults, there should not

---

150. Kirā I.45

151. KA VII.6.21
परस्यापसंधेयता दूष्यातिसंघानेन ।
स्थापयित्वा व्यतिक्रमः कृतविदूषणम् ॥

152. Kirā I.30

153. ibid. XVI.24

154. Kirā XIII.12
बलशालितया यथा तथा वा धियमुच्छेदपरामयं दधानः ।
नियमेन मया निबर्हणीयः परमं लाभमरातिमङ्गमाहुः ॥

be any forgiveness. In such a condition valour is an ornament of a warrior.[155] According to Balarāma, a mild policy towards an enemy who has inflicted insults repeatedly, is not useful. Even the magnanimous also do not bear repeated insults inflicted by their enemies. A dust when stamped under feet reaches the head of one who kicks; it is indeed superior to an inactive person who bears the hostile insults.[156] To emphasize this concept another beautiful simile is introduced. Though equally faulty, Rāhu swallows the mild moon immediately while the sun, flaming with fire is swallowed after a long time.[157] It reveals the fact that mildness is not proper before a valourous enemy. The persons who ignore the enemy, act like a fool, who setting fire to a dry grass lie against the wind.[158] One can not get peace without uprooting the enemy.[159] It is after destroying darkness that the sun shines with effulgence.[160] One should not be indifferent towards an enemy because he is single, for, if there lives a single enemy also, the king would never get stability and composure of the heart. For example Rāhu, the single enemy of the moon swallows the moon suddenly. An enemy, he may be significant or insignificant, must be destroyed. A wicked enemy who is worthy of destruc-

---

155. Śiśu II.44

156. Śiśu II.46
पादाहतं यदुत्थाय मूर्धानमाधिरोहति ।
स्वस्थादेवापमानेऽपि देहिनस्तद्वरं रजः ॥

157. ibid. II.49
तुस्येऽपराधे स्वर्मानुर्मानुमन्तं चिरेण यत् ।
हिमांशुमाशु ग्रसते तन्म्रदिग्नः स्फुटं फलम् ॥

158. ibid. II.42
विधाय वैरं सामर्षे नरोऽरौ य उदासते ।
प्रक्षिप्योदर्चिषं कक्षे शेरते तेऽभिमारुतम् ॥

159. ibid. II.34

160. ibid. II.33

tion by the fourth means viz. Daṇḍa, should never be made a target of the first three means. For instance, fever is never treated by sprinkling of the water.[161] the fame of an ambitious king climbs to heaven by the stair-case of the heads of enemies.[162]

It is important to state here that a king should recognize proper time and occasion while deciding the policy against an enemy. If the time is unfavorable, he should wait for the coming opportunity. Though insulted by the enemy, a king should not exhibit any outward, expression of anger etc. but should strike the enemy harshly, when he gets the opportunity. A disease, though not seen apparently, shows its symptoms and kills the patient, when the time comes.[163]

An enemy is always attentive in seeking weak-points of his opponents. In Raghuvaṁśa, it is described that when Daśaratha died, the kingdom was kingless and the prince was sent in exile, so it was a good opportunity like a bait to the enemies who were clever in seeking holes of others.[164]

The kings in the *Pañcamahākāvyas* were great enough to admire the valour of their enemy also.[165] They honoured the defeated kings. They protected the enemies who begged for protection (Raghu IV.33/35). But as victory was their extreme goal they meant enemy's defeat as the greatest gain (Kirā XIII.12). Attacking the weak-points of enemy was their policy (Raghu XV.17; XVII.61) They met the enemy in the

---

161. Śiśu II.54
162. ibid. II.52
163. ibid. I.84
164. Raghu XII.11
विप्रोषितकुमारं तद्राज्यमस्तमितेश्वरम् ।
रन्ध्रान्वेषणदक्षाणां द्विषामाभिषतां ययौ ॥
165. Raghu XII.89

same way in which manner the enemy wanted to meet them. They answered deceit by deceit (Kira I.30; Nai I.45/5.103) They did not divert from the right path, (Kirā XIII.42) but did not bear repeated wrongs from the enemies.

Thus in the interstate politics, the place of the king depends upon the maintenance of good relationship with allies and deciding policy against the enemies.

THE CONCEPT OF CAKRAVARTIN :

An idea of universal dominion was an animating ideal in indian political life and speculation. Raghu's conquest of all directions described in Raghuvaṁśa may be taken as modelled after the epic-ideal of world dominion. To become an emperor of the world was the foremost ideal of the kings in the *Pañcamahākāvyas*. The word 'Cakra' is used in the sense of *Rāṣṭra*.[166] So acquiring a position of the chief among the circle of states was the leading ambition of the kings. The highest extension of the idea of suzerainty was the concept of *'Cakravartin'*. The kings were obsessed by the idea of extendning the boundaries of their kingdom to the farthest limits of the earth.[167] The gods, Indra and others, were the masters of only one direction each, but the human kings were the masters of all directions.[168] Their mastery was over the sea-girt earth.[169] King Dilīpa governed the earth which was subject to no other rule and the encircling imparts of which were the sea-beaches and the seas were its moats, as if it was a single city.[170] Ruling all the world under the

166. Śiśu XVI.70
167. Raghu I.5, II.3, XVIII.22
168. Nai XIV.11
169. Raghu IX.11
170. Raghu I.30 Nai X.28

control of one royal umbrella was the strong ambition of the kings.[171]

The sacrifices *Rājasūya, Aśvamedha,* were symbolical of imperialism. Yudhiṣṭhira in Śiśupālavadha explains the intention of performing *Rājasuya.*[172] To set themselves as the peramount sovereign, the kings arranged military expeditions. While conquering other kings, a territorial aggrandizement was not their chief motif, but the honour and fame of the *Cakavartin* was desired by them.[173] Monior--Williams explains the word *Cakravartin,* as a ruler, the wheels of whose chariot will roll everywhere wihtout obstruction, the Emperor Sovereign of the world. [174] The wheel seems to be a symbol of universal dominion, power and influence.

A king was to conquer his enemies immediately after his coronation.[175] As Rapson mentions "It was always regarded as a legitimate object of the ambition of every king to aim at the position of a Cakravartin or supreme monarch. If the king is not actuated by this idea, he falls short of an ideal king according to the Hindu Rājadharma."[176]

Hindu *Cakravartin* ideal was not to establish only peace and harrmony on earth but to gain supremacy on earth; and high position in heaven. Cakravartin plays

---

171. ibid. II.47; XVIII.4
172. Śiśu XIV.5
सा विभूतिरनुभाव सम्पदां भूयसी तव यदायतायति ।
एतदूढगुरुभार भारतं वर्षमद्य भग वर्तते वंशे ॥
173. Raghu I.7
यशासे विजिगीषूणाम् ।
174. M. Monier williams, Sanskrit English Dictionary Published by Motilal Banarasidas, p. 381
175. Raghu IV.4; IX.10
176. VRR Dikashitar, War in Ancient India, Published by University of Madras, 1944; p. 336

the role of the preserver of dharmic order which was being disturbed and violated by the harassing enemies like Śisupāla, Tārakāsura etc. Their conquests were to attain a larger end viz. the realization and obtainment of Indrahood. Heaven was the ultimate goal and its attainment necessitates the conquest of earth. Dilīpa in Raghuvaṁśa, was not satisfied by performing one or two Horse-sacrifices but he has performed ninetynine Horse- sacrifices and has let loose the sacrificial steed, which was expected to be unobstructed, to perform hundredth horse-sacrifice to obtain Indrahood.[177]

Thus acquiring supremacy by arranging the expeditions and performing the Viśvajit and Aśvamedha, was the foremost ideal of the kings in the *Pañcamahākāvyas*.[178]

A THEORY OF MANDALA :

An ideal of the ambitious kings to acquire the position of *Cakravartin* gives rise to the theory of

---

177. Raghu III.38
नियुज्य तं होमतुरंगरक्षणे धनुर्धरं राजसुतैरनुद्रुतम् ।
अपूर्णमेकेन शतक्रतूपमः शतं ऋतूनामपविध्नमाप सः ॥

178. It is interesting to note one thing in this context. The kings known as *Cakravartins* were rulers directly of only a part of India, although they conventionally claimed soverigntly over the whole of the country. The idea of universal dominion has been an animating ideal in Indian Political life. Raghu's conquest of the quarters described in Raghuvaṁśa may be taken as modelled after the epic-ideal of world dominion.
The Buddhist concept of the world-conquest was intimately connected with the notion of righteous rule. Indeed when the wheel vanishes from Sight, a king is advised that only way it will return is by ruling in accordance with Dhamma and ensuring happiness of every creature within his kingdom. After following this advice the wheel reappears. (Dīgha Nikāya III.60).

Mandala. The idea of the extending state is favoured which follows the policy of self-aggrandizement. Immediately after the coronation, the kings arranged military expeditions to conquer the enemies. A neighbouring state was the possible enemy, because a geographical contiguity in them caused conflicts of interests between them. This theory of interstate relations holds that a kingdom is an ally or enemy according to its geographical position with respect to the intending conqueror. According to the conception of *Maṇḍala* a king was to regard one's own kingdom as the centre of twelve kings. In the centre of the circle stands *Vijigīṣu* or an intending conqueror. He was considered to be a king who desired to extend his territories by conquering the surrounding kings. The neighbouring states were possibly attacked by the *Vijigīṣu*. So they were the natural enemies of *Vijigīṣu*. After this *Arimaṇḍala*, stands the circle of allies, then enemies' friend and then friend of the friends of Vijigīṣu.

Behind the invader stands the rear enemy named *Pārṣṇigrāha*. Beyond this circle, There stands the circle of *Vijigīiṣu's* friend named *Ākranda*. Then follows the friend of the enemy named *Pārṣṇigrāhāsāra* and then stands friend of the friend, ie. Ākrandāsāra.

An *Udāsīna* was one, who was situated beyond the territory of the above kings and who was very powerful and capable of helping the enemy, *Vijigīṣu* or the *Madhyama* king, jointly or severally or resisting any of them individually.

A *Madyama* king was situated to afford help to both. He was situated close to *Vijigīṣu* and his enemy and was capable to help both. This *Mahyama king* was considered very important to *Vijigīṣu* as he acted as a strong buffer and was capable of resisting and helping both of them.

This theory of *Maṇḍala*, established by the ancient politicians, was no mere an abstract theory, but embodicd the experience of political leaders through countless generations. The poets of the *Pañcamahākāvyas* have established their heroes as the central monarchies of the *maṇḍala* of twelve kings.[179] The central sovereign was the most important as he wanted to establish his supremacy.[180] The central king was to arrange his relations with other states in such a way that foes and friends were interspersed around him and at no time he was rendered helpless. As *Vijigīṣu* was the leader of other kings, they helped him like other sentiments which help the Erotic.[181] He acts with steady wisdom and catches an opportunity. He conquers the circle of enemy- kings.[182] By his valour and other kingly qualities, he controls the world devoid of enemies.[183] A peculiarity of the invader is that, he is not contented by what is acquired by him. By his constant efforts he wishes to acquire more, like the moon which increases day after day getting no content.[184] Because a person who is satisfied by little gain does never prosper.[185]

There is always a danger of a possible attack by the immediate neighbour of the *vijigīṣu*. This immediate neighbour viz. *ari* or *pārṣṇigrāha* is named *'Anantara'*[186] because the border of his territory is closely atlached to the border of the a Vijigisu He has to keep a minute

---

179. Raghu IX.15; XVIII.20 Nai. VII.54
180. Śiśu II.81
181. Śiśu II.87
स्थायिनोऽर्थे प्रवर्तन्ते भावाः सञ्चारिणो यथा ।
रसस्यैकस्य भूयांसस्तथा नेतुर्महीभृतः ॥
182. Raghu IV.2; IV.4
183. ibid. VIII.27
184. Śiśu II.31
185. ibid. II.32
186. Raghu VIII.19 Kirā II.53

watch and control over this immediate neighbour for the safety of his own kingdom. It has always proved a profitable policy in warfare to embarrass an enemy either by inciting other powers to attack from the rear or by fomenting internal troubles within its territory. So the importance of the rear being kept safe has been always advocated. When king Raghu started for the expedition of conquest, he made full arrangment of the protection and security of his capital from the possible attack by the rearward enemy.[187] The king should also protect his internal constituents of the state against dissension. If the internal constituents of the state are shattered by dissension, then it is very easy for the immediate neighbouring enemy to take hold of the territory of his neighbour. A *Vijigīṣu* should decide a strategy by discrimination and with minute watch otherwise there causes a clash with the rearward enemy.[188]

A king having a position of *Madhyama* is capable to help *vijigīṣu* as well as his enemy. So the kings harassed by the enemies take shelter of the *Madhyama* king.[189] The *Udāsīna* king maintains an attitude of neutrality or policy of non-intervention. He is capable of helping the enemy, the invader and the madhyama king jointly or separately.

Thus the total number of kings in the *maṇḍala* is twelve and each possessing five elements of sovereignty viz. *Amātya, Koṣa, Daṇḍa, Durga, Janapada,* the aggregate of elements in the big circle of twelve kings is sixty. Ancient thinkers have discussed this theory of *mandala*

---

187. Raghu IV.26
188. Nai IX.134
189. Raghu XIII.7
पक्षच्छिदा गोत्रभिदात्तगंधाः शरण्यमेवं शतशोमहीध्राः।
नृपा इवोपप्लविनः परेभ्यो धर्मोत्तरं मध्यममाश्रयन्ते ॥

in details.[191] When one of these twelve kings augmented his power and means, he became superior to other kings and his suzerain power was acknowledged by one and all. This desire of acquiring central position in the circle of kings was the ideal of every king in the *Pañcamahākāvyas*. Having an ambition of conquering nine '*dvīpas*' is exhibited by all the kings.[192]

Thus, the theory of *maṇḍala* is based on the principle of balance of power. The theory of *maṇḍala* is not inflexible, but is shows the probable relationship and it also reveals that a geographical position is an important factor while determining relationship between two kings.[193]

SIX GUṆAS :

The relations between the various states in *Manḍala* were determined by six different ways known as *Ṣādguñyam*. Though the institution of war was recognized as the chief political weapon of the state in ancient India, it was looked only as a last resort. The sixfold policy was important essential of the art of diplomacy. When all expedients of conciliation, gift and dissensions failed and undertaking of a military expedition became imperative a king had to employ a sixfold policy towards his enemy. These measures consisted of *Sandhi* (Alliance), *Vigraha* (war), *Yāna* (marching), *Āsana* (Halting), Dwaidhībhāva (Dividing army or duplicity) and *Sañśraya* (Seeking protection).[194]

---

191. KA VI.2
192. Nai. 1.5.64. Raghu XVIII.14
193. Spellman, Political Theory of Ancient India, Published by Oxford University Press,1964, p.156
194. KA VII.1.6 to 12.
तत्र पणबन्धः सन्धिः अपकारो विग्रहः उपेक्षमाणमासनम् ।
अभ्युच्चयो यानम् परार्पणं संश्रयः संधिविग्रहोपादानं द्वैधीभाव इति षड्गुणाः ।

The conquering monarchs were well-versed in the employment of the six *guṇas*.[194] King Dilīpa became invincible to all by the application of six *guṇas*.[195] According to the need of time king Aja used six *guṇas* and gained success in administrative affairs.[196] Kauṭilya has stated a necessity for a king to be accomplished with six *guṇas*.[197] As universal conquest was not always possible, it was necessary for the king to conclude alliances or observe neutrality. The possible attitudes that the king could adopt were the six measures of polity.

Only recounting of the six measures is easy but the actual application of them is a difficult task.[198] It is difficult to furnish a solution of the intricate problems showing a proper time for conciliation etc.[199] Improper application of the *gunas* spoils the whole mission.[200] Uddhava, the prudent politician and minister of Kṛṣṇa observes that the six *guṇas* should be applied only after making a comparative estimate of one's own and enemy's strength. If the six *guṇas* be employed according to one's capacity, they work like medicinal tonic; and the seven limbs of the state become strong.[201]

An application of the six guṇas depends upon the policy employed by the enemy. For instance, in the

---

194. Raghu XVII.67
195. ibid. I.16
196. ibid. VIII.21
197. KA VII.3.1
     विजिगीषुः शक्त्यपेक्षः षाड्गुण्यमुपयुञ्जीत ।
198. Śiśu II.26/27.
199. Kirā II.3
200. Śiśu II.56
201. ibid. II.93
     षाड्गुण्यमुपयुञ्जीच शक्त्यपेक्षी रसायनम् ।
     भवन्त्यस्यैवमङ्गानि स्थास्नूनि बलवन्ति च ॥

manner Śiśupāla wanted to meet Kṛṣṇa, either in *Sandhi* or in *Vigraha*, Kṛṣṇa was ready to meet him in the same manner.[202] A king desirous of conquest should examine his might with that of his opponent. This principle, while employing the policy of *Yāna* was taken into account by the king Atithī. He formed a just estimate of his military power, circumstances, time and others of his own and that of his enemy and when he considered himself more powerful than his enemy he thought for expedition, otherwise he remained silent[203] Although he was powerful, his expeditions were especially on those who were in the reach of his power.[204] The ancient thinkers had stated the same policy about *Yāna*. According to Kauṭilya, a king desirous of victory should compare his might and other things with that of his enemy. Then he should attack with his valieant forces.[205] Manu states the similar principle[206] and adds that if a king finds himself unable, he should give up the idea of assault.[207] In the application of the policy of Yāna, there are diffeıent views and opinions, discussed in Śiśupālavadha. There are two conditions

---

202. Śiśu XVI.33
नरकच्छिदभिच्छतीक्षितुं विधिना येन स चेदिभूपतिः।
द्रुतमेतु न हापयिष्यते सदृशं तस्य विधातुमुत्तरम् ॥

203. Raghu XVII.59
परात्मनोः परिच्छिद्य शक्त्यादीनां बलाबलम्।
ययावेभिर्बलिष्ठश्चेत्परस्मादास्त सोऽन्यथा ॥

204. ibid. XVII.56

205. KA IX.1.1
विजिगीषुरात्मनः परस्य च बलाबलं शक्तिदेश-
कालयात्राकालबलसमुत्थान काल पश्चात्कोषक्षयव्ययलाभापदां
ज्ञात्वा विशिष्टबलो यायात् ॥

206. MS VII.171
यदा मन्येत भावेन हृष्टं पुष्टं बलं स्वकम्।
परस्य विपरीतं च तदा यायाद्रिपून्प्रति ॥

207. MS VII.172

for *Yāna* against an enemy, an increase of one's strength and distress of the enemy. Manu prescribes that one should declare war when calamity has befallen the enemy.[208] The school of Kāmanḍaka is not agree with the first view and it observes that expedition should be made when one is extremely strong and one should not consider either the enemy is in a condition of calamity or prosperity.[209] Different views about *Yāna* are considered by Balarāma.[210] According to him both these views are in favour of Kṛṣṇa, Kṛṣṇa's vast army is on the top of strength[211] and the enemy is in distress on account of the death of his friend Jarāsandha.[212] Though Balarāma wants to make an immediate attack on Śiśupāla, he is not favourable for the attack when the enemy is in distress. According to him the policy of attacking the enemy in distress brings shame to the chivalrous. A self-respected person attacks an enemy who is at the height of his power.[213] Balarāma, while stating his own view expresses the opinion that when the strength is immense, one should not consider the rules of *śāstras*.[214]

The *guṇa* named *Āsana* means holding a post against an enemy or staying quiet, waiting for the opportunity. If the time is unfavourable, it is preferable to pocket

---

208. MS VII.183
209. KN XI.1
210. Śiśu II.57
    स्वशक्त्युपचये केचित्परस्य व्यसनेऽपरे ।
    यानमाहुस्तदासीनं त्वामुत्थापयति द्वयम् ॥
211. Śiśu II.58
212. ibid. II.60
213. ibid. II.61
    नीतिरापदि मदगम्यः परस्तन्मानिनो ह्रिये ।
    विधुर्विधुन्तुदस्यैव पूर्णस्तस्योत्सवाय सः ॥
214. ibid II. 62

even insults without being perturbed, waiting for the proper time.[215] *Dwaidhībhāva* means the policy of duplicity. According to Kauṭilya, Kāmanḍaka *Dvaidhībhāva* means making peace with one and following hostile policy towards other.[216] According to Agnipurāṇa, duplicity means undertaking expeditions with only half of the army.[217] It means stationing of one's troops with duplicity. It also means dividing one's army and encountering a superior army in detachments, harassing the enemy by attacking them in small bands. Śiśupāla had employed the policy of duplicity. Outwardly he was speaking the terms of *Sandhi* but inwardly he was prepared for marching against Kṛṣṇa.[218]

The policy of *Samsraya* means seeking protection of the strong. Rāma allied himself with Sugrīva as he wanted to defeat the strong enemy like Rāvaṇa. Manu says that if a king fears that he may fall in the hands of the enemy then he should enter into an alliance with a virtuous sovereign.[219] the inferior kings cannot help because they are not capable of giving protection to other. But with a powerful backing even the meanest reach at the fulfillment of their work.[220]

Now we turn towards the first of the six *guṇas* viz. *Sandhi* which avoids war and creates friendly relations between two powerful states. It binds sovereigns in faith to one another and is a solemn promise given by

215. Śiśu II.84
216. KA VII.1.37
यदि वा मन्येत संधिनैकतः स्वकर्माणि प्रवर्तयिष्यामि
विग्रहेणैकतः परकर्माण्युपहनिष्यामि इति द्वैधीभावेन वृद्धिमातिष्ठेत् ।
KN XI. 24
217. AP 234.19
218. Śiśu XVI.34
219. MS VII.174
220. Śiśu II.100

the contracting parties to eachother to do or refrain from doing particular things.

Sandhi was done with equals and superiors. In Kirātārjunīyam it is stated that the unequal status of Arjuna and Kirāta was the barrier which compelled Arjuna to reject the offer of friendship with the latter.[221] Kauṭilya also recommends that peace may be made with equals and superiors while the inferior must be attacked.[222] While deciding the policy about peace or war, Daśaratha was kind-hearted to those who did not transgress his command but was ironhearted to those who were hostile towards him.[223] The haughty king of Lankā fearing the destruction of janasthāna made peace with the king of Pāṇdya, who was hard to overcome due to his obtainment of a missile from Śiva.[224]

In adversity a king should make peace even with a powerful and dangerous enemy; but he should be very careful after doing so. Because he, who does not protect himself after entering a treaty with a stronger enemy finds that treaty, creating injury, instead of benefit like the improper food that does harm to the body. One who having concluded a treaty with an enemy becomes satisfied, as if he has accomplished his objects, like one who is sleeping on the top of a tree and is awakened on having fallen therefrom.[225] The similar maxim is relevant in the employment of the policy of *Vigraha,* which is reflected in Śiśupālavadha.

---

221. Kirā XIV.22

222. KA VII.1.13/14
परस्माद्धीयमानः संदधीत । अभ्युच्चीयमानो विगृह्णीयात् ।

223. Raghu IX.9

224. ibid. VI.62

225. Ādi Parva 81 151; Critical edition by BORI
योऽरिणा सह संधाय शयीत कृतकृत्यवत् ।
स वृक्षाग्रे यथा सुप्तः पतितः प्रतिबुध्यते ॥

A person who is not watchful about his enemy is like a person sleeping in direction of wind where dry grass is placed in the fire.[226]

An application of *sandhi* depends upon benefit or degrading act done by a friend or an eney. For instance, Śiśupāla was an imborn friend of Kṛṣṇa but by his distressing actions he proved himself as an enemy of Kṛṣṇa. So one should make *Sandhi* with an enemy also but not with fraudulent relatives like Śiśupāla.[227]

In the case of a deceitful enemy, it is not proper to keep the agreement entered into with them, for in respect of enemies, the conquering kings effect breaches of peace under some pretex.[228] In Kirātārjunīyam, Draupadī reminds Yudhiṣṭhira of his high sense of duty. According to her it is not useful to upkeep the agreement of treaty done with a fraudulent enemy. The kings meet defeat who are unable to pay the fraudulent enemies in their coins. So the kings, intent on victory should break the agreement done with such enemies. In this connection Kauṭilya has made a monstrous suggestion that a conqueror may break off the terms of a treaty if it is convenient for him to do so.[229]

An agreement of treaty is done on specific terms. In Kirātārjuīyam the king of Kirātas wanted to make this type of treaty with Arjuna. If Arjuna admitted the lordship of the Kiratarāja then he was ready to offer Arjuna even earth by conqueing it.[230] But Arjuna was not a weaker king and he recognized that it was not a treaty of friendship but was a mere threatening.

---

226. Śisu II.42
227. ibid II.37
228. Kirā I.45
229. KA VII.6.21 कृतविदूषणम् ।
230. Kirā XIII.59

Sometimes a treaty with a stronger king is done by offering him one's daughter or sister in marriage relations. In Raghuvaṁśa, Kumuda, the king of Nāgas made this type of treaty with king Kuśa by offering his sister Kumudvatī in marriage. The king Kuśa was enraged and took the missile when he did not find his hereditary ornament dropped in the water and he suspected it to be taken by the snake Kumuda whose abode was below the deep pool. Kumuda prayed Kuśa to accept his sister in marriage[231] and by this relation Kumuda obtained a valorous king as his relative and Kuśa also was out of fear from the danger of serpents.[232]

Vigraha is an affair between two parties who having rival interests, settle their disputes by force of arms. When other expedients of polity do not bear satisfactory results, war becomes inevitable. In the concept of Vigraha there is postponement of actual fighting even after war is declared. A bargain is effected with little or even no profit, with an eye always to future permanent gain.[233]

Thus the six *guṇas* in their proper spheres offer success to the employer.

THREE POWERS OF THE KING :

An ambitious king conquers and rules over the earth by the three powers viz. *Prabhuśakti* means power of treasury and army, *Uṭsāhaśakti* means power of energy and enterprise and *manṭraśakti* means power of counsel.[234] These three powers of the kings are frequently referred in the *Pañcamahākāvyas*. Like the gem on the

231. Raghu XVI.85
232. ibid. XVI.88
233. MS VII.177
234. KA VI. 33
शक्तिस्त्रिविधा । ज्ञानबलं मन्त्रशक्तिः कोशदण्डबलं प्रभुशक्तिः । विक्रमबलं उत्साहशक्तिः ।

hood of a serpent, the three powers of king Atithī were unattainable by the enemies; but he attracted the three powers of the enemies as a magnet attracts an iron-ball.[235] Daśaratha with his three wives is described as Indra himself who came to earth with the three fold powers to govern his subjects.[236] The threefold kingly power brings an undecying store of wealth and prosperity[237] to a conquering king.

Prabhuśakti : *Prabhuśakti* comprises treasury and army. Statecraft is based on the good settlement of funds and force. A sound treasury is essential for the welfare of the state and for maintenance of army, by which the king protects his subjects from the external attacks of the enemy. An ambitious king, who neglects the *Prabhuśakti* means increasing power of enemy, his own riches soon pass away as if afraid of the public censure.[238] King Aja in Raghuvaṁśa, subdued the neighbouring princes by the influence of his regal power.[239] In Śiśupalavadha, Uddhava describes the enhancement of *Prabhuśakti* by the collection of taxes.[240] King Raghu, whose treasury was emptied in a sacrifice, remained *'Prabhu'* only by the title.[241] This shows *Prabhuśakti* as the power of prosperous treasury and army.

---

235. Raghu XVII.63
सर्पस्यैव शिरोरत्नं नास्य शक्तित्रयं परः।
स चकर्ष परस्मातदयस्कान्त इवायसम् ॥

236. ibid. IX.18

237. ibid. III.13
ग्रहेस्ततः पञ्मभिरुच्चसंचयैरसूर्यगैः सूचितभाग्यसंपदम् ।
असूत पुत्रं समये शचीसमा त्रिसाधना शक्तिरिवार्थमक्षयम् ॥

238. Kirā II.10

239. Raghu VIII.19

240. Śiśu II.89

241. Raghu V.22

Utsāhaśakti: *Utsāhaśakti* viz. the power of energy and enthusiasm is another essential power for an ambitious king. Activity of the strong is called the power of energy. An enterprising energy inspires the king for his undertakings as well as the expeditions of conquest.[242] By this power of enthusiasm a king gets a central place among the circle of twelve kings.[243] Other kings of the circle of the twelve kings around the ambitious and energetic king become subservient to him[244] If the king loses his enthusiasm, he becomes a target of another ambitious king,[245] so one should wipe out inactivity which otherwise will be helpful for the prosperity of the enemy himself.[246] Wealth is produced through enthusiasm.[247] Prosperity deserts inactive person. When the flame of a lamp ends, the light also leaves the abode, so when the power of energy leaves a king he becomes devoid of lustre and valour. The idle are defeated by the fortune as eunuchs are renounced by women.[248] People worship even a powerless king who makes efforts for achieving success, as they admire the new moon bearing natural and delightful lustre, though divested of former glory.[249]

---

242. Raghu IV.24
सरितः कुर्वती गाधाः पयश्चाश्यानकर्दमान् ।
यात्रायै चोदयामास तं शक्तेः प्रथमं शरत् ॥
243. Śiśu II.81
244. ibid. II.90
अनल्पत्वात्प्रधानत्वाद्वंशस्येवेतरे स्वराः ।
विजिगीषोर्नृपतयः प्रयान्ति परिवारताम्. ।
245. Kirā XVII.17
246. ibid. II.15
247. Ku I.22
248. KN XIV.8
249. Kirā II.11

Though being defeated by an enemy, king's power of enthusiasm exhibits his valour against the strong enemy and his fame and prowess shine like the rays of sun.[250] But a king devoid of unflinching energy can never attain success; on the other hand, with the help of enthusiasm an otherwise weak person also gets success.[251] "There is nothing impossible for an energetic king, is the confidence exhibited in the play Pratijnyāyougandharāyaṇa.[252] Thus Uṭsāhaśakti is considered to be an essential power of an ambitious king.

Manṭraśakti : *Manṭraśakti* viz. the power of counsel is the third strong power of an ambitious king. In Kirātārjunīyam, while opposing Bhīma's arguments Yudhiṣṭhira explains him the importance of counsel. He states- "A hasty action without deliberation becomes fruitless. One should not act without thought because want of thinking is a great source of calamities. The Fortune itself chooses a thoughtful person.[253] The power of thinking offers success definitely as the rich autunmal harvest is definite after a proper rainfall in the mansoons.[254] According to Kauṭilya, all the works should be preceded by deliberation.[255]

---

250. Kirā XVII.15
प्रत्याहतौजाः कृतसत्त्ववेगः पराक्रमंज्यायसि यस्तनोति ।
तेजांसि भानोरिव निष्पपन्ति यशांसि वीर्यज्वलितानि तस्य ।

251. KN XIV.9
श्रियो हि सततोत्साहो दुर्बलोऽपि समश्नुते ।

252. Pratinñāyougandharāyaṇa I.18
काष्ठादग्निर्जायते मथ्यमानाद्
भूमिस्तोयं खन्यमाना ददाति ।
सोत्साहानां नास्त्यसाध्यं नराणाम्
मार्गारब्धा सर्वयानाः फलन्ति ॥

253. Kirā II.30

254. ibid. II.31

255. KA I.15.2 मन्त्रपूर्वाः सर्वारम्भाः ॥

The power of counsel is able to avert the calamities and dangers of king.[256] The success of the power of deliberation depends upon the sharp intellect of a diplomat. With his sharp intellect he touches a slight part of the target but penetrates very deep inside of it. On the other hand a person having a common intellect touches the target broadly, but does not hit the mark.[257] Thus a deliberation through the sharp intellect surly gives success. Kauṭilya mentions the importance of deliberation. An arrow discharged by an archer may or may not kill any person but the intellect of a wise one would kill even a child in a womb.[258]

The deliberations were expected to conduct at specific place only. In Śiśupālavadha the place of counsel is described as having the pillors studded with jewels, but as the place was solitary there was no harm to the counsel.[259] In this connection many important suggestions are given by the ancient thinkers. According to Kauṭilya, the place of counsel should be concealed and should not be seen even by the birds.[260] Kāmanḍaka suggests that the place of deliberation should be poleless, windowless, without any vacant place inside the walls.[261] There used to be a separate consultation chamber called *Manṭraśālā*.

---

256. Śiśu XIV.56
257. ibid. II.78
258. KA X.6.51
अेकं हन्यान्नवा हन्यादिषुः क्षिप्तो धनुष्मता ।
प्राज्ञेन तु मतिः क्षिप्ता हन्याद्गर्भगतानपि ॥
259. Śiśu II.4
260. KA I.15.3
तदुद्देशः कथानामनिः श्रावी पक्षिभिरप्यनालोक्यः स्यात् ।
261. KN XII.47
निस्तम्भे निर्गवाक्षे च निर्भित्यन्यसंक्षये ।
प्रासादाग्रे त्वरण्ये वा मन्त्रयेद्‌भावभाविनौ ॥

In the deliberation one should not transgress the time-limit and one should not have a lengthy counsel as it discloses the secrets and spoils the whole plan.[262] After deliberation there should be a quick action, otherwise the counsel would not stay firm like a timid warrior on battlefield, though he is equipped with armour.[263] Counsel becomes fruitful with regard to that person only who does not transgress the opportune factors of time and place.

Keeping of secrecy in the deliberations is an important factor which should be always duly recognized by a diplomat. While getting an information of the plans and programmes of others, one should strictly observe secrecy about his own plans and programmes. The secret plans of the kings could be guessed from the successful results only.[264] The King Atithī in Raghuvaṁśa used to perform his missions, attacking the weak points of enemies and concealing the holes of his own.[265] Even after constant efforts to discover, one could not find a secret door to enter his secret deliberation.[266] The impenetratable secrecy of counsel is the protective armour of a king and his intellect is his weapon, so none is able to conquer such an extraordinary king.[267] A cleaver diplomat can work out the difficult task of finding out the weak points of the enemies and to conceal the secret steps of the policy

262. KA I.15.45/46
अवाप्तार्थः कालं न अतिक्रामयेत् ।
न दीर्घकालं मन्त्रयेत् न तेषां पक्षीयैयेषामपकुर्यात् ।

263. Śiśu II.29

264. Kirā I.20 Raghu I.20; XVII.53

265. Raghu XVII.61

266. ibid. XVII.50

267. Śiśu II.82
बुद्धिशस्त्रः प्रकृत्यङगो घनसंवृतिकञ्चुकः ।
चारेक्षणो दूतमुखः पुरुषः कोऽपि पार्थिवः ॥

of his own. The messenger sent by Yudhiṣṭhira in Kirātārjuniyam modestly says "It is difficult to penetrate in the policy of the kings and it is your majesty's greatness that the line of action of enemies, very intricate as to its real nature was known by me."[268] Two aspects of deliberation, ie to get knowledge of the secret policy of the enemy and at the same time to conceal one's own defects and holes are referred to compare with the skillful gestures in the science of archery.[269] So one should conceal his deliberation like a peacock who is silent in autumn.[270] According to Kauṭilya also a king should not open his secrets but he should know the weak points of other kings. He should conceal his secrets like a tortoise conceals his own limbs.[271]

The secrecy of the plans and deliberation is sometimes disclosed by the expressions and gestures of the envoy, minister or the king himself.[272] In the sixteenth canto of kirārjuniyam it is described that Indra, hearing the report about the penance being performed by Arjuna came to know that it was his own son, but still concealed signs of joy because the great personalities know the way of policy.[273] This political principle is finely expressed in the poetic imagery in *Naiṣadhīyacarita*. Nala's secret musings on Damayantī were manifested by the paleness of his visage. Cupid, the opperessor of Nala, is his enemy, so he wanted to divulge Nala's

---

268. Kirā I.6
269. ibid. XVI.23
270. ŚP (Critical Edition by BORI) 120.7
 नित्यं रक्षितमन्त्रः स्याद्यथा मूकः शरच्छिरवी ।
271. KA I.15.60
 नास्य गुह्यं परे विद्युश्छिद्र विद्यात्परस्य च ।
 गूहेत्कूर्म अिवाङ्गानि यत्स्याद्विवृतमात्मनः ॥
272. KA I.15.7
 मन्त्रभेदो हि दूतामात्यस्वामिनामिङ्गिताकाराभ्याम् ।
273. Kirā VI.38

secrets and is helped by his face.[274] Thus the secret plans are disclosed by the outward signs and gestures.

In the secret deliberation, an important part was played by the ministers, well-versed in state-craft. The kings used to consult with their ministers, deep-versed in polity.[275] The secrecy of the deliberation was well protected by the ministers. Sometimes the ministers deliberated the plans and performed their responsibility in the absence of a king. A well keeping of the secrecy of deliberation by the ministers of Agnivarṇa in Raghuvaṁśa is a fine illustration in this connection. When Agnivarṇa was seriously ill and there was no hope of his survival, the ministers kept the news secret. The news of the death of Agnivarṇa was not disclosed by the ministers until they placed the pregnant queen of the king on the royal throne.[276]

The whole process of deliberation comprises five parts. These are securing the means for beginning of the operation; Securing allies, good treasury and efficient army; Proper discrimination of favourable time and place; Means to meet emergencies or to avert dangers that may befall, and Accomplishment of the final object.[277] This fivefold deliberation is the basis of treasury and army.[278] It is the soul of the polity and the king with the fivefold deliberation containing all the means, gets no defeat.[279]

---

274. Nai III.107
275. Raghu VIII.17
276. ibid. XIX.54 to 57
277. KA I.15.42
कर्मणाभारम्भोपाय: पुरुषद्रव्यसंपद् देशकालविभागो
विनिपातप्रतीकार: कार्यसिद्धिरिति पञ्चाङ्गोमन्त्र: ।
278. Kirā II.12
279. Śiśu II.28
सर्वकार्यशरीरेषु मुक्त्वाङ्गस्कन्धपञ्चकम् ।
सौगतानामिवात्मान्यो नास्ति मन्त्रो महीभृताम् ॥

Thus these three powers are essential for an ambitious ruler. Though, these three powers are separately discussed, they work and bring success if applied in combination. They seem to be interdependent and interrelated. Their relative importance occurs frequently in the *Pañcamahākāvyas*. In Kirātārjunīyam, Bhīma urges a necessity of the power of energy for an ambitious king. A king, though devoid of *Prabhuśakti*, with his energetic action obtains his desired object. People worship even a powerless king if he has not abandoned enterprise for achieving success. The energetic actions of the intelligent king give rise to his regal power which is to be achieved in the near future.[280] Thus the power of energy and enthusiasm are essential requisites in comparison to *Prabhuśakti* because an energetic king can obtain funds and forces, sincerely making efforts. Enterprise of an energetic king leads to success when it is accompanied by a good counsel. Valour should be followed by policy. Policy devoid of valour is called timidness and valour unaccompanied by counsel is named as an act of a beast.[281] In *Śiśupālavadha* criticizing the arguments for the exhibition of valour, Uddhava says that valour should be supported by deliberation. A prudent king takes consultation of the wise before any enterprise and such a king never feels dejected.[282] Thus the valour of the kings was preceded by policy and deliberation.[283] A relative place of the three powers is described through a fine simile in Śiśupālavadha. A tree in the form of enterprise which

280. Śiśu II.28
प्रज्ञोत्साहवतः स्वामी यतेताधातुमात्मनि ।
तौ हि मूलमुदेष्यन्त्या जिगीषोरात्मसंपदः ॥

281. Raghu XVII.47

282. Śiśu II.77

283. Mallinātha's commentary on Raghu 1.19
नीतिपुरःसरमेव तस्य शौर्यमभूत् ।

has power of deliberation or intellect as a root produces fruits of regal power enhanced through taxes.[284] Thus an enterprising and ambitious king, though devoid of *Prabhuśakti* acquires kingdom relying on his power of deliberation viz. *Mantraśakti* Thus *Manṭraśakti* is the root of policy through which a king acquires his desired object. According to Kāmanḍaka the power of counsel is superior to the power of one's arms. It was the strength of deliberation only which made Indra successful in acquiring victory over the demons.[285] Kauṭilya himself holds a discussion about the relative superiority of these three powers and puts forth his opinion that *Manṭraśakti* is superior to both *Prabhuśakti* and *Utsāhaśakti*.[286]

A MAGICAL POWER OF THE KING REVEALED IN THE PAÑCAMAHĀKĀVYAS :

We have explained the significant place of three traditionally defined powers in the career of a conquering monarch. *Viṣṇudharmottara* adds the divine power viz. *daivīśakti* to the traditional three powers mentioned before and it states that all the energies issue forth from Viṣṇu without whose lustre, none is capable of protecting people.[287] In addition to these powers there

---

284. Śiśu II.89
करप्रचेयामुत्तुडग: प्रमुशक्तिं प्रथीयसीम् ।
प्रज्ञाबलबृहन्मूल: फलत्युत्साहपादप: ॥

285. KN XVI.57
आरिप्सुना मन्त्रबलान्वितेन प्रागेव कार्यो निपुणं विचार: ।
दोष्णां बलान्मन्त्रबलंगरीय: शक्रोऽसुरान् मन्त्रबलाद विजिग्ये ॥

286. KA IX.I.14/15/16
मन्त्रशक्ति: श्रेयसी । प्रज्ञाशास्त्रचक्षुर्हि राजाऽल्पेनापि
प्रयत्नेन मन्त्रमाधातुं शक्त: परानुत्साहप्रभावक्तश्च
सामादिभिर्योगोपनिषद्भ्यां चातिसंघातुम् ।
अेवमुत्साहप्रभावमन्त्रशक्तीनामुत्तरोत्तराधिकोऽतिसंघते ।

287. Viṣṇudharmottara II.71.11/12

is one more power of the king which can be named as magical power of the king. While discussing the topic of king's divine origin, It is mentioned before, that to save the people from 'Arājaka' the Creator himself created the king. As king's main duty consists in protecting his subjects, it is the very reason of his being created from the particles of *Lokapālas* or the divine protectors of quarters. The great poets of the *Pañcamahākāvyas* described the kings having divine origin and obtaining the powers from the divinities. The divinities offered their full co-operation, their lustre, valour and admiration to the earthly king, who was their essential part. Secondly, spiritual support of the preceptors was a significant power of the kings. It is mentioned before, that the spiritual power of the preceptors was able to protect the nation from the human and natural calamities. The preceptor was a *brahma* itself, placed like a shield before the king to protect him and his subjects. Defence of the kingdom, destruction of the enemies, offering of the ungained objects to the king were led by the spiritual power of the preceptor.

Yet there is one more remarkable power of the king which can be described as a magical power of the king. By this invisible power of king, the effects take place magically or without any seen efforts. There are lot of incidents described in the *Pañcamahākāvyas,* exhibiting the magical power of the king.

In Naiṣadhīyacarita, the power of being invisible was obtained by Nala from Indra.[288] Nala entered the palace of Damayantī in an invisible form. Damayantī was surprised to see the wreath thrown by her, went out of sight, as it was taken by invisible Nala. In Raghuvaṁsa it is described that prince Raghu, by his power of incarnation, saw the daughter of wishfulfilling

288. Nai VI.8

cow and by her favour he recognized the thief of his sacrificial horse.[289] The princes Rāma and Lakṣmaṇa having a practice of walking only on the pavements of gems in the royal palace, were not tired in the way of forest due to the effect of the power named 'Balā-ti-balā[290] In Kumārasaṁbhava it is described that the chief-martial Kārtikeya, only by his favourable looks released the serpent-nooses around the gods.[291]

Sometimes the royal ornaments also are described as endowed with special power. The ornament of kuśa named *Jaitra* was received by him hereditary; and which is described as 'charm of gaining victory.[292] A string of magical gems, named 'Cintāmani' is frequently referred in Naiśadhīyacarita. Nala's father-in-law offered him the wish-fulfilling wreath of gems. Nala's palace surpassed the mountain of gods by virtue of having objects coming at its will, by the power of gem.[293] King Vapuṣman, one of the candidates in Damayantī's *swayaṁvara*, was said to have a magical gift of medicinal herbs, affording luck.[294] In one place the gem is described as a magic-charm for the conquest of the world, acting like a comet on the throng of enemy kings.[295] In

289. Raghu III.41/42
तदङ्गनिष्यन्दजलेन लोचने प्रभृज्य पुण्येन पुरस्कृतः सत्ताम् ।
अतीन्द्रियेष्वप्युपपन्नदर्शनो बभूव भावेषु दिलीपनन्दनः ॥
स पूर्वतः पर्वतपशातनं ददर्श देवं नरदेवसंभवः ।
पुनः पुनः सूतनिषिद्धचापलं हरन्तमश्वं रथरश्मिसंयतम् ॥

290. ibid. XI.9

291. Ku XVII.7

292. Raghu XVI.74
जयश्रियः संवननं यतस्तदामुक्तपूर्वं गुरुणा च यस्मात् ।
सेहेऽस्य न भ्रंशमतो न लोभात्स तुल्यपुष्पाभरणो हि धीरः ॥

293. Nai XVIII.4

294. ibid. XI.69

295. ibid. XI.104
बालेऽधराधरितनैकविधप्रवाले पाणौ जगद्विजयकार्मणमस्य पश्य ।
ज्याघातजेन रिपुराजकधूमकेतुतारायमाणमुपरज्य मणिं किणेन ॥

Śiśupālavadha the Kausṭubha gem is described of which lustre spread to the ends of the quarters and which arose alongwith other jewels from the ocean.

All these instances and allusions reveal the fact that the kings were endowed with magical powers which they used not only for their personal interest but for the protection and welfare of the subjects. Admitting the fact that the gods themselves had the magical powers and they offered it to the kings, we can not neglect the additional magical power, which was a special feature of the kings themselves.

A reference in Naisadhīyacarita mentions king's power of showering rain. It is true that showering surplus water in deserts was a boon from god Varuṇa who favoured it to Nala, but in the very first canto of Naiṣadhīyacarita, that it was by his power that Nala showered rain and he also prevented the excessive rain throughout the entire earth.[296]

This reference leads the reader to think the origin of the magical power of the king from somewhat different standpoint. While stating the divine origin of the king, it is stated that the divinities offered the supernatural powers to the kings which they used for their subjects. Rain at proper time, plentyful crops, a good life were the expectations of the people from their kings. The kings fulfilled the desires of the subjects with their power. The theory forwarded by Frazer in his 'Golden Bough' is important in this context. It will not be out of place to state the theory in brief.

In his theory Frazer explains the origin of a king from a magician. According to Frazer, before the idea of religion comes the age of magic and the deliverer of magic got the chiefship in the primitive societies. The

---

296. Nai I.11
निवारितास्तेन महीतलेऽखिले निरीतिभावं गमितेऽतिवृष्टयः
न तत्यजुर्नूनमनन्यविश्रमाः प्रतीपभूपालमृगीदृशां दृशः ॥

chiefs were able to bestow upon their subjects and worshippers the blessings which were commonly supposed to be beyond the reach of mortals. A primitive man was not able to draw a distinction between the natural and supernatural. He believed in the unlimited power of the magician of influencing the course of nature by magic. The magic with its two types[297] when practised by the magician for the benefit of the whole community it was named public magic. A development of a such class of functionaries was of great importance for the political as well as religious evolution of the society. When the welfare of the tribe was supposed to depend on the performance of magical rites. the magician arose into the position of much influence and many of them have acquired the rank and authority of a chief or king.[298] Their principal art was that of rain-making. Their authority was rested upon their

---

297. The principles of thought on which magic is based are two. The first is that, like produces like and second that, things which have once been in contact with each other continue to act on each other at a distance after the physical contact has been severed. First is based on the law of similarly and the latter, the law of contact or contagion. By the application of the principle that like produces like, it was easy to injure or destroy an enemy by injuring or destroying on image of him, so does the man and he supposed that when it perishes, he must die. Frazer offers so many illustrations from all over the tribes in the world. The second type viz. the contagious magic contains the mistaken association of ideas.
G.J. Frazer, Golden Bough, (A Study of Magic and Religion) Abridged Edition,
Published by Macmillan and Co. Ltd. London 1993; p. 13 to 37

298. G.J. Frazer, Golden Bough (Abridged Edition) Published by MacMillan & Co. Ltd. London 1993; p.45

supposed power of making rain.[299] As the magician controlled the nature for the good of people, he reached the supreme power; so the public profession of magic has been one of the roads by which the ablest men have passed to the highest power of kingship.

A notworthy instance of the relic of the belief is that the English kings could heal scrofula by their touch. The belief that kings possess magical or supernatural powers by virtue of which they could fertilize the earth and confer their benefits on their subjects would seem to have been shared by the ancestors of all Aryan races from India to Ireland and it has left clear traces of itself in our own country down to modern times.[300] Thus the ancient Hindu law Book called the 'Laws of Manu' describes as follows the effects of good king's reign "In that country where the king avoids taking property of mortal sinners, men are born in due time and are long-lived. And the crops of the husbandmen spring up each as it was sown and the children die not and no mishaped offspirng is born.[301]

One more point in Frazer's theory is worthy to be noted here. Regalia, according to Frazer are the wonder-working talismans which the kings even of several modern civilized countries appear to have derived from their predecessors.[302]

The theory stated by Frazer is given in brief here. It is clear that the age of magic was before the origin and rise of religion. In course of time a faith in religion emerged. So this theory does notmake any contradiction

299. ibid. p.85

300. G.J.Frazer, Golden Bough (Abridged Edition) Published by MacMillan & Co. Ltd London 1933, p.89

301. MS IX.246/247

302. G.J. Frazer, Golden Bough (Abridged Edition) Published by MacMillan and Co. Ltd. London, 1933 p. 364.

with the theory of the divine origin of kingship, which is the outcome of the influence of dharma. It is not proposed here to go in details in Frazer's theory to search king's origin. The efforts are only to show that the relic of the magical power found in the kings in the *Pañcamahākāvyas* had a long trace in the pre- religion period. The rain-making and controlling power of the kings, the hereditary royal ornaments like Cintāmanī gem and ornament named 'Jaitra' which are described as a charm to give victory to the king are the relics of the magical powers described by Frazer and the wonder-working talismans alluded by him.

While stating the evolution of kingship N.N. Law has quoted Mahābhārata (1.136.35), Mahāvastu Avadāna (1.347) etc. In which good family, personal bravery, skill in leadership, protecting power etc. qualities are mentioned essential for leadership.[303] So the theory of the origin of a king from a magician is only one of the ways to kingship and not the only way towards the throne.

Thus it is clear that there is defiantly a magical power in the king which is different from the magical power offered to him from the divinities and which had a long source in the remote period of magic which became gradually apparent and religion evolved.

303. N.N. Law, Aspects of Ancient Indian Polity, Published by Orient Longmana, 1960, p.97

CHAPTER V

A COMPARATIVE STUDY OF KIRĀTĀRJUNĪYAM AND ŚIŚUPĀLAVADHA

FROM THE POLITICAL POINT OF VIEW :

Kirātārjunīyam and Śiśupālavadha, the two *mahākāvyas*, resemble each other in many aspects. From the literary point of view, it is clear that Māgha followed Bhāravi, not only in the style and structure but also in the arrangement of the similar subject matter. In Kirātājunīyam the events take place as follows. A messenger sent by Yudhiṣṭhira brings a report of Duryodhana's good administration, hearing which, Draupadī gets enraged. She vehemently attacks the inactive policy of Yudhiṣṭhira and states necessity of applying of fraud against the wicked enemies. Bhīma whole heartedly supports Draupadī on the point of self-respect. Yudhiṣṭhira who is against any hasty action states on importance of forbearance. Then comes the great sage Vyāsa who advises for the increasement of valour and strength to face the strong enemy. Then follows Arjuna's departure for the propitiation of penance, his control over the passions, sending of messenger to Arjuna by the king of the Kirātas, his threatening and lastly a tough fight between Arjuna and the king of Kirātas and an obtainment of the desired divine weapons. Similar order is followed by Māgha in the first canto of Śiśupālavadha. After the advice by sage Nārada to Kṛṣṇa to kill the wicked enemy Śiśupāla, we come across the discussion of deciding the two problems whether to attack Śiśupāla or to join the Rājasūya sacrifice of Yudhiṣṭhira. Balarāma and Kṛṣṇa give priority of uprooting the wicked enemy but after the wise consultation by Uddhava, a decision of attending Yudhiṣṭhira's sacrifice is fixed. Śiśupāla is inflamed by the great honour offered to Kṛṣṇa and sends an envoy who inwardly threatens Kṛṣṇa and declares war. After a tough fight Śiśupāla is killed.

Here it is not concerned to show the places of similarity from the point of style and structure but to reveal the resemblance in the political ideas and arguments and to compare the ideas.

The arguments of Draupadī and Bhīma in Kirātārjunīyam and that of Balarāma in Śiśupālavadha are based on the importance of self-respect. According to Draupadī straight- forwardness is a useless policy against a wicked enemy like Duryodhana.[1] A king can never win back his lost kingdom through peace-policy. Foremost importance in the political life of the king should be given to self-dignity. So it is not proper for the spirited king like Yudhiṣṭhira to bear insults inflicted by an enemy. To a man having a high sense of self-respect, whose wealth in the form of valour is not snatched by the enemies, even defeat is as good as a festival[2]. Draupadī also states the importance of anger which can be reckoned as a virtue if it is used in a proper manner. People regard only such a person whose anger does not prove futile.[3] Bhīma supports her arguments highly praising her speech. According to him

---

1. Kirā I.30
2. ibid. I.41
   द्विषन्निमित्ता यदियं दशततः समून्मूलयतीव मे मनः।
   परैरपर्यासितवीर्यसम्पदां पराभवोऽप्युत्सव अेव मानिनाम् ॥
3. Kirā I.33
   अवन्ध्यकोपस्य विहन्तुरापदां भवन्ति वश्याः स्वयमेव देहिनः।
   अमर्षशून्येन जनस्य जन्तुना न जातहादेन न विद्विषा दरः ॥

it is not proper for self-respected person to bow before an enemy and silently bear the insults. The nature of the spirited persons never allow them to bear the superiority of others.[4] Balarāma expresses the same attitude of the High-spirited. He states that even dust is worthier than such a person who silently bears insults.[5] People take advantage of the mild behaviour of the person as moon is swallowed earlier by the demon than the lusterous Sun having a similar fault.[6] Both Bhīma and Balarāma had a profound belief in their valour through which prosperity is possible. So due to their opinion, one should obtain prosperity depending on the valour of his arm. An enemy should be conquered by the fourth means only where mild policy is useless.[7] Thus declaration of war against the wicked enemy is the chief thread of the argument of Bhima, Draupadī and Balarāma.

Bhīma and Balarāma exhibit good deal of their knowledge in the political field. They consider themselves as the foremost experts in polity. According to Bhīma the science of statecraft, though difficult, is practised as a lake can be entered, if it has steps.[8] A man, versed in the four sciences is expected to guide others but as Bhīma opines, Yudhiṣṭhira is not able to select the right course of action.[9] He also states the

4. Kirā II.20
ज्वलितं न हिरण्यरेवसं चयमास्कन्दति भस्मनां जनः ।
अभिभूतिभयादसूनतः सुखमुज्झन्ति न धाम मानिनः ॥

5. Śiśu II.46

6. ibid II.49

7. ibid. II.54/55

8. Kirā II.3
विषमोऽपि विगाहयते नयः कृततीर्थः पयसामिवाशयः ।
स तु तत्र विशेषदुर्लभः सदुपन्यस्यति कृत्यवर्त्म यः ॥

9. ibid. II.6
चतुसृष्वपि ते विवेकिनी नृप विद्यासु निरुढिमागता ।
कथमेत्य मतिर्विपर्ययं करिणी पङ्कमिवावसीदति ॥

relative value of the two powers viz. energy and enterprise. According to him people admire the rising king having enterprise.[10]

According to Balarāma the whole science of polity rests on the rise of self and fall of the enemy.[11] His profound study of the political knowledge is clearly exhibited when he states the opinions of the political thinkers and declares his own view. Regarding the policy of expedition there are different opinions in the ancient thinkers. Balarāma has mentioned these opinions. According to Kāmandaka one should attack the enemy when one is sufficiently strong and one should not think about enemy's calamity or prosperity.[12] According to Manu one should declare war when the enemy is in a clamity.[13] Here Balarāma seems to be accepting both the views when he describes the topmost strength of his victorious army[14] and also, Śiśupāla's calamity on account of the death of his friend Jarāsandha. Apparently Balarāma opines that a spirited person prefers to attack the enemy who is at the top of his power and attacking the enemy in a clamity brings shame to such person.[15] But truly speaking Balarāma is eager to apply his strength immediately

---

10. ibid II.11
11. Śiśu II.30
    आत्मोदयः परज्यानिर्द्वयं नीतिरितीयती ।
    तदूरीकृत्य कृतिभिर्वाचस्पत्यं प्रतायते ॥
12. KN XI.1.2
13. MS VII.183
    अन्येष्वपि तु कालेषु यदा पश्येद्धुवं जयम् ।
    तदा यायाद्वि गृहयैव व्यसने चोत्थिते रिपोः ॥
14. Śiśu II.58/59
15. ibid. II.61
    नीतिरापदि यद्गम्यः परस्तन्मानिनो ह्रिये ।
    विधुर्विधुन्तुदस्येव पूर्णस्तस्योत्सवाय सः ॥

against Śiśupāla who is in a calamity.[16] His prudence in the political knowledge is seen in his suggestion of cutting off the daily supplies as eatings, grass, fuel, aid of friends etc. of the enemy, through which it becomes easy to conquer the enemy.[17]

Thus many aspects of the political knowledge are exhibited in the arguments of Bhīma and Balarāma. But their political knowledge is used for their urge on the declaration of war. Self-respect is the main stand of their argument. But they neglect the fact that while deciding a policy against a strong enemy, one should discriminate the more and the less dangerous. Having the knowledge of polity also, Bhīma and Balarāma seem to be more partial of exhibiting their strength and valour for the self-respect and totally neglect the time-factor. They mainly rely on the emotional side which has a secondary value in a field of polity. The drawbacks of the one-sided policy stated by Bhīma and Balarāma in Kirātārjunīyam and Śiśupālavadha are clearly explained by Yudhiṣṭhira and Uddhava respectively. Their profound knowledge of polity and their vision visualized the unseen points in the political field which were neglected by persons of mediocre intellect.

Both are against taking any hasty action of declaring war against the enemy, without considering the pros and cons of the whole situation. Yudhiṣṭhira and Uddhava refute the arguments by Bhīma and Balarāma respectively which are apparently logical but are not fit

---

16. Śiśu II.63
इन्द्रप्रस्थगमस्तावत् कारि मा सन्तु चेदयः ।
आस्माकदन्तिसांनिध्या द्वामनीभूतभूरुहः ॥

17. ibid. II.64
निरुद्धवीवधासारप्रसारा गा इव व्रजम् ।
उपरुद्धन्तु दाशार्हाः पुरीं माहिष्मतीं द्विषः ॥

in the present situation of things which they have to face.

According to Yudhiṣṭhira a want of discrimination or thoughtlessness is a source of many dangers. While refuting the argument of Bhīma he says that enterprize without the backing of counsel is useless. It leads to destruction. The power of discrimination gives success to the person, like a rich and fruitful grains is definite after a proper rainfall.[18] Valour without diplomacy gives no success. Uddhava, the great politician and eminent minister of Kṛṣṇa states the way of success through the accompaniment of the power of counsel with enterprize. These two provide the means of success to the king desirous of victory.[19] A combination of counsel and enterprize makes the king chief among the circle of the twelve kings.[20] Thus a consultation with others and not taking a hasty action is emphasized by both Yudhiṣṭhira and Uddhava.

According to Uddhava the point of self-dignity is no doubt important, but for a true politician it is necessary to neglect it, judging the whole situation. If the time is unfavourable, one has to bear insults inflicted even by an enemy and has to wait for a proper opportunity.

Yudhiṣṭhira and Uddhava urge and explain the importance of forbearance in a political field. Draupadī has mentioned forbearance as a merit behoving only to sage free from worldy gains and unfit for an ambitious king. Yudhiṣṭhira argues that forbearance is a great virtue which gives success to one's undertakings. It is

---

18. Kirā II.31
19. Śiśu II.76
    प्रज्ञोत्साहवतः स्वामी यतेताधातुमात्मनि ।
    तौ हि मूलमुदेष्यन्त्या जिगीषोरात्मसंपदः ॥
20. ibid

indestructive itself but destroys the enemy.[21] Uddhava is well aware of the importance of forbearance in the field of polity. Just as a host of fleeting emotions works for on sentiment, so the other kings help their leader having forbearance.[22]

Bhīma and Balarāma had exhibited their knowledge about the relation of friends and foes, but Balarāma forgot the other side of keeping friendship, which is reminded by Uddhava. The wise politician Uddhava directed another side of the relation with friends. Balarāma, while stating the strong enmity of Śiśupāla, urges for the declaration of war against him. But Uddhava reminds him of the risk of losing a real friends like Yudhiṣṭhira, not attending his sacrificial function and involving all other kings in the war. Uddhava reminds that Kṛṣṇa and Yudhiṣṭhira are the best friends, so Kṛṣṇa cannot afford to lose friendship of Yudhiṣṭhira in the cost of declaring war against Śiśupāla. In Kirātārjunīyam also, Yudhiṣṭhira's 'wait and see' policy, exhibits another aspect of the behavior of friend and foe. According to him Duryodhana's strength is relied upon his friends who are apparently devoted to him. They are really attached to Pāṇḍavas and they will declare their real support at the proper time. So at the time of war, Duryodhana's support and strength is surely to be decreased by losing friendship or these so-called friends, who are likely to be estranged by the haughty and arrogant nature of Duryodhana.[23] This outstanding vision of the eminent politicians like Yudhiṣṭhira and Uddhava is able to forecast the policy

21. Kirā II.43
उपकारमायतेमृशं कर्मफलस्य भूरिणः।
अनपायि निर्वर्हणं द्विषां न तितिक्षासममस्ति साधनम् ॥
22. Śiśu II.87
23. Kirā II.44 to 46

effected by the nature of friends and allies, which is only theoretically explained by Bhīma and Balarāma.

A thorough reading of the arguments and advise by Yudhiṣṭhira and Uddhava makes one to think over one more point which is relevant in connection with this topic. Yudhiṣṭira's diplomacy and the 'wait and see' policy aims at the haughtiness of Duryodhana which itself gives him proper opportunity. Yudhiṣṭhira urges for the value of forbearance and his stand of catching proper opportunity is relied upon the explosion of haughtiness of Duryodhana. Yudhiṣṭhira infers that proud Duryodhana would surely insult the other kings. Even an ordinary person cannot tolarate insulates; so it is not possible that the valorous kings would bear a loss of their dignity. Thus the anger of Duryodhana would certainly alienate his supporting kings and it will cause the destruction of Duryodhana.

But this above mentioned argument of Yudhiṣṭhira is unable to forward certain plan before the confused Pāṇḍavas. It is realised only on the bursting out of anger of Duryodhana and it does not offer any time limit when the estrangement of the other kings would take place and when Duryodhana's strength would become weak and upto which period Pāṇḍavas have to wait for the proper opportunity. All the arguments of Yudhiṣṭhira are based on the explosion of the haughty spirit of Duryodhana which seems contradictory to the report brought by his own emissary. According to the report of the messenger Duryodhana has controlled his anger and other passions and he rules through a righteous path of *Nīti.* He tries to outshine Yudhiṣṭhira by his merits.[24] The messenger also mentions Duryodhana's desire of abiding by the laws of Manu,

24. Kirā I.8
तथापि जिह्मः स भवज्जिगीषया तनोति शुभ्रं गुणसम्पदा यशः ।
समुन्नयन्भूति मनार्यसङ्गमा द्वरं विरोधोऽपि समं महात्मभिः ॥

his benign treatment at attendants, friends and relatives[25] and to his political generosity to his dutyful servants. Yudhiṣṭhira has not given any specific reason which would cause Duryodhana to leave his righteous path. Though Yudhiṣṭhira's suggestious mind and political conviction enable him to foresee the political turn of events for Duryodhana, without a definite reason for it, it seems to be an inactive 'wait and see' policy.

In comparison with Yudhiṣṭhira's policy, Uddava's valid reasoning in Śiśupālavadha stands many steps higher in prudency and knowledge of polity. He gives proper reasons for the political forecast of the declaration of war by Śiśupāla and not by Pāṇḍavas. He knows that keeping a good relationship with the friends is more important than merely acquiring victory over the enemy. So he defers war on definite grounds. A king who understands an importance of time and occasion does not apply force or peace extremely. If the time is unfavourable one has to wait for the coming opportunity. According to Uddhava's guess this opportunity will definitely arise in Yudhiṣṭhira's sacrifical ceremony where Śiśupāla will not bear the honour of *'Agrapūja'* offered to Kṛṣṇa, his foremost enemy, and will himself declare war against Kṛṣṇa. An enmity between Kṛṣṇa and Śiśupāla is increased by their deeds. Śiśupāla is already enraged by the abduction of Rukmiṇi, his betrothed by Kṛṣṇa. Thus enraged Śiśupāla will start the game of war, catching the opportunity of his insult. Thus attending Yudhiṣṭhira's sacrificial function, two birds are to be killed by one stone, viz. keeping of friendship and defeat of the enemy.

These arguments by Uddhava hold definite plan of action which seem to be lacking in Yudhiṣṭhira's policy. Uddhava's expert knowledge of polity is revealed when he suggests an application of four political expedients.

---

25. Kirā I.10

He mainly relies on the policy of seduction. According to him if the eighteen *Tīrthas* of the enemy are detected by the spies, then it is easy to uproot the enemy. So a seduction among the important functionaries through the spies, who are in the pay of both sides, is an effective policy. Thus Uddhava's political wisdom is revealed in his suggestion of the political means of success without bloodshed.

While comparing the counsels consulted by Yudhiṣṭhira and Uddhava it seems that the speech of Yudhiṣṭhira, though backed by *Nīti* is a speech of a straightforward and righteous administrator who is not ready to apply a 'tit for tat' policy. While Uddhava as a prudent politician is concerned even with the minute aspects of the policy and does not hesitate to advise the application of seduction to uproot the strength of the enemy. His intellectual capacity of thinking in the political field suggests some definite plans which are the outcome of a wise consillor. Kauṭilya the great politician mentions Uddhava's views in a name of Vātavyādhi. Uddhava's suggestions are so convincing that Kṛṣṇa at once takes a decision of attending Yudhiṣṭira's sacrificial ceremony.

The mission of the two great sages viz. Vyāsa in Kirātārjunīyam and Nārada in Śiśupālavadha is worthwhile of comparison. Vyāsa, whose intellectual vision sees that Duryodhana's wicked policy will end in the declaration of war, states a necessity of valour and strength of arms. According to his advice success in the battlefield mainly depends upon the superiority of weapons.[26] As the enemy is superior in valour and strength, it is essential to acquire divine weapons to increase the strength of Pāṇḍavas. It is creditable that an ascetic like Vyāsa, free from wordly affairs gives a valuable advice to an administrator and also helps in

26. Kirā III.17

directing the means for acquiring the desired object. Nārada's advice to Kṛṣṇa in Śiśupālavadha is no doubt important as he states the intention of the birth of Kṛṣṇa for the destruction of the wicked. He reminds Kṛṣṇa of his previous births in which his chief function was to destroy the harassing powers and to protect the subjects.[27]

In comparison to Vyāsa's politically important advice, Nārada's suggestion seems to be a real devotee's praise to the incarnation of the Lord to pray him for the destruction of the wicked. The speech of Vyāsa directly leads Arjuna to acquire the divine weapons and draws the attention to the fact of acquiring military equipments, while Nārada's speech acomplishes the task of reminding the Great Ruler his duty of protection of the subjects and destruction of the enemy. It results in the discussion of giving priority to attend Yudhiṣṭhira's Rājasūya sacrifice and not to take a hasty action of waging war against Śiśupāla. Thus both these great personalities, free from worldly desire, perform the mission due to their affection towards the kings and due to the admiration for merits.[28]

Now comes the turn of Duryodhana and Śiśupāla, who are painted as wicked enemies but reveal a good deal of their political knowledge. Duryodhna shines foremost as an able administrator who knows many of the political principles and follows them in his life. He fully knows to win the people of the conquered territory, which was snatched by him from Pāṇdavas through deceitful means, but he was desirous to maintain it by righteous means. It is mentioned before that the righteous reign of Duryodhana, from which we come

---

27. Śisu I.35 to 42
28. Kirā III.12
तथापि निध्नं नृप तावकीनैः प्रह्वीकृतं मे हृदयं गुणौघैः ।
वीतस्पृहाणामपि मुक्तिभाजां भवन्ति भव्येषु हि पक्षपाताः ॥

to know his profound knowledge of internal administration as well as of international relationship.[29] In comparison to Duryodhana Śiśupāla reveals less number of aspects of his political wisdom. His extreme enmity to Kṛṣṇa is based on valid reasons, so not bearing the honour of Kṛṣṇa offered by Yudhiṣṭhira, he wages war against Kṛṣṇa for the self-dignity. He exhibits his strength and valour by sending a messenger to Kṛṣṇa and creates a background for declaring war.

Sending of an envoy by the opposite party for the declaration of war is the similar aspect in Kirātārjunīyam and Śiśupālavadha. Envoy is an important factor in political field by whose work the policy of *Sandhi* or *Vigraha* takes place.[30] All the qualities of a good envoy are visible in both envoys. The messenger in Śiśupālavadha speaks the words having double meaning through which he apparently seems to be praising Kṛṣṇa but inwardly threatens Kṛṣṇa describing the valour and strength of Śiśupāla. In Kirātārjunīyam Arjuna praises the speech of the envoy in which all the merits are present. In his speech the messenger exhibits the application of four expedients in their due order. He praises Arjuna and his penance, suggests superiority of his master, gains of obtaining such strong friends, advice of asking for the arrow and wealth and lastly threatening Arjuna showing him the vast standing army of Kirātarāja. Through his excellent speech he urges Arjuna not to leave the path directed by ancient thinkers.[31]

---

29. Kirā I.21
न तेन सज्यं क्वचिदुद्यतं धनुः कृतं न वा कोपविजिह्ममाननम् ।
गुणानुरागेण शिरोभिरुह्यते नराधिपैर्माल्यमिवास्य शासनम् ॥

30. MS VII.66

31. Kirā XIII.42
स्मर्यते तनुमृतां सनातनं न्या यमाचरितमुत्तमैर्नुभिः ।
ध्वंसते यदि भवादृशस्ततः कः प्रयातु वद तेन वतर्मना ॥

Thus both these *mahākāvyas* have a good deal of political ideas which are applied in proper circumstances. Sometimes possessed of the virtue of *Ksātra dharma*. Bhīma and Balarāma desirous to present their self-dignity and destruction of the enemy lack political wisdom which is directed by the wise politician and minister like Uddhava. It is discussed before that the policy applied by Uddhava in Śiśupālavadha seems to be more convincing due to his definite plan and programme than the consultation of Yudhiṣṭhira.

CHAPTER VI

THE ART OF WAR AND MILITARY ORGANIZATION

THE INTENTIONS BEHIND THE WARS DESCRIBED IN THE PAÑCAMAHĀKĀVYAS :

While enumerating the intentions behind the wars, several motives are seen to be reflected in the *Pañcamahākāvyas,* which stimulated the kings to take arms against their enemies.

Cast-ridden society was one of the prominent intentions behind the wars fought. A prominent duty of the *kṣatriya* caste, living on arms, was protection of the society.[1] Valour was an essential quality of Kṣatriyas and it found its outlet in protection of the people on one hand and the conquest of the world on the other. As the prescribed duties of each caste were strictly observed, each person was to realize his own responsibility and duty. An observance of one's own *dharma* was the highest ideal before the people. For a *kṣatriya* king, it was not a mere instrument of diplomacy, but it was a bounden duty for him and to die on the battlefield was the greatest glory that a *kṣatriya* could achieve. A close relationship seems to be established between war and '*svadharma*'. Achieving victory or meeting death, both were profitable for a warrior. A conquest in the battles gave the kings fame and glory

1. Raghu XVI.80 Nai IX.150

which was their foremost ideal. In the opening verses of Raghuvaṁśa it is described that the victory achieved by the conquering kings was aimed for the sake of glory.[2] It was strongly believed that observation of *svadharma* was the easiest way to heaven.[3] Running away from battlefield by the warrior was highly condemned.[4] but a warrior who got an opportunity to die on the battlefield was praised. He was eagerly received by nymphs in the heaven,[5] and he acquired a place in the orb of sun.[6] Ancient thinkers had given a touch of sanctity to the idea of wars by respeating the dictum that dying in a battle was an act of highest merit for a kṣatriya and the kings who died in the battlefield, obtained salvation.[7] Dying at home by some disease was counted as great sin.[8] According to Kauṭilya, heaven which is attainable by the *brāhmaṇas* after great penances and performance of several sacrifices, is attained in no time by a *kṣatriya* simply by dying on the field of battle.[9] So a warrior was always in preparedness for war and responded when challenged without caring for victory or death. Thus for the warriors of military class, observing the caste- rules, it was inevitable to risk their lives in the battles. This framework and moral backgroud of society was a prominent instinct behind the wars.

---

2. Raghu I.7 Kirā XVI. 9
3. Nai V.15 Śiśu XVIII.14
4. Kirā XV.15; XI.78
5. Raghu VII 51/53
6. Nai XII.98
7. MS VII.87/89
8. ŚP (Critical Edition by BORI) 98.23
   अधर्मः क्षत्रियस्यैष यद्शय्यामरणं भवेत् ।
9. KA X.3.30
   यान् यज्ञसंघैस्तपसा च विप्राः स्वर्गेषिणः पात्रचयैश्च यान्ति ।
   क्षणेन तानप्यतियान्ति शूराः प्राणान् सुयुद्धेषु परित्यजन्तः ॥

An ambition of the ancient kings to extend boundaries of their kingdoms made the wars frequent. Their ideal was to set themselves as the paramount sovereigns for which they frequently arranged military expeditions. It is discussed while explaining the concept of *'Cakravartin'*. The idea of universal dominion has been an animating ideal before every king. Raghu's conquest of the quarters which is described in details in Raghuvaṁśa, may be taken as modelled after the ideal or world-dominion. Thus wars were fought and territories were conquered, as the object was to bring the whole country under one scepter. It was only through wars, the other states accepted influence of the paramount ruler.

Great sacrifices were perfomrmed by the conquerors to confirm officially with a seal upon their overlordships. We have discussed this point in earlier pages. In the *Aśvamedha* sacrifice a horse was to be let loose, guided by armed princes and wherever it roamed unobstructed, the whole territory came under that king's control. Sometimes the steed was obstructed and challenged by the kings and wars ensued.

While reading the account of the kings in Raghuvaṁśa the reader comes across a fact which exhibits an inevitability of frequent wars. Each and every king of the succeeding generation in the Raghu-race arranged an expedition of conquest to declare his sovereignty. Was it necessary to arrange everytime such expensive expeditions on the neighbouring countries, which were already conquered by their ancestors. If the sacrifices were performed for solemnization of the power acquired and not for the acquisition of power then what was the necessity to the successor of the previous emperor to be aggressive everytime by harassing the neighbouring countries, who had admitted the overlordship of the emperor in a previous attack? The answer to this question can be given by the political point of view. It was necessary for the ruler to renew the seal of his sovereignty. For example, after the successful reign of Dilīpa, his son Raghu received the kingly office, but having heard about him that he was established on the throne, the fire of jealousy that was long smoking in the bosoms of rival princes burnt aglow.[10] So it was very much necessary for the conquerors to be watchful in the case of enemies by making exhibition of their strength. Secondly, when one thinks of a psychological tendency of the kings one can recognize that they had a great confidence in the valour of their arms, which was exhibited by arranging the expeditions of conquest. The kings were not contented in ruling the already acquired kingdom but were desirous of exhibiting their valour which was shown by their ancestors. In Kirātārjunīyam, Bhīma expresses this tendency. He says to Yudhiṣṭhira— If you get back your kingdom being restored to you by your enemy, then vain will be the arms of your younger brothers which have already displayed their valour. A great person, overpowering the valour of the world by his might does not wish to attend prosperity by other's favour. Self- respect is the wealth to such a person seeking imperishable glory and mere wealth is an object of secondary consideration for him.[11] This tendency of exhibiting valour leads to frequent expeditions of conquest.

Acquisition of religious merits by performing the great sacrifices was an important cause of war. It is mentional in Raghuvaṁśa that the sacrificial horse sent by Dilīpa was stolen by Indra and he refused to return

---

10. Raghu IV.2
दिलीपानन्तरं राज्ये तं निशम्य प्रतिष्ठितम् ।
पूर्वं प्रधूमितो राज्ञां हृदयेऽग्निरिवोत्थितः ॥

11. Kirā II.17/19

it back to prince Raghu. So Raghu prayed him to offer atleast the merit of the sacrifice to his father.[12] Moreover, the pride and vanity of the conquering monarchs did not end in performing a single Horse-sacrifice; but they were eager to obtain the status of Indra, the lord of gods, by performing hundred Horse-sacrifices. The incident of sending the sacrificial[13] horse by Dilīpa for the hundredth horse-sacrifice shows this fact. Indra, who was the only person entitled for the epithet *'Śatakratu'* was not ready to leave his monopoly which was being seized by Dilīpa.[14] A terrific war between Raghu and Indra was fought after which Raghu got an assurance of religious marit of the sacrifice from Indra.

Haughtiness and spirits of jealousy were the provocative causes for war. An instance of the first type is of Paraśurāma in Raghuvaṁśa and of the latter is of Śiśupāla in Śiśupālvadha. Paraśurāma's father Jamaḍagni was killed by Haihaya king; so to take revenge of his father's murder, he took the vow of the destruction of *kṣatriya* race in twenty-one generations[15] Paraśurāma openly declared enmity with dauntless spirit.[16] As Paraśurāma came to know the rise of *kṣātratejas* in the form of Rāma, he threatened Rāma by his fierce appearance and challenged him for war.

In Śiśupālavadha, it seems that the roots of enmity between Śiśupāla and Kṛṣṇa were hidden in the jealous nature of Śiśupāla which resulted in a furious war.[17]

---

12. Raghu III.65
अमोच्यमश्वं यदि मन्यसे प्रभो ! ततः समाप्ते विधिनैव कर्मणि ।
अजस्रदीक्षाप्रयतः स मदगुरुः क्रतोरशेषेण फलेन युज्यताम् ॥
13. ibid. III.38
14. ibid. III.49
15. ibid. XI. 66.67
16. ibid. XI.74
17. Śiśu XV.1

In the ceremony of Rājasūya sacrifice performed by Yudhiṣṭhira, he offered the first place of honour to Lord Kṛṣṇa.[18] Jealous Śiśupala could not bear the insult of ignoring others , including himself, for the honour. He abused Bhīṣma, Yudhiṣṭhira and Kṛṣṇa in ugly words. He exhibited his extreme jealousy in counting the valorous acts of Kṛṣṇa as minor acts. Kṛṣṇa remained silent as he wanted to keep the promise to Śiśupāla's mother of bearing hundred wrongs of Śiśupāla.[19] Bhīma could not bear the abusive words of Śiśupāla and declared war against Śiśupāla and other kings.[20] Thus the jealousy of Śiśupāla resulted in a provocation of war.

Svayaṁvara was a favourite form of choosing a husband from assembled princes, for a princess in royal dynasty. But sometimes the defeated princes unanimously declared war against the successful prince, who had to prove his worth as a proper choice by exhibiting his valour. In the *svayaṁvara* of Indumatī, she selected prince Aja as her consort. But this selection aroused the anger of the unsuccessful princes and the haughty host of kings arrested Aja on his return journey.[21] Aja accepted their challenge and a terrific fight ensued.

A forcible abduction of a maiden gives rise to a war. A hostility between Rāma and Rāvaṇa took place on account of kidnaping of Sītā by Rāvaṇa. In *Janasthāna* Rāma defeated the demons led by Śūrpaṇakhā, who was punished and disfigured by Lakṣmaṇa. Rāvaṇa by

---

18. Śiśu XV.2

19. ibid. XV.42

20. ibid. XV.46

21. Raghu VII.34/35
प्रमन्यवः प्रागपि कौसलन्द्रे प्रत्येमात्तस्वतया बभूवुः ।
अतो नृपाश्चक्षमिभिरे समेताः स्त्रीरललाभं न तदात्मजस्य ॥
समुद्वहन्तं पथि मोजकन्यां रूरोधः राजन्यगणः स द्रुप्तः ।
बलिप्रदिष्टां श्रियमाददानं त्रैविक्रमं पादमिवेन्द्रशत्रुः ॥

abducting Sītā took revenge of the wrongs done by Rāma to his kinsmen. Rāma had to fight a war against Rāvaṇa which resulted in defeat and death of Rāvaṇa.

In Kirātārjunīyam, Bhāravi emphasizes the justifiability of war with all his poetic fervour and strength. Through the mouth of Draupadī, he preaches the cult of war. She argues that a self-respected person should not bear insults from the enemies. She urges to declare war against Kauravas. According to her, it is not necessary to keep an agreement and promise with the fraudulent enemy.[22] It is not a wrong policy for the kings, intent on victory, to make breaches of peace and declare war. This line of policy leads to warbreak.

A prominent duty of the king is to protect the subjects from the distress and harassment of the wicked enemies by declaring war against them. King Rāma sent Śatrughna against Lavaṇa who had distressed the hermits living on the banks of Yamunā. Śatrughna returned with success after a tough fight with the demon.[23] To uproot the enemies, the supreme divinities had to take an embodiment as human rulers on the earth. In Śiśupālavadha, the sage Nārada specifically refers to the previous births of Viṣṇu, in which he had destroyed the enemies like Hiraṇyakaśipu, Rāvaṇa, etc.[24] and in this birth it is the turn of wicked Kaṁsa and Śiśupāla for whose destruction Viṣṇu has incarnated himself in a human form viz. Kṛṣṇa.[25] Rāma in Raghuvaṁśa and Kumāra in Kumārasaṁbhava perform the similar functions of destroying Rāvaṇa and Tārakāsura respectively. Thus the great fights between Kṛṣṇa and Śiśupāla, Rāma and Rāvaṇa, Kumāra and

---

22. Kirā I.45
23. Raghu XV 15 to 25
24. Śiśu I.42/48/68
25. ibid. I.36/38; XIV.42

Tārakāsura are all caused for the release of the people from the distress inflicted by the wicked personalities.

In short, a desire to obtain imperial status, war-glory, acquiring religious merit, vanity, jealous nature, abduction of a maiden, protection of the oppressed subjects, control of the harassing enemy etc. are the dominating causes of war. The inspiration of military spirit among children is seen in the very cradle, through their mothers. They took pride in being called progenitors of brave sons.[26] The *kṣatriya warriors* did not get satisfaction unless they fight in wars.[27] they were eager for the victory in the battlefield.[28] The valorous kings used their valour for increasing their empires, stabilizing them and making a welfare state for their subjects.

DIGVIJAYA YĀTRĀ :

Generally months from *Mārgaśīrṣa* to *Chaitra* were regarded as the best months for undertaking military expedition. Winter was declared as the proper time for starting a military expedition. This season of autumn makes the rivers fordable and the roads mud-dried and inspires the conquering monarch to start an expedition of conquest.[29] Astronomical considerations also weighed in deciding the time for the march. When an expedition was decided, astrologers were consulted to ascertain the most auspicious moment for the formal departure of the army.

Before starting on a military expedition, the king was to keep his eye on the security of his kingdom.

---

26. Ku XII.59
27. Nai XI.111
    वैरिश्रियं प्रतिनियुद्धमनाप्नुवन्यः किंचिन्न तृप्यति धरावलयैकवीरः ।
    स त्वामवाप्य निपतन्मदनेषुवृन्दस्यन्दीनि तृप्यतु मधूनि पिबन्निवायम् ॥
28. Kirā XVI.9
29. Raghu IV.24

He was to see that the capital fortresses as well as the frontier fortifications were well guarded and defended.[30] It was also seen that there were no internal troubles within the state and no apprehension of an attack from the rear. It has always proved a profitable policy in warfare to embarrass an enemy either by insisting on other powers to attack it from the rear or by fomenting internal troubles within the territory. Hence it was important to secure the rear at the time of expedition. It has been most zealously advocated by the ancient thinkers on polity. A calamity arising in the rear is indeed a matter of great anxiety. Kauṭilya holds that as between a small disturbance in the rear and a large gain in the front, the small disturbance in the rear is of great importance.[31] Raghu started his expedition only after taking such precaution.

At the commencement of the expedition, the king was blessed and showered with fried grains by the women of advanced age.[32] Propitious rites and ceremonies were performed on the eve of expedition. According to Kāmandaka the king should worship the gods and twice-born ie. *brāhmaṇas* while commencing the expedition[33] The kings used to offer gifts to the *brāhmaṇas* and petitioners.[34]

Among the propitious rites the ceremony of *Nīrājanā* was an important rite to be performed before the commencement of the expedition. It was a military and religious ceremony performed by the king or generals of armies before they started for battles. This rite consists of purifying the various component parts of the army

30. Raghu IV.26
31. KA IX.3 अल्पः पश्चात्कोपो महान पुरस्ताल्लाभ इति अल्पः पश्चात्कोपो गरीयान् ।
32. Raghu IV.27
33. KN XIX.2
34. Śiśu XVII.24

during the recitation of sacred texts. Ceremonial waving of lights to various arms and weapons, horses and elephants and to the banners was the chief part of this ceremony.[35] Before starting for the expedition of conquest Raghu performed the lustration ceremony of his horses and duly offered oblations to the holy fire.[36] This lustration chiefly consist of sprouts, bark of benign trees, sprouts of Yava grass and Durvā shoots.[37]

Purification of the army, elephants and horses was the chief purpose behind this rite. though this rite was chiefly meant for horses, it was performed for elephants also as adds Mallinātha.[38] This ceremony of weaving of lights was performed to obtain victory over the enemy as remarks Mallinātha in his commentary.[39] So this rite was meant for bringing victory. The military character of the ceremony finds prominence in Bṛhatsaṁhitā (Cha 44) which prescribes *Nīrājanā* of horses, elephants and men in the month of *Aśvina* or *Kārtika* and lays stress on the rites connected with the horses in particular. The priest pierces the earthen figure of the foremen with a spear and the king sets out on his expedition.

Gradually, this Nīrājanā ceremony lost its military character, but continued as a propitious rite. For instance, in Naiṣadhīyacarita, *Nīrājanā* means a vassel waived round the face of a person to ward off the evil eye.[40] The reference is to a custom of warding off the

---

35. Nai I.10
अनल्पदग्धारिपुरानलोज्ज्वलैर्निजप्रतापैर्वलयज्ज्वलद्भुवः।
प्रदक्षिणीकृत्य जयाय सृष्टया रराज नीराजनया राजघः॥
36. Raghu IV.25
37. ibid. XVII.12
38. Commentary of Mallinātha on Raghu IV.25
वाजिग्रहणं गजादीनामप्युपलक्षणम् तेषामपि नीराजनाविधानात्।
39. ibid. on Śiśu XVII.16
नीराजनात् स्याद्विजय अित्यागमः।
40. Nai II.26

evil eye by waiving round the face of a person a vessel smeared with cow-dung and containing flour-water.[41] The military significance was soon lost but only the lustration of lights continued intact. Rucipati in his commentary on Anargharāghava (2.10) attaches the similar connotation to the word.[42]

ETHICAL STANDARDS IN THE WARFARE :

The code of war in those days was fully developed. War was fought according to certain specific rules and principles. The soldiers were expected to fight in a disciplined manner. The hardness of diplomacy was modified by the influence of moral sense of humanity.

Hindu science of warfare reflected in the *Pañcamahākāvyas* valued both *Nītī* and *Śaurya* viz. Ethical principle and valour.[43] Waging of war without due consideration to morality was nothing less than a beasty action. So the fighting parties were expected to observe the rules of warfare very strictly.

Fighting with persons in unequa circumstances was prohibited. Foot-soldiers had to fight with foot-soldiers only;[44] A horse-rider should have a similar combatant, elephant-rider had to fight with an elephant-rider and a chariot-warrior should face only the chariot-warrior.[45] Thus a war was fought between the warriors of equal

41. Nai VII.43
42. Commentray on Anargharāghava (II.10) by Rucipati,
नीराजना शान्तिकर्म । तेजोञ्छन इति प्रसिद्धम् ।
43. Raghu XVII.47
कातर्यं केवला नीतिः शौर्यं श्वापदचेष्टितम् ।
अतः सिद्धिं समेताभ्यामुभाभ्यामन्वियेष सः ॥
44. Ku XVI.2
पत्तिः पत्तिममीयाय रणाय रथिनं रथी ।
तुरङ्ग तुरङ्गस्थो दन्तिस्थं दन्तिनि स्थितः ॥
45. Śiśu XVIII.2; XIX.66

footing.[46] In Kirātārjunīyam, it is described that, after the loss and destruction of all the weapons, Arjuna started for wrestling, seeing which his rival also came on equal footing keeping a side his bow and arrow.[47] In the fight between Rāma and Rāvaṇa, described in Raghuvaṁśa Indra offered a chariot to Rāma standing on foot after observing his opposite party seated in a chariot.[48] Thus ordinarily the rules of equal equipment of the warriors were adhered to by all means. But sometimes in a promiscuous battle[49] the rules of equality in the use of different divisions of army were not observed by the warriors. A fight between a warrior on the horse with a warrior on elephant could take place.[50] But such cases were rare.

It was observed that a warrior in armour could not fight with the rival who was not clad in a coat of mail. The warriors wore the armour, not because of fear, but to obey the ethical code of wearing an armour.[51]

Warriors were very sympathetic towards their wounded opponents. A wounded soldier, who was unable to strike at his enemy in return, was not attacked again by the enemy.[52] The code of chivalry also demanded that an emeny who was not engaged in fight with one, but was engaged in conflict with another was not attacked without warning. Not only this but the

---

46. Raghu VII.37
47. Kirā XVII.1
48. Raghu XII.84
49. Śiśu XVIII.18
50. ibid. XVIII.23
51. ibid. XVII.21
52. Raghu VII.47
    पूर्वं प्रहर्ता न जघान भूयः प्रतिप्रहाराक्षममश्वसादी
    तुरंगमस्कन्धनिषण्णदेहं प्रत्याश्वसन्तं रिपुमाचकाङ्क्षः ॥

warriors were expected to allow the enemy an opportunity to recover and to be refreshed.

In the tumultuous battle also, the warriors expressed their condolence, by sitting near the killed warrior. At that time the noise of the bells also was stopped.[53] It exhibits a high ethical standard of the ancient warfare. Wounded and armless opponents were exempted from the staughter. A person who asked for mercy was not killed.[54] The running army of Kirātarāja was chased by Arjuna very slowly, giving them a chance of escaping.[55] The confiding enemies were promised of safety.[56] If a warrior from the enemy was captured, he was not killed but was kept alive[57] for there was a possibility of getting some important news from the opponent. A subdued enemy coming for protection was never attacked.[58]

Thus these ethical rules of warfare were not in vogue in theory only, but they exhibited a humane ethical standard. Sometimes these ethical rules were trangressed by the warriors. The main target of fighting the battle was to gain victory. So it was natural that sometimes an advantage of the situation was taken by the warriors setting aside the ethics of war. For example, in the fight between the demon named Lavaṇa and Śatrughna described in Raghuvaṃśa, Śatrughna assailed

---

53. Śiśu XIX.80
अन्धौ विपन्नेऽनेकेन नरेणेह तदन्तिके ।
अशौचि सैन्ये घण्टाभिर्न रेणे हतदन्तिके ॥

54. Kirā XV.4

55. ibid XV.6
त्रासजिह्मं यतश्चैतान् मन्दमेवान्वियाय सः ।
नातिपीडायितुं मग्नानिच्छन्ति हि महौजसः ॥

56. Raghu IV.35

57. Śiśu XVIII.66

58. ibid. XIX.13

Lavaṇa finding him without his pike; for success attends those who strike at the vulnerable points of the enemy.[59] Thus in some places the moral standards seem to be surpassed by the chief target of getting victory. This principle of attacking an enemy in his weak points is not accepted even by a malicious person like Śiśupāla. According to him the valorous person does not attack the enemy in his loophole like a thief.[60]

Though we come across some rare cases of neglecting the ethical rules of warfare, these cases do not make less the importance and influence of the moral side of warfare; because waging of war without regard to moral standards degraded the institution into mere animal ferocity.[61] In this connection we may say that our texts lean towards *smṛti* tradition which teaches a high ethical standard and rules of warfare.[62] It was recogniszed by the victorious warriors that unrighteous way bars the merits of a conquering king.[63] So much importance was given to observe the ethical standards in the warfare by the conquering monarchs.[64] Wars were fought at any cost but with any method.

The mbitious kings in the *Pañamahākāvyas* were strictly observing the code of warriors because they were desirous of *Dharmavijaya*. Kālidāsa specifically speaks of

---

59. Raghu XV.17 Nai XVII.23
60. Śiśu XVI.52
    प्रहितः प्रधनाय माधवानहमाकारयितुं महीभृताः ।
    न परेषु महौजसश्छलादपकुर्वन्ति मलिम्लुचा इव ॥
61. V.R.R.Dikshitar, War in Ancient India, Published by University of Madras, 1994. p.58
62. MS VII.91 to 94. SN IV.II 76 to 78
63. Kirā XIII.29
64. Śiśu XIX.60
    आपदि व्यापृतनयास्तथा युयुधिरे नृपा ।
    आप दिव्या पृतनया विस्मयं जनता यथा ॥

the kings as 'dharmavijayī'.[65] They conquered the world through righteous warfare and they were satisfied with the acknowledgment of their overlordship. This conquest was only for the purpose of earning reputation and the victorious monarchs were not in favour of annihilating the captured foes or annexing their territories. Though the kings in the *Pañcamahākāvyas* accepted the idea of conquest, after conquering the territories, the kings restored peaceful relations with the subdued enemy. In Raghuvaṁśa, we see Rāma, giving the kingdom of Lankā back to Vibhīṣana, the brother of the conquered monarch. So it was an important practice of Hindu international morality that a king having conqered the capital of his foe invested there a prince of royal race. Manu also states that a victorious king should install the successor of the dead king.[66]

It was a well established maxim of the ancient Hindu statecraft that a victor should continue the laws, beliefs and customs of the vanquished people and instead of destroying the defeated dynasty, he should be content with their submission and tribute. This policy is described as one of 'uprooting' and 'replanting'.[67] As Dr. R.N. Dandekar remarks : Extension of imperial power with a view to impose to culture of the conqueror on the vanquished people and the exploit them economically was almost unknown in ancient India. It was sheerly for the exhibition of the conqueror's valour -Parākrama that several states were brought under the control of a single authority."[68] The conquering

---

65. Raghu IV.43
गृहीतप्रतिमुक्तस्य स धर्मविजयी नृपः।
श्रियं महेन्द्रनाथस्य जहार न तु मेदिनीम् ॥

66. MS VII.202

67. Raghu IV.36/37

68. R.N. Dandekar, The Age of the Guptas and other Essays, Ajanta Publications, Delhi 1982, p.5

monarchs followed the maxim that a defeated king should neither be deprived of his life nor be dethroned. He should be forced to accept the suzerainty of the conqueror and if he agrees to do so he should be allowed to rule as usual. This was the Kautilyan ideal of *dharmavijaya*.

In 'dharmavijaya' a conquering king was satisfied with the acknowledgment of his overlordship by the inferior. In 'Lobhavijaya' the aim of the conqueror was to covet the territory and treasure of the enemy and in the *Asuravijaya* the enemy was captured and deprived of his kingdom, treasure sons and wives or he was slain and his country was reduced to ashes.[69] Thus, the first mode of conquest was always preferred by the monarchs in the *Pañcamahākāvyas*. They did not desire to conquer the earth by unfair means. They knew that the unrighteous conquest was temporary, uncertain and unstable and it does not lead to heaven.[70] As the kings wanted to establish their overlordship through the conquest, they were contented by the tributes offered by the defeated kings. King Raghu in his world-conquest took away the wealth but not the territory of king of Mahendra. He captured him but subsequently released because he was compassionate towards the bowing kings. Only hearing of the valour of Raghu the kings could not bear his lustre and they offered tribute of pearls to Raghu. He assured safety to them who begged

---

69. Commentary of Vallabha on Raghu 4.43
यः शत्रुं निर्जित्य तदीयां नृपश्रियं नीत्वा तस्मिन्नैव स्थाने स्थापयति स धर्मविजयी । यः शत्रुं निर्जित्य तदीयां श्रियं मेदिनीं च गृहीत्वा प्राणैर्न विकुरुते स लोभविजयी । यः शत्रुं हत्वा तदीयां श्रियं मेदिनी च गृह्णाति सः असुरविजयी इति ।

70. ŚP (Critical Edition by BORI) 97.2
अधर्मयुक्तो विजयो अध्रुवोऽस्यवर्ग्य अेव च ।
सादयत्येष राजा नं महीं च भरतर्षभ् ॥

for it.[71] Thus Raghu conquered the earth fixing the pillars of his victory, accepting the tributes from the defeated and making a seal of his overlordship on the conquered territories. Thus raising a mountain of fame was their ideal; and they were satisfied only with the acknowledgement of their unchallenged mastery over the earth.[72]

The feudatories accepted the administration and orders of the conquerors, like a flowery garland on their heads. They bowdown to the commands by the monarch like the orders by god Indra.[73] They offer precious tributes to him. The conquering monarchs accepted the medium policy, not too harsh, not too mild, to control the feudatories.[74] The feudatory kings saved themselves by following the course of a cane.[75] This bending down like a cane made them safe from the monarch. The practice and usage of the feudatories with the conquerors which is frequently described in the *Pañcamahākāvyas* clearly exhibit the monarchs as *dharmavijayī*.

Dharmavijaya was an arbitrary division from the moral and religious stand-points which were highly valued by the monarchs in the *Pañcamahākāvyas*. So the monarchs desirous of dharmavijaya strictly followed the code of ethics enjoined upon warriors. The experts in the polity used to teach the princes both good and bad modes of warfare but the princes employed only the

---

71. Raghu IV.64
अपनीत शिरस्त्राणाः शेषास्तं हि शरणं ययुः ।
प्रणिपातप्रतीकारः संरम्भो हि महात्मनाम् ॥

72. ibid

73. Nai XII.18; XII.80 Ragu VI.33; IX.13; XVIII.79

74. Raghu VIII.9

75. ibid. IV.35

former mode of warfare and never the latter.[76] The kings fought always in the right way though they were skillful in the art of fraudulent warfare.[77] The kings of the solar race were confident about their valour and the right path of warfare that the goddess of victory always blessed them. It seems that *Kūtayuddha* though deprecated as unrighteous, became an accepted mode of warfare under *Hindu* Military science and a regular training was imparted to the warriors of this type.

In this context, it is worthy to note that this policy of righteous warfare was handled by the kings with limitations, so much so that it might not conduce to a defeat. World-conquest was their ideal. The kings were prudent enough to pay the enemy in his own coin. If the enemy resorted to unrighteous and intriguing methods of war, they could also resort to similar methods and struck the enemy down. One is not to be blamed for employing unfair means against a deceitful enemy. If the enemy practised unrighteous warfare the defender must also resort to it. This was the policy of the conquerors. So the warriors were taught every mode of warfare. For the defence purpose the unrighteous warfare was permissible and the defender resorted to it only if, he found the opponent resorting to it. Otherwise it was forbidden. In Śiśupālavadha, Kṛṣṇa becomes ready to meet Śiśupāla in the same manner in which he wanted to meet.[78] In the tough battle the weapons of Śiśupāla proved to be futile against Kṛṣṇa and Śiśupāla followed the way of fraudulous

---

76. Raghu IV.10
नयविद्भिर्नवे राज्ञि सदसच्धोपदर्शितम् ।
पूर्व अेवाभवत्पक्षस्तन्नाभवदुत्तरः ॥

77. ibid. XVII.69
कूटयुद्धविधिज्ञेऽपि तस्मिन्सन्मार्गयोधिनि ।
भेजेऽभिसारिकावृत्तिं जयश्रीर्वीरगामिनी ॥

78. Śiśu XVI.33

warfare by employing missiles.[79] So Kṛṣṇa had to resort to the same method only to give an answer to the enemy in his own coin. This policy, which may be named as defensive policy, advocated while attacking the antagonists, is accepted by the ancient thinkers on polity. According to Kāmandaka a king should fight openly and fairly if the circumstances are in his favour. He should have recourse to the war of intrigues only if the case be just the contrary.[80] Thus, though the defenders of righteous warfare, the kings were ready to fight the unrighteous warfare, to acquire the ultimate goal viz. victory in the war. In Kirātārjunīyam, Draupadī, the strong supporter of this 'tit for tat policy', could not bear the peace-policy of Yudhiṣṭhira. According to her, the unrighteous means also are to be used by one to face the deceitful enemy.

This unjust method of warfare viz. *'Kūṭayuddha'* was the common practice of the treacherous enemies demons and Rākṣasas. In Kirātārjunīyam it is described that the demon named Mūka came to attack in the form of a bear.[81] As demon named Subāhu was wandering by same intrigue and was killed by Rāma by his sword.[82] Lakṣmaṇa firstly heard a sweet sound of the demoness Śūrpaṇakhā but then heard her dreadful sound like a she-jackal and recognized that the was a demoness.[83] Afterwards, Rāma was deceived by Rāvaṇa who through Mārīca taking a deceitful form of a deer, kidnaped Sīta[84]

79. Śiśu XX.32

80. KN XIX. 54
विशिष्टो देशकालाभ्यां भिन्नारिप्रकृतिर्बली ।
कुर्यात्प्रकाशयुद्धं च कूटयुद्धं विपर्यये ॥

81. Kirā XII.37; XIII.9

82. Raghu XI.29

83. ibid. XII.39

84. Raghu XII.53

In the actual battle of Lankā, Rāvaṇa again showing an illusive cut-off head of Rāma, frightened Sītā[85]

Thus war of intrigues was a common method of the deceitful enemies; and it was necessary for the righteous kings to be expert in Kūṭayuddha to react the treacherous enemies.

SENĀPATI :

Senāpati or commander-in-chief was an important officer of the army. He was the chief of the heads of various units of the army.[86] A significant place of Senāpati seems from the fact that a poetic muse of Kālidāsa inspired him to compose Kumārasmhbhava, which exhibits a necessity of a divine commander-in-chief for gods. Without an able leader it was difficult for the gods to acquire success against Tārakāsura. The gods were in need of a competent leader, who could assure them victory against their enemy. When the kingdom of gods was overrun by Tārakāsura, they prayed for the rise of their Saviour, that came to them in the form of Kumāra, who proved to be a prudent leader of the gods.

The qualifications of the commander-in-chief are clearly revealed in the *Pañcamahākāvyas*, prominently in Kumārasaṁbhava. The commander-in-chief should create a faith among the followers.[87] the gods believed that Indra would gain success under the command of a leader of the army.[88] Senāpati leads the army and protects it himself staying with the army like a shadow

85. ibid. XII.72 to 74.
86. Ku XV.7
87. Ku XIII.15
88. ibid XII.52
गोप्तारं सुरसैन्यानां यं पुरस्कृत्य गोत्रभित् ।
प्रत्यानेष्यति शत्रुभ्यो बन्दीमिव जयश्रियम् ॥

of a great tree staying with it.[89] It is very necessary for a Senāpati to have a great confidence about his own power.[90] A competent general is able to guess the power and capacity of the opposite side. Only a sight of the leader creates an enthusiasm and hope of success among the warriors. His presence on the battlefield causes to increase the power of they army.[91] The soldiers bear courage by the stimulating words of the leader and rise up for war like getting support of the shore.[92]

The leader makes an encouraging speech, reminding the soldiers of their duty as warriors. In Kirātārjunīyam we come across a model speech of the Senāpati to the dipressed army losing courage due to defeat from the skilled warrior Arjuna. He addresses the army not to leave the battlefield, because the consequences of fleeing from the battlefield are infamy and reproach. He says the lustrous swords laugh at you. There is no greater sin for a warrior than flight from the battlefield. The enemy is a mere human being, so it is not proper to runaway in the fear of the enemy. It is better not to enter the battlefield than to flee away from the fight. The enemy is devoid of any war- vehicles, so there is nothing to be afraid of. Your lord is supporting you. Why then are you leaving your valour and self- respect ? Our enemy, being alone, is not trembling at all. So it is not proper for you to abandon valour and courage which has reached the apex.[93] These words of en-

---

89. Kirā XV.33
स बमार रणापेतां चमूं पश्चादवस्थितम् ।
पुरःसूर्यादपावृत्तां छायामिव महातरुः ॥

90. Ku XIII.16
शक्तिर्ममासावहतप्रचारा प्रभावसारा सुमहःप्रसारा ।
स्वर्लोकलभ्या विपदावहाऽरेः शिरो हरन्ती दिशतान्मुदं वः ॥

91. Ku XIII.51; XV.51

92. Kirā XV.31/32

93. Kirā XV.7 to 28

couragement pleased the army like a shower of snow.[94] Thus protection and encouragement of the frightened army is the chief duty of a *Senāpati.*

A Senāpati should be trained in the knowledge of the science of warfare. By employing the unknown means and policies he creates dissension in the enemy-circle.[95] Kauṭilya, while stating the qualifications and duties of Senāpati has specially mentioned the tactics of dissension According to him Senāpati must be thoroughly versed in all kinds of tactical and strategical modes of warfare, skilled in handling weapons of war and deciding action or inaction in the circumstances of situation. He must also study the advantage or otherwise of the ground, the time and strength of his force, sow seeds of dissension among the enemy-troops. He should collect his own army engaged in different directions, order an advance or retreat and assail fortresses.[96]

In the battlefield the commander aims at the strategical position of the army in its various divisions. He employs different troops in their proper places. This highest military officer viz. commander-in-chief was variously known as *Senāpati, Vāhinīpati, Camūpati,* etc. He should pay a special heed to the maintenance of

---

94. ibid. XV.30
मुनीषुदहनातप्तांल्लज्जया निविवृत्सतः।
शिवः प्रल्हादयामास तान्निषेधहिमाम्बुना ॥

95. ibid. XVII.27
विभेदमन्तः पदवीनिरोधं विध्वंसन चाविदितप्रयोगः।
नेताऽरिलोकेषु करोति यद्यतत्तच्चकारास्य शरेषु शंभुः ॥

96. KA II.33.9/10
तदेव सेनापतिः सर्वयुद्धहरणविद्याविनीतो हस्त्यश्वरधचर्या
संपुष्टश्चतुरसङगस्य बलस्यानुष्ठानाधिष्ठानं विद्यात् ।
स्वभूमिं युद्धकालं प्रस्थनीकमिन्नभेदनं भिन्नसंधानं
संहतमेदनं भिन्नवधं दुर्गवधं यात्राकालं च पश्येत् ॥

discipline in his army not merely in camping and marching but also in the thick of battle.

A ceremony of Abhīṣeka took place in the case of commander-in-chief. We come across a graphic picture of the commencement of marching of the army under the leadership of Kumāra.[97] His coronation for commandership also is described in Kumārasaṁbhava.[98] The marching army was led by Kumāra who wore the dress fit for a commander-in-chief. He received blessings of elder persons. He was connated by the tears from his mother's eyes. The king of the gods, as a special honour to the commander-in-chief, exchanged the garments which is called Niruñchana The Creator admired Kumāra and offered him blessings. All the gods offered best wishes to him. The sage Nārada also made *'Niruñchana'* to Kumāra. Some honourable sages performed holy rites. Kumāra bowed down to sage Kāśyapa, other ascetics, chaste women and queen of Lord Indra. All of them offered him blessings for acquiring victory.

Then the *Abhiṣeka* ceremony was performed. The great archer Kumāra mounted the great chariot named *Vijitvava*..[99] The golden umbrella was held by th gods on his head. he was fanned by the *Chowri*. The *Siddhas* and *Kinnaras* were singing panegyrics of the *Senāpati*. He was followed by Indra who was properly dressed and was mounted on *Airāvata* elephant. All other gods as Agni, Yama, Varuṇa, Marut, Kubera followed their *Senāpati*.

Thus a much praiseworthy and honourable position was offered to the commander-in-chief, who was the doner of victory to his army. Killing of the Senāpati

---

97. Ku XII.56
98. Ku XIIIth Canto.
99. ibid. XIV.2

was regarded in the Mahābhārata as the most eventful incident. The warrior, who killed the commander of enemy's force and rode upon chariot of his fallen antagonist, was regarded as Viṣṇu in prowess and Bṛhaspati in intelligence.[100] The commander-in-chief is required to be confident, endowed with intelligence and fertitude, devoted and able. Leadership is one of the requirements on which depends the success in battlefield. Unity of the army in the battlefield is a very important requirement[101] which is effected by the commander-in-chief. He thus occupies an important position in the military department of the state.

ARMY was accorded a recognised position in the state organism. Army was counted as one of the seven limbs of the body politic. It is stated before that acquiring the title *Cakravartin* war the foremost ideal of the kings in the *Pañcamahākāvyas*. So the frequency of arranging expeditions of conquests and other causes of was necessitated the building of army-organization on most scientific lines. For the above-mentioned purposes and for the protection of the subjects, a huge standing army was a requisite of king's administration.[102] For maintaining internal peace also military organization was necessary. In the commencement of the expeditions, the capitals of the kings were well protected. A relation of the army to the state is compared by ancient thinkers, with that of the mind to a man. As without mind human organization can not work, so without army, state organization comes to a stand-still.[103]

---

100. ŚP (Critical Edition by BORI) 99.41
यस्तु सेनापतिं हत्वा तद्यानमधिरोहति ।
विष्णुविक्रमक्रामी बृहस्तपतिसमः ऋतुः ॥

101. Śiśu XVII.59

102. Nai XVI.9

103. ŚN IV.466

The soldiers and warriors in the army were highly qualified. They proved their valour in the battlefield. They were mighty in spirit, regarding personal honour as their wealth. They were distinguished in battles and wished to accomplish the objects of their kings at the cost of their lives. They were loyal to their masters. As the army was properly paid and honoured with money gifts[104] there was no discontent in them. The kings were aware of the fact that, if army properly paid and rewarded and if it had not any financial difficulty, it could exhibit valour at its best. The kings appreciated the services of the soldiers after their respective duties and felt regret if any of the soldiers died without felicitation and honour by his hands[105] The warrior also considered it as his defeat if he died in the battlefield without having hououred by his master.[106] The qualifications of the army are stated by Kauṭilya. According to him it was the best army well trained in all arts and modes of warfare and also in the handling and application of weapons and which never loses its sense of obedience and loyalty to the king.[107] In Agnipurāṇa it is stated that a good army should be hereditary, loyal, compact regularly paid and must belong to the families famous for bravery.[108]

Traditionally the army consisted of four component parts. viz. Infantry, Cavalry, Elephants and war-cars. The term *Caturaṅgabala* and the allusions to the four divisions of army are profusely available in the

---

104. Kirā I.19
महौजसो मानधना धनर्चिताधनुर्भृतः संयति लब्धकीर्तयः।
नसंहतास्तस्य नभिन्नवृत्तयः प्रियाणि वाञ्छन्त्यसुभिः समीहितुम् ॥

105. Śiśu XIX.57

106. ibid. XIX.58

107. KA IX.2

108. AP 239.31 to 33.

Pañcamahākāvyas.[109] In Raghuvaṁśa an army is mentioned with its six parts.[110] So we should consider here the six divisions along with the traditional four divisions. The constituents of the army are described in the descriptions of the battles. So in dealing with the epics, one must make due allowance for the poetic effusions.

Infantry was an efficient and strong part of army. It was believed that victory ever attends the army where foot-soldiers are numerically strong.[111] The vastness of the army was frequently compared to that of an ocean. Being the most numerous part of the army, the foot-soldiers sometimes decided the fortunes of battles by the sheer weight of their numbers. In Śiśupālavadha the infantry is described as armed with swords and shields.[112] The types of warriors due to their holding of various weapons are mentioned. A warrior, who used *Śakti* or lance was named as *Śāktika*[113] A killer of thousand of men in the battle was attributed as *Sahasrapūraṇa.*[114]

Cavalry was a second prominent constituent of the army.[115] It represents mobility of the army. Enemies at the distance easily come within the grasp of the warrior.

---

109. Raghu IV.30; Kirā VI.16; Nai XII.66; Śiśu XV 77 to 80; XVI. 69; XII.23.

110. Raghu IV.26 XVII.67
स गुणानां बलानां च षण्णां षण्मुखविक्रमः ।
बभूव विनियोगज्ञः साधनीयेषु वस्तुषु ॥

111. AP 228.7
सेना पदातिबहुला शत्रूञ्जयति सर्वदा ।

112. Śiśu XVIII.4; XIX.21; XIX.25

113. ibid. XIX.59

114. ibid. XIX.51

115. Raghu IV.62; IV.71
सङ्ग्रामस्तुमुलस्तस्य पाश्चात्यैरश्वसाधनैः ।
शाङ्र्गकूजितविज्ञेयप्रतियोधे रजस्यभूत् ॥

Ascending of the mountains was done with army of horses. Chargers or war- horses were well-known for speed.[116] There is a poetic description of the speed of the horse engaged in war.[117] Kāmbojan horses exceeded other horses in speed The horses from the North-East of India were celebrated for their horse-breed.[118] The countries famous for horses were *Āratta*[119] and *Bālhi.*[120] Horses were classified according to their breed. In the war, the horse of good breed was not afraid of advancing as long as the rider was on its back, fighting with lances.[121]

Horses were considered auspicious or inauspicious according to the colour of their body and a location of twist on their body. An excellent horse bears various locks of hair on its body.[122] The horse typed as Śrīvṛkśakī was considered very auspicious granting wealth and good progeny. In Śukranīti we get an elaborate list of the characteristics of a noble horse and of the various auspicious and inauspicious marks.[123] Horses are described as the sons of Lakṣmī[124]

As horse was an important factor of the royal possession of army, it was necessary for the king to

---

116. Nai XI.127
अेतद्वलैः क्षणिकतामपि भूखुराग्रस्पर्शयुषां रयरसादसमापयद्भिः।
द्ववपेयकेवलनभः क्रमणप्रवाहैर्वाहिरैलुप्यत सहस्त्रगर्वगर्वः॥
117. ibid. XII.99
118. Raghu V.73
119. Śiśu V.10
120. ibid. V.54
121. ibid. XVIII.23
कुन्तेनोच्चैः सादिना हन्तुमिष्ठान्नाजानेयो दन्तिनस्त्रस्यति स्म।
क्मोदारं कीर्तये कर्तुकामान्किंवा जात्याः स्वामिनो ह्लेपयन्ति॥
122. Śiśu V.4
123. ŚN IV.7. 42 to 52 75 to 110.
124. Śiśu XV.78

know Hypology or the science of horses. In Śiśupālavadha and Naiṣadhīyacarita many details of great advance about the science of horses are frequently seen. King Nala was the expert in knowing the instincts of horses. [125] A regular training was given to horses to prepare them for war. A trained horse is termed as *Sthūrīprṣtha* while the untrained horse is called *Durmukha*.[126] The trainer of the horse should be skilful in using the various types of bridles.[127] The horses prepared for war were well equipped and decorated. Armours were placed on the bodies of the horses.[128] Saddle[129] and bridle[130] were the equipments used for horses. Small jingling bells were tied round the horses neck.[131] A chowrie was tied on both the sides of horses neck. Golden rings were placed on the leathern straps.[132] Beautiful trappings were placed on the body of the horse.[133]

Various gaits of the horses are described in *Śiśupālavdha*. The gait in general is named as *Dhārā* Other gaits also are mentioned as *Mukha, Vikrama, Dhaurita, Urmi* etc.[134] The horses were being actually taken out to practice the movements. Galloping of the

---

125. Nai V.60, XIII.43
126. Śiśu XVIII.22
127. Śiśu v.60
   अव्याकुल प्रकृतमुत्तरधेयकर्मध्चारा: प्रसाधयितुमव्यतिकीर्णरूपा: ।
   सिद्धं मुखे नवसु वीथिसु कश्चिदश्वं वल्गाविभागकुशलो गमयाम्बभूव ॥
128. Raghu IV.56
129. Śiśu V.53
130. ibid. V.56
131. ibid. V.58
132. ibid. XVIII.5
133. ibid. XVII.36
134. Śiśu V.60; V.4; XVII.36; XVIII.5

horse and other movements are referred in Raghuvaṁśa and Naiṣadhīyacarita.[135]

Like the horses elephants also played a major part in the warfare described in the *Pañcamahākāvyas*. Elephants, was a prominent part of the army and it had occupied a first rank in the military service.[136] Elephants were specially trained by the professors of elephantine science.[137] Elephants were taught placing a golden mount in the middle of the ground.[138] Elephant trainers developed a code of technical terms in various parts of the country. Māgha has a reference to driver's speaking words of encouragement do the elephants.[139] Rivers were crossed with the army on a bridge made of elephants.[140]

The elephants resembling mountains in their height, were strong enough to bear the yoke of war.[141] Elephants were occasionally employed to batter the gates of forts.[142] It was the most important function of the war-elephants. These animals were particularly trained for this purpose. At a given signal from their leader tney rushed impetuously towards the walls and pressed themselves against them. A prominent position of the

135. Raghu IX.51 Nai I.73
136. Raghu IV.40; VI.54; VII.59
137. Raghu VI.27, Kirā XVI.2 Nai XII.82
138. Śiśu XIX.65
139. ibid. XVIII.10
घण्टानादो निस्वनो डिण्डिमानां ग्रैवेयाणामारवो बृंहितानि ।
आमेतीव प्रत्यवोचन् गजानामुत्साहाय वाचमाधोरणस्य ॥
140. Raghu IV.38; XVI.33
141. Kirā XVI.2
मदस्रुतिश्यामितगण्डलेखाः क्रमन्ति विक्रान्तनराधिरुढाः ।
सहिष्णवो नेह युधामभिज्ञा नागा नगोच्छ्रायमिवाक्षिपन्तः ॥
142. ibid. XVI.36
महास्त्रदुर्गे शिथिलप्रयत्नं दिग्वारणेनैव परेण रुग्णे ।
भुजङ्गपाशान्भुजवीर्यशाली प्रबन्धनाय प्रजिघाय जिष्णुः ॥

elephants seems from their being in front of the army.[143] Elephants rush as eager for the commencement of the battle. On the boundry line of the vanguard, numerous trumpeting elephants gaily put forth, their roar.

Elephants, classified as *'Gambhīravedin'* are specifically referred in Raghuvaṁśa. After planting a sharp goad in the head of the elephant, it does not mind the pricking of the goad.[144] According to Rājaputrīya quoted by Mallinātha,[145] it means an elephant, which does not know even when there is some injury to the sting or a flow of blood from the body or a slight cut of flesh.

So it is on elephants that the destruction of an enemy's army depends. Elephants form a chief beauty of the army. Elephants are a decoration of the camp and they acquire desired victory to the king.[146] For, elephants being of large bodily frame are able not only to destroy the arranged army of the enemy, his fortifications and encampments but also to undertake works that are dangerous to life.

In the tumult of war, elephants fight furiously. A fight between two elephants is mentioned frequently.[147] Sometimes the elephants, feared by the war- harangues by the warriors, turn away, not controlled even by goad. Like horses, elephants were bedecked with ornaments

---

143. Raghu VI.54, Nai XIII 22.23.24

144. Raghu IV.39 स प्रतापं महेन्द्रस्य मूर्ध्नि तीक्ष्णं व्यवेशयत् ।
अङ्कुशं द्विरदस्येव यन्ता गम्भीरवेदिनः ॥

145. Quoted by Mallinātha from Rājaputrīya.
त्वग्भेदच्छोणितस्त्रावान्मांसस्य क्रथनादपि ।
आत्मानं यो न जानाति स स्याद्गम्भीरवेदिता ॥
चिरकालेन यो वेत्ति शिक्षां परिचितामपि ।
गम्भीरवेदी विद्धेयः स गजो गजवेदिभिः ॥ मृगचर्मीये ।

146. KA II.2.13 हस्तिप्रधानो विजयो राज्ञः ।

147. Śiśu XVI.69, XVIII.32. XIX.66

and jingling bells.[148] Collyrium paints were applied to the large bodies of the elephants and their heads were painted with vermilion paint or red chalk.[149] A golden chain was tied around the neck of the elephant.[150] An elephant is said to live for 120 years. There are twelve stages in his life each of ten years. The fourth stage is the prime youth of an elephant.[151] Other stages as *bālaka,*[152] *Viṣka*[153] also are referred. The elephant named Vyāla is very strong and cruel.[154]

The elephants were not killed except in wars.[155] As the elephants played a great part in the battles, the kings were very grateful to them as they assisted the kings in the battles.[156] Rutted elephants which were gifted as presents from the kings, was a sign of prosperity of the monarch.[157] Daśaratha's army with elephants and horses dashing forth with great speed only proclaimed his victory.[158] While describing the campaigns of Raghu, the mighty elephant forces of Kalinga and Aṇga kings are described.[159]

War-cars was the fourth limb of the ancient army. The chariot was carried by a charioteer, but charioteering

---

148. Raghu XII.41 Śiśu XIX.36/80 Ku XIV.26; XIV.47
149. Nai XII. 36; XIII.23 Śiśu XVII.13
150. Śiśu XVII.69
151. ibid. XVIII.6
    सान्द्ररत्ववकास्तल्पलाश्लिष्टकक्षा आङ्गीं शोभामाप्नुवन्तश्चतुर्थीम् ।
    कल्पस्यान्ते मारुतेनोपनुन्नाश्चेलुश्चण्डं गण्डशैला इवेमाः ॥
152. ibid. V.47
153. ibid. XVIII.27
154. ibid. XVIII.48
155. Raghu IX.74
156. ibid. IX.65
157. Kirā I.16
158. Raghu IX.10
159. Raghu IV.40/83; VI.54

also formed a part of warrior's military training. King Nala was fond of driving a chariot and he was an excellent charioteer.[160] Charioteer in india had an honorable position. Even the charioteers acted as councillors of the masters. They had occupied a place of honour on different occasions. Sumantra, the charioteer of Daśaratha enjoyed a great esteem with the royal household.

A chief duty of a charioteer was to lead the war-chariot and to shield his master. When the swoon caused by the strike of enemy's weapons was over, the warriors were kept secure in their chariots by the charioteers.[161] In the battlefield the charioteer drives the chariot at proper place.[162] A great skill of a charioteer consists in leading the horses in his charge in such circles as to avoid the shafts of the enemies from any quarter. "His true art says Hopkins, "consisted in wheeling and turning in bringing the car rapidly about so as to attack the antagonist with such speed from all quarters that the chariot seemed to advance from all sides at once.[163] The warchariot is equipped with weapons. (Ku XV.31). The chariot is distinguished by the top of its banner.[164] We come across the poetic description of the running chariots, the dust arising by the wheels and covering the sky.[165] Thus chariot was a very important apparatus of war. It attracted the minds of warriors. Well-known warriors were the chariot-

---

160. Nai V.60; XVI.24
161. Raghu VII.44
162. Ku XV.44
163. Hopkins, Quoted by V.R.R. Dikshitar, War in Ancient India, Published by University of Madras, 1944.
164. Raghu VII.60
165. Kirā XVI.6 Raghu IV.82 Ku XIV.19

fighters. The chariot fighters were known as *Mahārathas.*[166]

Though it was accustomed to use the term 'fourfold army' in the context of the ancient army, one cannot neglect, one more important department of the army viz. Navy which is specially mentioned in Raghuvaṁśa. There are many references to ships employed as instruments of war. Kālidāsa clearly refers to the fact that Raghu routed the forces of Baṅga which were ready with their navy.[167] In his expedition of world conquest, Raghu marched on Pearsia through the land route and not by sea-route; it shows that latter was a more common route. The actual way of crossing rivers appears to have been by maans of boats. The armies were transported across the rivers by means of boats.[168] In Śiśupalavadha also we find an elaborate description of the crossing the river by the army. Firstly elephants, then horses, was the order of crossing the river.[169] In the world conquest, Raghu erected the triumphal columns in the stream of Ganga , which shows his victory over the water.

The ancient thinkers had taken for granted the necessity of naval department. According to Manu, boats should be employed for military purposes, when the theatre of hostilities abounded in water.[170] When

166. Mallinatha on Kirā XVI.14
आत्मानं सारथिं चाश्वान् रक्षन्युध्येत यो नरः।
स महारथसंज्ञः स्यादित्याहुर्नीतिकोविदाः॥

167. Raghu IV.36
वङ्गानुत्साय तरसा नेता नौसाधनोद्यतान्।
निचरवान जयस्तम्भान्गङ्गास्त्रोतोन्तरेषु सः॥

168. Raghu IV.31 Śiśu XII.71

169. Śiśu XII.72/73

170. MS VII.192
स्यन्दनाश्वैः समे युद्धेयदनूपे नौद्विपैस्तथा।
वृतगुल्मावृते चापैरसिचर्मायुधैः स्थले॥

Kauṭilya mentions a special *Nāvādhyakṣa,* he seems to have taken for granted that kings possessed an elaborate naval department, During the epoch of the imperial Guptas a naval force was maintained by the state as is evident from the inscriptions. The *Allahabad Praśasti* of Samudragupta refers to his conquest of several islands.[171]

All these evidences clearly show that the tradition of the naval fight was unanimous. In *ŚāntiParavan* a verse mentions navy as one of the limbs of complete army.[172] A reference of *Auḍaka Durga* also reveals the fact that there is a necessity of the organization of a naval force. Thus naval warfare was not unknown in ancient India, though it was not as widely practised as land warfare. But the military significance of the rivers was rightly understood by Indians. the balloon-shaped boats were also used for navigation.[173]

There are also allusions to the use of flying machines, but they are not connected with actual warfare.

(1) When Rāvaṇa was flying with Sītā in his aerial-car to Lankā, Jatāyu, a giant bird charged him and his car and this led to a duet between the bird and the Rākṣasa-king.

(2) After the great victory of Rāma Vibhīṣaṇa presented him the *puspaka Vimāna.* Rāma flew to his capital Ayodhyā pointing to Sītā from above the places

---

171. Corpus. Ins. Ind. III p.14 quoted by V.R.R. Dikshitar, War in Ancient India Published by University of Madras 1944; p.289

172. Ś P (Critical Edition by BORI) 59.41
रथा नागा हयाश्चैव पादाज्ञाश्चैव पाण्डव ।
विष्टिर्नावश्चराश्चैव देशिकाः पथि चाष्टकम् ॥

173. Raghu XVII.68

of encapment, the town Kiṣkindhā and others on the way.[174]

Due to another classification of army, it is mentioned as sixfold army.[175] This classification is based on the source of recruitment. These are as follows: Hereditary troops *(Maula)*, Mercenaries (Bhṛṭa) Gild levies (Śreṇies), Soldiers supplied by feudatory chiefs or allies (सुहृद्बलम्)Troops captured or won over from enemies (द्विषद्बलम्) forest tribes.(अटवीबलम् ।)

The large army of the conquering monarchs was consisted of the abovementioned sources. Rāma fought the great battle of Lankāa, with the great monkey army which was given by Surīva, the friend of Rāma.

In the description of warfare, there is no direct reference of the department of commissariat. But cutting off the supplies of the opponents was an accepted method of strategy, which is stated by Balarāma in Śiśupālavadha.[176] It shows the presence of the department of commissariat The services of the Commissariat were valuable when the cities or fortresses were besieged.

Thus the army with all these divisions, was a prominent part of king's *daṇḍa* power. The minute details about the constituents of the army, shows that the science of warfare was much advanced in the period of the *Pañcamahākāvyas*.

ON THE BATTLEFIELD :

Though the accounts of battles described in the *Pañcamahakāvyas* were in a most conventional way, they create a live picture of the battlefield, before our eyes.

---

174. Raghu XII.103; XIII.1
175. ibid. IV.26; XVII.67
176. Śiśu II.64

At the time of war-breaking a formal declaration of hostilities was made by means of war-drums, *dundubhi* and other martial musical instruments. The army waited until the war-drums were beaten. Conches were blown and banners were unfurled which signalized the start of the hostilities.[177] The soldiers get together after hearing the noise of conch.[178] Conches were blown even in th midst of battles. The warriors return hearing the noise of the conch. Warriors wear their armour in battles.[179]

The valour of the warriors is exhibited on the battlefield. The battlefield seems to be a pleasure-place for them. As a wall between two infuriated elephants is common to both so in tough fight the future fortune of victory becomes common to both the parties on account of displaying valours. In the case of Arjuna, the armour which was loose for him due to the weakness on account of the performance of penance, became fit for him because of the commencement of battle.[180] In the thick of the battle the warriors make loud noise and harangues.[181] The trumpet sound is mingled with the noises. It is again mixed with the noise by huge chariots and elephants having bells around their necks.[182] There seems to be a competition of the noise of wheels of chariots, horses and infuriated elephants.[183]

The warriors utter the names of their respective masters. In the thick dust, the distinct knowledge of

177. Raghu VII.38
178. ibid IX.64
179. Kira III.58; XVI.12 Raghu XII.86; VII.48/56/66
180. Kirā XIV.48
181. Raghu XVII.50
182. Ku XIV.26
183. Kirā XVI.8

one's party is due to the uttering of the names.[184] The warriors start the fight uttering their own names.[185] A presence of bards on the battlefield is important for creating and increasing enthusiasm in the soldiers. They sing the songs of victory.[186] the eager warriors hear their praise, standing a bit before the bards and prepare for war.[187] By the fearful harangues the elephants are infuriated and do not mind the goads.[188] the lustre of the warrior resembles that of god 'Śiva' in the sacrificial ceremony of King Dakṣa.[189]

The battlefield appears to be a drinking-room of Death.[190] After cutting of the heads of the warriors, seeing their dancing bodies, the horses are feared and throw away the warriors on their back.[191] The vultures with their sharp points of nails catch the falling elephantmen.[192] A *bali* is offered asif to the city of battlefield.[193] The body of the thousand-killer dances after cutting of his head also.

The heavenly nymphs claim for the dying valorous warrior. The warriors are eager to test their loyalty for their master by not remaining in the rear of the battle.[194]

---

184. Raghu VIII.41
रथो रथाङ्गध्वनिना विजज्ञे विलोलघण्टावक्वणितेन नागः ।
स्वभर्तृनामग्रहणाद् बभूव सान्द्रे रजस्यात्मपरावबोधः ॥
185. Ku XV.48
186. Śiśu XVIII.16
वीर्योत्साहश्लाघि कृत्याऽवदानं सङ्ग्रामाग्रे मानिनां लज्जितानाम् ।
अज्ञातानां शत्रुभिर्युक्तमुच्चैः श्रीमन्नाम श्रावयन्ति स्म नग्नाः ॥
187. Ku XVI.4
188. ibid. XVI.23
189. Śiśu XIX.54
190. Raghu VII.49 Kirā XVI.16
191. Kirā XV.26
192. Raghu VII.46
193. Kirā XVII.62
194. Śiśu XIX.30

A warrior is very eager to acquire fame, which he considers to be more valuable than his life.[195]

FLAGS AND BANNERS :

Flag was a distinctive mark of a warrior. *'Dhvaja' 'Ketu' 'Patākā* were the expressions which were employed for flags. The war-chariots were marked with ensigns and banners.[196] On the top of the staff was placed the *'dhvaja'* or *'Ketu'* bearing an image. Flags were with various marks on them to distinguish them from others.[197] Every leader had his own insignia to distinguish on division from the other. This device avoided confusion in the ranks, both during the march of the army and in action in the battlefield. The enemies whose flags were previously marked were recognized by their opponents.[198] The cars were distinguished by the top of the banners.[199] Sometimes the staffs of the flags were made of gold.[200]

Flags and banners were such an essential feature of the army that in latter times the army came to be designated as *Dhvajinī*[201] or *Patākinī*. The row of the

---

195. ibid. XVIII.15
रोदोरन्ध्रं व्यश्नुवानानि लोलैरडगस्यान्तर्मादितैः स्थावराणि ।
केचिदगुर्वीमित्य संयन्निषद्यां क्रीणन्ति स्म प्राणमूल्यैर्यशांसि ॥

196. Nai XVII.6
ततान विद्युता तेषां रथे पीतपताकताम् ।
लब्धकेतुशिखोल्लेखा लेखा जलमुचः क्वचित् ॥

197. Śiśu V.20

198. Raghu VII.44
प्रहारमूर्च्छापगमे रथस्था यन्तॄनुपालभ्य निवर्तिताश्वान् ।
यैः सादिता लक्षितपूर्वकेतूंस्तानेव सामर्षयता निजघ्नुः ॥

199. ibid. VII.60

200. Ku XIV.14

201. Raghu IV.2; VII.40
Kirā XIII.9; XIV.26/27/58/62/64; XV.32
XVI.10/13; XVII.31

flags on the chariots is so large that the warrior seems to be menacing his enemies as it were with his flags.[202] The flags were so important that once a banner was captured or struck claim was made for success in the battle over the enemy.

VYŪHA (BATTLE ARRAY) :

An arrangement of the army in various shapes is called Battle- array. In Raghuvaṁśa one finds a mention of the array as both the armies arranged together for battle.[203] In Śiśupālavadha are the names of the arrays as *Śarvatobhardra, Cakra, Gomūtrikā,* crocodile shaped array etc.[204] When the battle order was so arranged as to face in all directions it was called *Śarvatobhardra*. Kauṭilya mentions that if the danger be apprehended from all sides it was necessary to form this type of array.[205]

An array was commonly divided into two parts : wing and centre. In the arrays, all the divisions of forces were arragned in such a way that there was a unanimous effect of opposition. So the arrays were formed for offering organized attacks. If the road on the route of the march was sufficiently broad it was recommended that the front ranks should march in a crocodile like order. Śiśupāla arranged this crocodile type of array which was broad in front and back.

The array should be formed into a perfect battle order even on the march. Though the arrays were practically in parts, yet all of them were not engaged at one and the same time. In Manusmṛti we find an

---

202. Raghu IV.28
203. ibid. VII.54
204. Śiśu XIX.41; XVI.67
205. KA X.2.9
पुरस्तादभ्याघाते मकरेण यायात् पश्चाच्छकटेन,
पार्श्वयोर्वज्रेण समन्ततः सर्वतोभद्रेण अेकायने सूच्या ।

information of different battle orders.[206] The epics give the impression that after the plunge into the fight, no battle-order whatever was maintained. As soon as the armies meet, there was complete disorder.

IMPORTANCE OF FORTIFICATIONS :

Impregnable forts and a highly trained army were the capital means of defence for the kingdom. *Ṛgveda,* the oldest literary record in India testifies to the prehistoric origin of the art of fortification. The *Dasyus* were the excellent builders of forts and had numerous forts. Śambara was said to have had ninety[207] or hundred[208] forts.

The forts are classified according to their location. The watery and mountain fortifications served the best as defences.[209] Manu has mentioned the mountain fort as the best means for defence.[210] A deep ditch around the fort was dug out to obstruct the passage of the enemy.[211]

A king who had a fort to shelter himself was considered as a strong and efficeint monarch. The real strength was in the fort. A king with meagre force could become powerful on account of the invincibility of the strong forts.

On account of forts, the sieze-warfare became an important part of the Indian warfare. Treasury and army

---

206. MS VII.187/188/191

207. Rg. I. 130.7

208. ibid. II.14.6

209. Nai VII.18 Śiśu XVIII.24

210. MS VII.71
सर्वेण तु प्रयत्नेन गिरिदुर्गं समाश्रयेत् ।
अेषां हि बहुगुण्येन गिरिदुर्गं विशिष्यते ॥

211. Raghu XII.66
श्रुत्वा रामः प्रियोदन्तं मेने तत्संगमोत्सुकः ।
महार्णवपरिक्षेपं लङ्कायाः परिखालघुम् ॥

were safely kept in the forts. The forts were fully equipped with the implements of war. It is from the fort that secret war, upkeep of the army, reception of allies and driving out of enemies were successfully carried out by the kings. So a king without a fort is compared to a snake without poison or an elephant without rut.

Defeat of a king, fortified in his metropolis was very difficult. The metropolis in ancient India was invariably surrounded by fortifications, either natural or artificial. These forts were very difficult to be assailed by the enemies,[212] and were specially prepared for the battle.[213] Various tactics were played by the enemies to open the gates of the forts. Generally elephants were employed for tattering the gates of the fort.[214] The most usual tactic employed by the attacking foes in such cases was to cut off the supplies of provisions and arms by stationing posts of all the passages of the forts.[215]

Like the water and mountain forts, we come across the reference of *Vanadurga* which is mentioned as inaccessible due to the impenetrable clusters of wood.[216] the forest fortifications were intended to ward off dangers arising from unknown wilds and woods.[217] According to G.T.Date, in the classification of forts the addition of '*Naradurga*' by Manu (7.70) is unnecessary

212. Raghu XVII.52
दुर्गाणि दुर्ग्रहाण्यासंस्तस्य रोद्धुरपि द्विषाम् ।
न हि सिंहो गजास्कन्दी भयाद्गिरिगुहाशयः ॥
213. Śiśu I.45
214. Kirā XVI.36
215. Śiśu II.64
216. Nai II.4
स गरुद्वनदुर्गदुर्ग्रहान्कटु कीटान्दशतः सतः क्वचित् ।
नुनुदे तनुकण्डु पण्डितः पटुचञ्चूपुटकोटिकुट्टनैः ॥
217. KA II.3.2 MS VII.69
वनदुर्गमटवीस्थानम् आपद्यपसारो वा ।

as arrays or *Vyūhas* form an important section of military science known to ancient Indians.[218]

Thus the fortresses were the most powerful defensive weapons, known to the people in ancient India; and conquering of the enemy's forts was the surest means to defeat him.[219]

WEAPONS AND MISSILES :

A success of the battle depends upon superiority of men and means viz. weapons.[220] In the various battles described in the *Pañcamahākāvyas,* we find a great deal of information about weapons and missiles and also about the science of Archery. the weapons are classified under two heads. Weapons of throwing and weapons of striking.[221] The missiles come under the category of throwing weapons because they are thrown with the help of incantations.

The throwing weapons are arrows, disc, lances, darts etc. the weapons of striking are sword, iron-clubs, mace and others. The weapons and missiles alluded to in the *Pañcamahākāvyas,* with all their wealth of details regarding military matters are stated here.

Bow and Arrows: Bow was regarded as the foremost sign of valour for warriors.[222] They relied on their bows

---

218. G.T. Date, Art of War in Ancient India Published by Oxford University Press 1929, p.33

219. Nai I.22

220. Kirā III.17
लभ्या धरित्री तव विक्रमेण ज्यायांश्च वीर्यास्त्रबलैर्विपक्षः ।
अतः प्रकर्षाय विधिर्विधेयः प्रकर्षतन्त्रा हि रणे जयश्रीः ॥

221. Śiśu XVIII.11
यातैश्चातुर्विध्यमस्त्रादिभेदादव्यासङगैः सौष्ठवाल्लाघवाच्च ।
शिक्षाशक्तिं प्राहरन्दर्शयन्तो मुक्तामुक्तैरायुधैरायुधीयाः ॥

222. Kirā XIII.14
इति तेन विचिन्त्य चापनामप्रथमं पौरुषचिह्नमाललम्बे ।
उपलब्धगुणः परस्य भेदे सचिवः इवाददे च बाणः ॥

for acquiring victory.[223] The bow was made from a cane of high quality.[224] It was tested at the beginning of the battle (Śiśu XVIII.9). Various kinds of arrows are alluded. Some are of semicircular in shape.[225] Warrior's head was cut by such arrow.[226] the crescent shaped arrows were named as Bhalla.[227] The thin arrows, shot through a tube, rightly piercing the mark were called *Nālīka*[228] The razor-tipped arrows also were used by the warriors.[229] The foreparts of the arrows thrown by Śiva were golden.[230] The tips of the arrows were sharp pointed.[231] A butt(पुङ्ख) was often added to the shaft for the purpose of making securer notch.[232] It is specifically mentioned that the arrows employed were pure and poisonless.[233] It was forbidden by the ancient thinkers also to use poisonous or fire emitting weapons, in a righteous warfare.[234] The shaft of an arrow bore the name of a archer inscribed upon it.[235] A good arrow bears the qualities as straightness of tip, purity of iron and long wings.[236]

---

223. Raghu XII.44
224. Kirā XVI.28
225. Śiśu XVIII.53 Raghu XII.96 Ku XVI.28
226. Ku XVI.49
227. Śiśu XIX.17
228. Śiśu XIX.61 Nai II.28, XXI.151
229. Raghu IX.62; XI.29 Nai XI.123
230. Kirā XV.43
231. Śiṣu XVIII.74
232. Raghu II.49/64, IV.63/77
233. Śiśu XVIII.13; XX.11 Kirā XVI.14
234. MS VII.90
    न कूटैरायुधैर्हन्यायुध्यमानो रणे रिपून् ।
    कर्णिभिर्नापि दिग्धैर्नाग्नि ज्वलित तेजनैः ॥
235. Raghu III.35; VII.38 Śiśu XIX.110
236. Śiśu XX.9
    ऋजुताफलयोगशुद्धिभाजां गुरुपक्षाषयिणां शिलीमुखानाम् ।
    गुणिना नतिमागतेन सन्धिः सह चापेन समञ्जसो बभूव ॥

The science of archery had a significant place and importance in the warfare described in the *Pañcamahākāvyas.* the kings were clever in archery.[237] Śrikṛṣṇa in Śiśupālavadha, always aimed at minute target in archery, though his charity had a larger target.[238] Daśaratha was expert in aiming the target by the sound from that direction.[239]

The power of the arrows is difficult to be perceived, able to avert the danger and reached upto the end of the target at a distance.[240] The lustrous row of the arrows running in a straightforward direction pierces the target.[241] The deadly activity of the arrows consists in direct hitting, noiseless course and the reaching of the edge of the archer's ears.[242] In Kirātarjunīyam, the expert archery of Arjuna and Śiva is well described. Arjuna's bow was twanging constantly. The speed of the arrows was so tremendous that its slipping from the bow and piercing the target was not seen at all. It appeared that it pierced the target before reaching it.[243] While discharging the arrows his neck and shoulders were steady, his posture was without any strain and

---

237. Raghu VI.55

238. Śiśu XIX.99
अक्षितारासु विव्याध द्विषतः स तनुत्रिणः।
दानेषु स्थूललक्ष्यत्वं न हि तस्य शरासने॥

239. Raghu IX.73
कुम्भपूरणभवः पटुरुच्चैरुच्चकार निनदोऽम्भसि तस्याः।
तत्र स द्विरदबृंहितशङ्की शब्दपतिनमिषुं विससर्ज॥

240. Kirā XIV.52
गतैः परेषामविभावनीयतां निवारयद्भिर्विपदं विदूरगैः।
भृशं बभूवोपचितो बृहत्फलैः शरैरुपायैरिव पाण्डुनन्दनः॥

241. ibid. XIV.57

242. NI XII.44

243. Kirā XIII.27
अविभावितनिष्क्रमप्रयाणः शमितायाम अवांतिरहसा सः।
सह पूर्वतरं नु चित्तवृत्तेपतित्वा नु चकार लक्ष्यभेदम्॥

there was not any change or defect on his face.[244] His aim was not disturbed while changing the posture, his excellence in discharging the arrows on steady or unsteady target was the same.[245] The arrows were so speedy that they were as if coming from so many bodies created by the power of his penance.[246] Lord Śiva, the opponent of Arjuna, was an expert archer.[247] He was clever in seeking the deficiency of eney and covering even a great fault of his own.[248] Another peculiar posture named Vīrāsana in archery is mentioned in Śiśupālavadha.[249] The chest of the archer should be expanded, with bent shoulders, raised head and both the fists forward and backward, quite firm.

An archer with his expert actions in archery exhibits his command on his bow.[250] The arrows are so speedy and sharp that after piercing the warriors, they drop downwards without any stain of blood.[251] The whole battle appears to be speedy due to the speed of the arrows.[252] A single archer is able to check the opposite party.[253] Thus the entire military science of archery is centered round the bow. Bow was used as the main offensive weapon. Some technical terms in the science

---

244. ibid. XVI.21
245. ibid. XVI.22
246. ibid. XIV.60
247. Kirā XV.36
परिमोहयमणिन शिक्षालाघवलीलया ।
जैष्णवी विशिखश्रेणी परिजह्वे पिनाकिना ॥
248. ibid. XVI.23
परस्य भूयान्विवरेऽभियोगः प्रसह्यः संरक्षणमात्मरन्ध्रे ।
भीष्मेऽप्यसंभाव्यमिदं गुरो वा न संभवत्येष वनेचरेषु ॥
249. Śiśu XX.20
250. Śiśu XIX.97; XX.8 Nai XII.49/64
251. Ku XVI.9
252. Kirā XV.51 Raghu VII.45
253. Śiśu XX.17

of archery are mentioned in Śiśupāpālavadha. A man who lives by the bow is called *'dhānuṣka'* (II.27, The skilled archer is described as *'Laghusandhāyin* (XIX.97). The place where the archer or the hunter lies secretly in wait for an animal is named *Upaśaya* (II.80) *Varanḍaka* is a mound of earth which is used as a place for practicing the various skills in archery. (XIX.65).

Disc- It was a sharp circular weapon with rezorlike edges.[254] It could be hurled from a long distance. It cut off some limb of the enemy. Disc was a famous weapon of god Viṣṇu.[255] Kṛṣṇa cut the head of Śiśupāla by disc named Sudarśana.[256] *Lances* were generally used by horse-soldiers.[257] *'Sakti* is a kind of lance made of iron having a long and pointed dart.[258] It furnished with eight bells, giving cut a terrible roar, made full or art and guile and destructive to enemy's life. It flies rapidly leaving behind it a fiery track. Kumāra holds the weapon named *Śakti.*[259] Noose was the weapon of Varuṇa[260] and *Vajra* was the deadliest weapon of god Indra.[261] *Śataghnī* was one more sharp weapon used by the warriors. It was a projectile weapon. In Raghuvaṁśa, Kālidāsa describes Rāvaṇa hurling a Śataghnī towards Rāma but it was soon split into pieces by Rāma's crescent shaped arrows.[262] It has pointed iron spikes.

---

254. Raghu VIi.46
255. Ku II.49; XVI.17 Śiśu XII.3
256. Śiśu XX.78
257. Kirā XVI.4
258. Śiśu XIX.59
    स्खलन्ती न क्वचितैक्षण्यादभ्यग्र फलशालिनी ।
    अमोचि शक्तिः शक्तीकेलोहजा न शरीरजा ॥
259. Ku XIII.22
260. NaiXVII.10 Śiśu XVIII.57
261. Raghu IX.12 KU II.20
262. Raghu XII.95/96

It's name shows that it is a hundred-killing weapon. It was generally placed on the walls of forts. It surpasses the power of hundred kings.[263]

The striking weapons were of various kinds of swords and clubs. Sword was the prominent weapon of warriors on which they relied for victory. Sword was the foremost way of acquiring desired object viz. success in battlefield. In Śiśupālavadha their is a poetic reference of the mode of carrying the sword.[264] Sword was used in a close combat. *Nistriñśa* was a short sword.[265] *Tomara* was a kind of dart with a wooden handle having a hook at the end. A warrior cuts the sword of his opponent by his own and acquires success.[266]

Various kinds of swords as Kaukṣeyaka (Śiśu XVIII.17 Ārdhāsi (Śiśu XVIII.47 also are mentioned. Clubs as Musala,[267] Parigha[268] are mentioned. Mace was specielly used by god Keubera.[269] Balarāma is attributed as Musalapāni, for holding his special weapon mace. Battle-axe was regarded as a weapon of Paraśurāma.[270] A valorous warrior like Arjuna, after losing all his weapons fought with stones and trees.[271] Stones were thrown by means of sling from the mountain-tribes towords the enemies. Generally the wars were fought with *śastras* or non-missiles but in the indiscriminative

---

263. Nai XII.58
264. Śiśu XVII.25
सुमेखलाः सिततरदन्तचारवः समुल्लसत्तनुपरिधानसंपदः ।
रणैषिणां पुलकमृतोऽधिकंधरं ललम्बिरे सदसिलताः प्रिया इव ॥
265. Kirā III.57
266. Śiśu XIX.48/49
267. ibid. II.70
268. ibid. XV.57
269. Ku II.22 Nai XIII.16; XVII.9
270. Raghu VI.42; XI.78
271. Kirā XVII.60

warfares the missiles were brought into operation to bring about wholesale annihilation of enemies.[272]

The developed science of missiles was taught in those days by brāhmaṇas and was given as preceptor's gift.[273] The divine and superhuman weapons were in the reach of human beings after practising severe penances. A theme of Kīrātārjunīyam is the acquirement of the divine missile named Pāśupatāstra after a severe penance by Arjnuna. Acquisition of the powerful means in the form of divine missiles was a need of warriors, which was prescribed by their preceptors. The great sage Vyāsa urgefully states that the kingdom is to be regained by Pāṇḍavas by valour alone and the enemy is stronger in valour, missiles and army. So measures must be employed to gain superiority in missiles.[274] The attainment of supreme excellence in the science of missiles is stated as success incarnate.[275] The missile had its presiding deity, who duly worshipped by the *Manṭra* proves efficacious and remains subservient to the will of the *sādhaka*. There is a graphic description of the obtainment of the lore of *Manṭra* from Vyāsa to Arjuna. the lore viz. *Manṭra* having Indra for its deity, bright like a spark of fire, issuing from the mouth of the great sage passed to that of Arjuna. By the power of his penance the sage at the very moment imparted Arjuna, the fittest recipient, the powers of contemplation by which he being enlightened by the real knowledge his eyes seemed to be brightened after a long time.[276] The high inspiration of his mind was increased by the

---

272. Raghu IV.77
273. ibid. XI.21
274. Kirā III.17
275. Kirā III.23
महत्वयोगाय महामहिन्नामाराधनीं तां नृप ! देवतानाम् ।
दातुं प्रदानोचित भूरिधाम्नीमुपागतः सिद्धिमिवास्मि विद्याम् ॥
276. ibid III.25/26

lore, which indicated a great gain of success.[277] The sage directed Arjuna the regulations to be observed in the period of penance and offered his blessing to Arjuna to secure success in penance.

The missiles are hard and huge in shape.[278] The expert in the science of missiles is capable of throwing as well as withdrawing it. After a severe penance Arjuna praised Śiva to favour him with the science of missiles which gives victory over the enemy.[279] Lord Śiva the presiding deity of the *Pāśupata* missile incarnated before Arjuna in a lustrous bodily form and favoured him by *Pāśupata missile.*

In the use of these deadliest missiles the policy of the warriors was not always defensive but sometimes in the discriminative wars the warriors had to take an offensive step. In the Lankā war Rāma employed the unfailing *Brahmāstra* which was as if a medicine for extricating the thorn of grief for his his beloved.[280] the missile thrown with proper spell and charm was successful in felling Rāvaṇa's head. Prince Aja in the fight with the host of princes employed the missile named Gāndharva which was not wholesome destructive but had a quality of causing slumber to the enemy.[281] Rāma, who was skilled in the use of missiles killled the demons by projecting wind-missile against them.[282] The skilled warriors knew to employ counteracting missiles against the missiles projected by the

---

277. ibid. III.27
278. ibid. VI.40
279. Kirā XVIII.44
280. Raghu XII.97
     अमोघं संदधे चास्मै धनुष्येकधनुर्धरः ।
     ब्राह्ममस्त्रं प्रियाशोकशल्यनिष्कर्षणौषधम् ॥
281. ibid. VII.61
282. ibid. XI.28

enemies. the serpent missile projected by Meghanāda was made futile by Rāma by employing *Garuda* missile.[283] King Kuśa also employed the Garuda missile against the serpent Kumuda but immediately counteracted it when he saw that Kumuda was returning the ornament alongwith his sister.[284] In Kirātāruniyam, we come across a graphic description of the fight of missiles employed by Kirāta and Arjuna. Arjuna was thinking of projecting missiles towards the Kirāta to avert his valour. He projected the sleep-missile which pervaded the whole army of Kirāta. But Śiva in the guise of Kirāta, by the lustre of his third eye averted the darkness of sleep. Then Arjuna projected the serpent missile by which the sky prevailed with fire-flames. But Śiva defeated the serpent missile by counteracting Garuda missile, just like a leader who averts dissension caused by the enemy. Then the fired missile projected by Arjuna was defeated by *Varuṇāstra.* thus all the missiles employed by Arjuna were counteracted by Kirāta.[285]

In the fight between Kṛṣṇa and Śiśupāla, Śiśupāla started the war of missiles by projecting sleep-missile. It affected the army of Kṛṣṇa but not Kṛṣṇa himself, whose *Kausṭubha* jem averted the darkness of sleep.[286] Then was the fight of serpent missile and Garuda missile and of fire missile with Meghāstra, which was projected by Kṛṣṇa.[287]

---

283. Raghu XII.76
गरुडापातविश्लिष्टमेघनादास्त्रबन्धनः ।
दाशरथ्योः क्षणक्लेशः स्वप्नवृत्त इवाभवत् ॥

284. ibid. XVI.80
विभूषणप्रत्युपहारहस्तमुपस्थितं वीक्ष्य विशांपतिस्तम् ।
सौपर्णमध्यं प्रतिसंजहार प्रह्वेष्वनिर्वन्धरुषो हि सन्तः ॥

285. Kirā XVI.25 to 57

286. Śiśu XX.37

287. ibid. XX.65

Thus the science of missiles was a prominent part of warfare. The wars with the help of spells and charms was also favoured by the kings. The spells and Mantras recited by the preceptors were able to quell the enemies.[288] The arrows of the kings were supported by the spells of their preceptors.[289] A guess about the use of guns in ancient warfare is supported by the reference in Naiṣadhīyacarita. There, the nostrils of Damayantī are compared to guns.[290] Frequent references to *Āgneyāstra* as a powerful weapon of destruction suggests the idea of gun. But according to G.T.Date the points of doubtful significance cannot be treated as corroborating evidence. He has refuted the theory of existence of gunpowder, in ancient India, raised by Oppert.[291] Whatever may be the fact the missiles used by the warriors were destructive and were resulted in a discriminative warfare.

OMENS :

An influence of the superstitious beliefs in good and ill omens, seems not only in the lives of the common people but the omens influence the activities of the royal authorities in their personal lives as well as on their administrative works.

The omens good and bad were based on the appearance and movements of heavenly bodies, the behaviour of plants, birds and animals, the spontaneous expressions of one's own limbs and dreams.[292]

---

288. Raghu I.61

289. ibid. XVII.38
वसिष्ठस्य गुरोर्मन्त्राः सायकास्तस्य धन्विनः ।
किं तत्साध्यं यदुभये साधयेयुर्न संगताः ॥

290. Nai II.28; XXI.151

291. G.T. Date, Art of War in Ancient India, Published by Oxford University Press, Bombay 1929, p.40/41

292. Ramashraya Sharma, a Socio-Political Study of Vālmīki Rāmayaṇa, Published by Motilal Banarasidas 1971, p.177

At the birth of the prince or princess, the nature exhibits good signs. At the very moment of Raghu's birth, the quarters became fair and bright, the breeze began to blow in a pleasant manner. The sacrificial fire with an encircling flame on the right received the offerings.[293] Everything had an augury of good. The atmosphere at the day of birth of Pārvatī was prosperous with spotless quarters. The wind was devoid of dust and decorative with the showers of flowers.[294]

When king Dilīpa reached the hermitage of Vaśiṣṭha, he experienced good signs which were indicative of the success of the desired object. The wind was blowing favouravbly. The sage Vaśiṣṭha, who had a good knowledge of omens addressed that the king, whose hope for desired object was not destined to be fruitless, because at the very mention of the name of the divine cow, she made her appearance.[295]

Throbbing of the right hand was expressive of a good omen. In the *swayaṁvara* ceremony of Indumati, Aja was doubtful as to whether she would choose him or not but the throbbing of his right hand removed his doubt.[296]

The gales of the winds blowing in opposite direction was an indication of ill-omen, because king Daśaratha asked his spriritual advisor regarding its pacification.[297]

---

293. Raghu III.13/14

294. Ku I.23
प्रसन्नदिक्पांसुविविक्तवातं शङ्खस्वनाऽनन्तरपुष्पवृष्टि ।
शरीरिणा स्थावरजंगमानां सुखाय तज्जन्मदिनं बभूव ॥

295. Raghu I.86/87

296. ibid. VI.38

297. ibid XI.62
तत्प्रतीपपवनादि वैकृतं प्रेक्ष्य शान्तिमधिकृत्य कृत्यवित् ।
अन्वयुङ्क्त गुरुमीश्वरः क्षितैः स्वन्तमित्यलंघयत्स तद्व्यथाम् ॥

The demoness Śūrpaṇakhā whose nose and ears were mutilated was an ill-omen to the demons who attacked Rāma.[298] Throbbing of the right eye was an indication of the ill omen for women. The great misfortune in the form of abandonment, that was to stare for Sīta and which Lakṣmaṇa kept concealed from her, was suggested by the throbbing of her right eye and her tender face faded away in consequence of dejection caused by that ill-omen in her heart of hearts, she prayed for the welfare of her husband.[299]

Dropping tears, when one is about to depart was meant to be inauspicious.[300] In Kirātarjunīyam, Draupadī who at the time of departure of Arjuna, though manifestly longing to see Arjuna, could not close her eyes suffused with tears, as she was afraid to violate the auspiciousness of the hour.[301] A dove perching on the roof of a house was regarded as an evil omen involving risk of fire.

The time of an expedition of conquest was fixed by seeing the auspicious position of the planets. The ill omens, before the commencement of the battle, suggested the coming defeat. In Kumārasaṁbhava and Śiśupālavadha we come across the series of ill omens on the way to the enemy of gods viz. Tārakāsura and Śiśupala respectively, indicating their common distress. Unfinely and furious tempest,[302] attack of the dark dreadful serpents, vomiting poisons from their tongues,[303] furiously burning orb of the Sun, terrific cry of

298. Raghu XII.43
299. ibid. XIV.49/50
300. Nai IX.106
301. Kirā III.36
302. Ku XV.15
303. ibid. XV.16

the jackals, fall of a mete or from the sky,[304] Sudden fall of a lightning without clouds, showering of blood, bones and bouring charcoals from the sky,[305] earthquake and storm in the ocean,[306] crying of the dogs facing onwards to the sun[307] were the ill omens. Due to these illomens the experts of the omens prohibited Tārakāsura, from going to the war, but he did not care for the advice. His royal emblems exhibited bad signs. The royal umbrella diverted its position at an upward direction; his crown broke down scattering its pearls.[308] the poisonous black serpents embrassed the flag of the chariot,[309] a sudden burns of the yoke, chowries, bow, arrows and quiver,[310]all these ill omens indicated a destruction of Tārakāsura. In Śiśupālavadha also, the description of the ill omens experienced by the wives of the warriors of Śiśupāla indicated his total defeat. Stumbling, falling and breaking of a glass from the hand, weeping of the wives, a sneeze at the time of departure, breaking of stars.[311] etc.

There is a reference of dream of Kuśa in Raghuvaṁśa. The presiding deity of the city of Ayodhyā in the form of an auspicious lady entered into the inner apartment of Kuśa and narrated him the distressed condition of Ayodhā which was minded due to the absence of the king, as Kuśa had built a new capital named Kuśāvatī. When in the morning, King narrated the account of the dream to the *brāhmaṇas,* they

---

304. ibid XV. 17
305. ibid. XV.20
306. ibid. XV.21
307. ibid. XV.23
308. ibid. XV.27
309. ibid. XV.31
310. ibid XV.31
311 Śiśu XV. 57/81/83/85/86/88/91

congratulated the king on his having been chosen as a husband by the hereditary capital.[312]

Thus not only common people but the royal personalities strongly believed in the omens and they changed sometimes their programmes according to the indication of the omens.

312. Raghu XVI.24
तदद्भुतं संसदि रात्रिवृतं प्रातर्द्विजेभ्यो नृपतिः शशंसः।
श्रुत्वा त अेनं कुलाराजधान्या साक्षात्पतित्वे वृतमभ्यनन्दन्।

CONCLUSION

A critical investigation of the political ideas in the light of *Pañcamahākāvyas* leads to some definite conclusions.

As, monarchy was a dominant form of government, the concepts of the science of polity were centred around the king. That is why, a critical interpretation of the various aspects of the king and kingship is dealt with in forgoing pages with due details. They are as follows:

The principle of divine origin of king and kingship prominently reflected in the *Pañcamahākāvyas*. It provided the kings with a controlling power for their administration.

The virtues and merits of the administrators bear purely political value. For instance, their charity in the garb of religious ceremonials leads to social welfare of the subjects and exhibits an attitude of equanimity towards the subjectṣ, offering each member of the society a chance to participate in the ceremonials. The virtue of self-respect does not remain an idealistic merit of the king, but it becomes an essential requisite for a conquering monarch to increase his domain.

Dharma was a non constitutional check to control king's powers. As an employer of *daṇḍa* power, the king had no rights to make the laws and rules, but he was to execute them only. *Dharma* was not merely an ethical set of virtues but was a strong directive for the rulers. It effected and affected in various ways and offered mixed results.

The duties of the kings, which were molded in *dharma* and in the social structure of *varnāśrama* were the effective controllers to save the king from being a tyrant.

A strict observance of the rule of *varṇāśrama* leads to the smooth succession of the royal throne. Secondly, it ensured harmony in the individual aims as well as the aims of the society.

Judicature in ancient India was influenced by *dharma*. The laws and rules were formulated in consideration of the caste of an offender. The king was expected to be impartial and equanimous merely in the execution of them.

Observance of penances was considered as an accepted path to acquire and increase the *Kṣātra* power.

Polity was influenced by the spiritual support of the priests and preceptors. *Brāhmaṇas* known for their spiritual attainments and *kṣatriyas* reputed for their valour, employed their merits for the welfare of the state.

Thus, the concept of *dharma* was immensely embedded in the concept of polity; and we can not consider the political aspects without the due investigation of the social and religious aspects.

The ministry was a strong support to king's power. The administrative decisions were solely dependent upon the consultation of the ministers. In the absence of the kings, on some occasions the ministers took important decisions e.g. consecration of the queen of the dead king, was a bold decision taken by the ministers. It shows that ministers shared great power in administration.

These powers of the king were accepted traditionally. One more power of the king viz. the magical power, may be stated as a new fourth power of the king. While discussing the theory of divine origin of kingship, it is stated that the divinities offered many of the supernatural powers to the kings; but inspite of these powers from the divinities, there are some allusions to show the magical power of the king. While investigating this power, a partial help of the theory forwarded by G.J. Frazer in his 'Golden Bough is taken here.

The aspects of diplomacy are discussed in a comparative study of the two *mahākāvyas* viz. Kirātārjunīyam and Śiśupālavadha. They exhibit advance political tactics employed by the diplomats. The art of diplomacy reflected in the *Pañcamahākāvyas* leads to some important conclusions; It was not a wrong policy for the kings, intent on victory, to make breaches of peace and declare war.

A cut-off the supplies of the enemies, at the time of war, employment of seditious means, employment of the double paid spies were the purely diplomatic tactics.

It has always proved to be a profitable policy in warfare to embarrass an enemy either by insisting on other powers to attack him from the rear or by fomenting internal troubleș within the territory.

The kings, though accustomed to the means of diplomacy were prudent to give a first chance to their opponent to start the game of hostility.

In the art of war, a prominence was given to archery. The unrighteous methods of warfare were not disregarded outright, but the kings, as a defensive policy, employed the deceitful means to pay the enemies in their coins. In the traditional fourfold army, there seems to be a creditable addition of navy in the warfare.

Thus, the polity reflected in the *Pañcamahākāvyas* holds two ways of traditions. Their kings personal lives were strictly controlled by the principles of *dharma* and *nīti*. They offered value to the ethical standards prescribed by *smṛti* tradition. But the provinces of diplomacy and interstate relationship were clearly influenced by the Arthaśāstra of Kauṭilya. We find a clear reflection of these two paths in the *Pañcamahākāvyas*.

BIBLIOGRAPHY

ORIGINAL TEXTS :

Agnipurāṇa
Aitereya Brāhmaṇa
Bhaṭṭikāvya
Jaminīya Brāhmaṇa
Kāmandakīya Nītisāra
Kautilīya Arthaśāstra
Kirātārjunīyam
Kumārasaṁbhava
Mahābhārata (Critical Edition by BORI)
Munusmṛti
Naiṣadhīyacarita
Nāradasmṛti
Nītivākyāmṛta
Pañcatantra
Raghuvaṁśa
Śatapatha Brāhmaṇa
Śiśupālavadha
Śrīmadbhagavadgītā
Śukranītisāra
Vālmīki Rāmāyaṇa
Viṣṇudharmottarpurāṇa
Yājñavalkya Smṛti

MODERN WORKS CONSULTED :

1. Aiyangar K.V.Rangaswami

   1) Some Aspects of Ancient Indian Polity, Madras University, 1935.

2) Indian Cameralism, Adyar Library,1949.

2. Altekar A.S.
State And Government in Ancient India,
Motilal Banarasidass Delhi, 1962.
3. Basu Praphullachandra
Indo-Aryan Polity, P.S.King & Sons, London, 1925
4. Bhandarkar D.R.
Some Aspects of Ancient Hindu Polity
Banaras Hindu University, 1929.
5. Charavarti P.C.
The Art of War in Ancient India,
Oriental Publishers, Delhi 6, 1972.
6. Chaudhuri P.K.
Political Concepts in Ancient India
S.Chand & Company Ltd. New Delhi, 1977
7. Dandekar R.N.
The Age of the Guptas and Other Essays
Ajanta Publications, Delhi 1982
8. Date G.T.
The Art of War in Ancient India,
Oxford University Press, Bombay 1929.
9. Datta Bhupendra Nath
Studies in Indian Social Polity,
Purabi Publishers, Calcutta,1944
10. Dikshitar V.R.R.
1) War in Ancient India,
University of Madras, 1944.
2) Hindu Administrative Institutions,
University of Madras, 1929
3) The Mauryan Polity,
University of Madras (Historical Series) 1932.

11. Frazer J.G.

The Golden Bough, A Study in Magic and Religion (Abridged Edition),

Mac Millan & Co.Ltd. London, 1933

12. Ghoshal S.N.

Kālidāsa - An Estimate of His Literary Merit (Alfred Hillebrandt), World Press, Calcutta 1971

13. Ghoshal U.N.

A History of Indian Political Ideas,

oxford University Press, 1959.

14. Gonda J.

Ancient Indian Kingship from the Religious Point of View, E.J.Brill, London, 1966

15. Handiqui K.K.

Naiṣadhacarita of śrī Harṣa.

Deccan College, Poona 1965.

16. Hopkins Edward W.

The Social and Military Position of the Ruling Caste in Ancient India,

Bharat-Bharati, Oriental Publishers & Book-sellers, Varanasi 5, 1972.

17. Indra

Ideologies of War and Peace in Ancient India,

Vishveshvaranand Institute Publications,

Hoshiarpur, 1957.

18. Jani A.N.

Naiṣadhacaritam - A Critical Study,

Oriental Institute, Baroda, 1957

19. Jauhari Manorama

Politics and Ethics in Ancient India,

Bharatiya Vidya Prakasana, Varanasi, 1968

20. Jayaswal, K.P.

Hindu Polity, Butterworth & Co. India Ltd. Calcutta,1924.

21. Kale M.R.
Raghuvaṁśa of Kālidāsa (Cantos I-V), Motilal Banarasidass, Delhi, 1972

22. Kane P.V.
The Kauṭilīya arthaśāstra, University of Bombay, 1960.

24. Law N.N.
1) Aspects of Ancient Indian Polity, Oriental/Longmans, Calcutta, 1960.
2) Interstate Relations in Ancient India, Oriental Series, Calcutta, 1920.

25. Majumdar B.K.
The Military System in Ancient India, World Press Ltd. Calcutta, 1955.

26. Majumdar R.C.
1) Indian Religion, University of Calcutta, 1963
2d) Ancient India, Motilal Banarasidass, Banaras, 1952.

27. Mirashi V.V. & Navlekar N.R.
Kālidāsa - Date, Life and Works, Popular Prakashan, Bombay 1969.

28. Mishra B.B.
Polity in the Agni Purāṇa, Punthi Pustak, Calcutta, 1965.

29. Mookerji Radhakumud
Local Government in Ancient India, Oxford, 1920

30. Nandargikar G.R.
The Raghuvaṁśa of Kālidāss, Motilal Banarasidass, Delhi, 1977.

31. Oppert Gustav
On the Weapons, Army Organisation and Political Maxims of the Ancient Hindus, Published by the New Order Book Co. Ellis Bridge, Ahmedabad, 1967.

32. Pratapgiri Ramamurthi
The Problem of the Ancient Polity, Longmans, Green and Co.Ltd. Calcutta, 1955

33. Rao.M.V.K.
Studies in Kauṭilya, Munshiram Manoharlal Publishers, Delhi,1979.

34. Roy B.P.
Political Ideas and Institutions in Mahābhārata, Calcutta,1975.

35. Saletore B.A.
Ancient Indian Political Thought and Institutions, Asia Publishing House, Bombay, 1963.

36. Shama Shastri R.
Evolution of Indian Polity, University of Calcutta, 1920.

37. Sharma Ramashraya
A Socio-Political Study of the Vālmīki Rāmāyaṇa, Motilal Banarasidass, Delhi 1959.

38. Sharma R.S.
Aspects of the political Ideas and Institutions in Ancient India, Motilal Banarasidass, Delhi, 1959.

39. Singh Ram Charitra Prasad
Kingship in Northern India, Motilal Banarasidass, Delhi, 1968.

40. Sinha N.K.P.
Political Ideas and Ideals in Mahābhārata,

Oriental Publishers and Distributors, Delhi, 1976

41. Spellman John W.
Political Theory of Ancient India,
Oxford University Press, London, 1964.

42. Suryakanta
1) Kālidāsa's Vision of Kumārasambhava
(A Study of the Kumāra Problem)
Meherchand Lachhmandas, Delhi, 1963.
2) The Kumārasaṁbhava of Kālidāsa,
Sahitya Akademi, New Delhi, 1962

43. Tenkshe S.A.
Contribution of Māgha to Sanskrit Literature,
Venus Prakasana, Poona, 1972.

44. Upadhyaya B.S.
India in Kālidāsa, Published by Kitabistan,
Allahabad, 1947.

45. Upadhyaya Geeta
Glimpses of Political Thought in Sanskrit Kāvya,
Chaukhambha Orientalia, Varanasi, 1979

मराठी व हिंदी :

1. अळतेकर अ.स.
प्राचीन भारतीय शासनपद्धति, भारती भंडार, लीडर प्रेस,प्रयाग 1948.

2. अळतेकर मा.दा.
कालिदासाची सृष्टी

3. करंदीकर अ.ज.
अशोक ते कालिदास, अ.ज.करंदीकर पुणे 1962

4. घिल्डियाल अच्युतानंद
प्राचीन भारतीय राजनैतिक विचारक, विवेक

घिल्डियाल बन्धु, वाराणसी, 1972

5. नरहर रतिभानुसिंह

प्राचीन भारत का राजनैतिक एवं सांस्कृतिक इतिहास,

किताबमहल, इलाहाबाद, 1971

6. मिराशी वा.वि.

कालिदास, व्हीनस प्रकाशन, पुणे, 1967

7. वाटवे के.ना.

संस्कृत काव्याचे पंचप्राण, मनोहर ग्रंथमाला, पुणे 1947

8. शर्मा मनमोहनलाल जगन्नाथ

महाकवि माघ (उनका जीवन तथा कृतियां) नवयुग प्रकाशन, दिल्ली, 1963.

9. शुक्ल चंडिकाप्रसाद,

नैषध परिशीलन, हिन्दुस्थानी एकेडमी, इलाहाबाद, 1960.

10. भारतीय राजनीतिकोश (कालिदास खण्ड)

JOURNALS :

Annals of Bhandarkar Oriental Research Institute, Pune

1) (42) 1961, p.141-159
Betai Rameshchandra S. Individual & Society.
2) (30) 1949, p.332-345
Karmarkar R.D. The Aśvamedha :
Its Original Significance.
3) (12) 1930-31, p.1-24
Shamashastri R.
Forms of government in Ancient India.
4) (15) 1933-34, p.137-158
Altekar A.S., Ideal,Merits and Defects of Ancient Indian Educational System.

The Journal of the Ganganth Jha Research Institute, Allahabad.

Vols. XXIII (January 1967-December)

Mishra Rudrakanta, A Critical Evaluation of the theory and practice of kingship as Revealed in Raghuvaṃśa.

Indian Historical Quarterly

1) Vol. III September 1925

Vol.IV December 1925

Basak Radhagovinda, Minsters in ancient India.

2) 1925, p.94

Banerjee N.C. Policies and Political

History in Mahābhārata.

3) (27), 1951

Sharma Dasharath, Arthaśāstra Material in Raghuvaṃśa.

4) (2), 1926

Ganguli J.N.C. Principles of Hindu Taxation

Journal of the Bihar Research Society

Vol.LXI 1975

Sohoni S.V., Some Aspects of Kālidāsa's

Description of Raghu's Digvijaya.

Bhāratīya Vidyā Journal, Bombay

(20-21) 1960-61, p.340-352

Dandekar R.N. The system of government under the Guptas.

Journal of the Banaras Hindu University, Varanasi.

4(1), 1939, p.251-284

Upadhyaya B.S. The State, King and Some

Other Incidents of Polity in Kālidāsa.

Sir Monier - Williams

A Sanskrit-English Dictionary

Published By Motilal Banarasidass, 1979

INDEX